Forgotten Capitals

Forgotten Capitals and the Historical Lessons They Teach

Derek Dwight Anderson

ISBN: 9798334400986

Cover design by the author

Cataloging Data

Forgotten Capitals and the Historical Lessons They Teach /
Derek Dwight Anderson

Includes bibliographic references.

1. Capitals (Cities)--History. 2. Cities and Towns—History.
3. History, Modern

G140.A53 2024
307.7609—dc23

Amazon KDP
Seattle, Washington

For additional resources and information visit: forgottencapitals.com

For all those who care enough not to forget the past.

CONTENTS

ACKNOWLEDGMENTS

It's been four years since I published my first book in 2020, and no one I know would describe that period as having been easy. COVID and cancer, climate change and January 6th, wars and death, have all combined to frustrate and obfuscate, dishearten and disgust. I have been quite fortunate to have had this project to distract me and fulfill me, just as I have been lucky to have benefitted from the assistance of so many.

Because I know that libraries, archives, and museums stand at the foundation of all historical research, I would like to begin by thanking the librarians and archivists, guards and custodians, curators and fundraisers who are affiliated with:

- Clark Library, University of Portland, Portland, OR
- Church History Museum, Salt Lake City, UT
- Doe-Gardner Library, University of California-Berkeley, Berkeley, CA
- Gleeson Library, University of San Francisco, San Francisco, CA
- Green Library, Stanford University, Stanford, CA
- Main Library, University of Iowa, Iowa City, IA
- Marriott Library, University of Utah, Salt Lake City, UT
- Northern Facility Library, University of California, Richmond, CA
- Museum of Republika Srpska, Banja Luka, Bosnia Herzegovina.
- Perry-Castañeda Library, University of Texas-Austin, Austin, TX
- Portland State University Library, Portland, OR
- San Francisco Public Library, San Francisco, CA
- San Rafael Public Library, San Rafael, CA
- Sausalito Public Library, Sausalito, CA
- Territorial Statehouse State Park Museum, Fillmore, UT
- Underwood Law Library, Southern Methodist University, Dallas, TX
- Widener Library, Harvard University, Cambridge, MA
- Wilson Library, University of Minnesota-Twin Cities, Minneapolis, MN

And a special thanks to those at the Lied Library at the University of Nevada-Las Vegas, who allowed me to visit in spring 2021, when so many other academic libraries were closed to independent scholars. Without UNLV, I would not have been able to measure the viability of this project initially or to finish it so quickly.

Dr. Aleksandar Jankovic of the University of Banja Luka not only shared his some of his research with me prior to its publication, but he also generously met with me to offer his perspective on Bosnia and Herzegovina's ethos. I continue to appreciate his time and thoughtfulness, especially since our meeting delayed a family vacation. Dr. Rainer F. Buschmann of California State University-Channel Islands interpreted the content of a baffling photograph for the Rabaul chapter; Park Manager Carl Camp of Utah's Territorial Statehouse Museum took the time to resolve several factual discrepancies I had encountered; and Kathleen Weessies of Michigan State University provided access to a street map of Enugu in 1974 that helped me to understand the city's layout just after the Nigerian Civil War. I am so quick to remember the assistance of Amy Santos of the University of Texas-Austin, who helped me obtain special technological permissions and got the dreaded microfilm machine to work so that I could retrieve material that was otherwise unavailable.

I hope that readers appreciate this book's illustrations, which is why I am immensely grateful to all those who share images on Wikimedia Commons. This is especially true of those who provide a direct way to thank them, such as Peter Milošević. Kaylee Andersen of the Papua

New Guinea Association of Australia, Steven Schreiber of NorkaRussia.info, and Alexander Spack of Wolgadeutsche.net were particularly generous and encouraging. *Forgotten Capitals* is a better book because of their kindness. There have also been numerous institutions whose digitized works influenced me or provided me with illustrations, including:

- The Church of Jesus Christ of Latter-Day Saints, Salt Lake City, UT
- Digital Collections, Harvard University, Cambridge, MA
- Leiden University Libraries, Leiden, The Netherlands
- Library of Congress, Washington, DC
- Metropolitan Museum of Art, New York, NY
- National Archives and Record Administration, Washington, DC
- Nationaal Archief, The Hague, Netherlands
- New York Public Library, New York, NY
- Rijksmuseum, Amsterdam, Netherlands
- Smithsonian Institution, Washington, DC
- Wellcome Library, London, U.K.

My colleagues and students at Marin Academy, both past and present, continue to provide the necessary emotional and practical support all creative endeavors take. I would particularly like to extend my gratitude to Anayansi Aranda-Yee, Travis Brownley, Julia Carlisle, Candace Chen, Tim Conn, Jen Coté, Bill Henley, Pam Maffei, Kim Martin, Anita Mattison, Betsy Muir, John Petrovsky, J O'Malley, Aurora Robathan-Wu, Brian Rowett, Lisa Shambaugh, Jon Denton-Schneider, Mark Stefanski, and Marie Dalby Szuts for their faith and interest during the past four years. You've all been so good to me.

Friends and family members, including Omid Ahmadian, Dorothy Anderson, David and Jan Anderson, Mikell Bodner, Shannon Bouchard, Karen Bouwer, Georgi Coventry, Chad Dawson, Leonard Girard, Helen Harper, Mae Henley, Heather Hoag, Joan Hoff, Pam Jacklin, Rob and Sandy Jacklin, Emily Kosokar, Susan and Bob Lankford, Taylor Lankford, Linda Ojeda, Kathy Nasstrom, Rob Pierce, Debi Reiter, Chiquita Rollins, Ginger da Silva, Brendan Schmonsees, Brian Schmonsees, Linda Steck, Johanna Stefanski, Tobi Szuts, Joshua Tanzer, Terri Vehnekamp, and Marlene and Thomas Woodward have nourished and engaged, blessed and inspired. I feel so lucky to have your support.

And what would my life be like without Joni, Valerie, and Marty, each of whom bring me such tremendous joy? Joni, thank you for the never-ending optimism; Valerie, thank you for the never-ending conversation; and Marty, thank you for the never-ending love. This book would not have been possible without the three of you.

INTRODUCTION

During an expedition cruise on the west coast of Greenland in July 2022, I met a gregarious programmer in his mid-thirties who consulted with the Pentagon. He had a keen interest in history and had read widely about war, economic policy, and politics. As he spoke at length about topics as diverse as Alexander the Great, Adam Smith, and Trumpian Populism, I noticed that he struggled to draw meaningful historical conclusions, despite all of his expertise and curiosity. Instead, this once-fit football player had to fall back upon cliches and platitudes, tropes and truisms. As the week in the ice progressed, I thought about how many other readers of history hunger to put the specifics of what they learn into a more meaningful context. Like my own students, these adults long to find revealing patterns in the human experience, but labor to do so. They want to be able to say something more enlightening than "history repeats itself" and "to the victors go the spoils." This book seeks to help such individuals realize more complex conclusions, while exploring nine fascinating but forgotten cities at a particular moment in time.

I have dedicated my professional life—both as a teacher and as a writer—to examining history in unconventional ways. My first book, *Improbable Voices* (2020), imparted a history of the early modern and modern world through the words and actions of twenty-six people who are not household names. *Forgotten Capitals and the Historical Lessons They Teach* continues my mission to push readers to reconsider whose history matters and why it matters. My hope is to shed light upon the margins: by using the unusual window these nine cities provide, I hope to offer readers a richer understanding of the world's collective modern history, while allowing them to explore, in some depth, the inherent tension between particular historical circumstances and broad commonalities in the human experience.

This duality reminds me of a thin book published in 1968 by Will and Ariel Durant. After spending the better part of forty years writing their ten-volume history of Western civilization, the couple wrote *The Lessons of History*, which in many ways stands as their conclusion to their monumental series.[1] As is true of the work of so many historians, the Durants' opus is a product of its time and, therefore, runs the risk today of being dated, but I am loath to discount it because *The Story of Civilization* offers me a baseline against which change can be measured. The Durants made historical conclusions in 1968 based on the previous forty years of their research and writing; by comparing their ideas to mine in 2024, perhaps we can understand ourselves a bit better and shed light on how the past half century has changed our perception of the past. The Durants concluded, in part:

- "Man, not the earth, makes civilization." In other words, environmental factors are not the primary drivers in human history.

- "Life is competition." "Life is selection." "Life must breed." The Durants hold that these Darwinian ideas are central to the development of human civilization.

- "A knowledge of history may teach us that civilization is a co-operative product, that nearly all people have contributed to it; it is our common heritage and debt." "It is not race that makes the civilization, it is the civilization that makes people."

- "The conservative who resists change is as valuable as the radical who proposes it...out

---

[1] The Durants published an eleventh volume, *The Age of Napoleon*, in 1975.

i

of this tension, as out of the strife of the sexes and the classes, comes a creative tensile strength…and movement of the whole."

- "History as usually written…is quite different from history as usually lived."

- "Religion has many lives, and a habit of resurrection." "As long as there is poverty there will be gods."

- "The concentration of wealth is natural and inevitable, and is periodically alleviated by violent or peaceable partial redistribution."

- "The fear of capitalism has compelled socialism to widen freedom, and the fear of socialism has compelled capitalism to increase equality."

- "Democracy is the most difficult of all forms of government since it requires the widest spread of intelligence." "The road to dictatorship will be open to any man who can persuasively promise security to all."

- "War is one of the constants of history…Peace is an unstable equilibrium."

- "Nations die."

I think that's an impressive list—one that was supported with evidence taken from antiquity to the early nineteenth century and from around the world. The Durants weighed the historical evidence they had and developed meaningful conclusions from what they found. I have attempted to do the same thing with *Forgotten Capitals*. There are a few things to note, however: 1) my conclusions differ from those of the Durants; 2) my conclusions are not the only ones that might be taken from the experience these nine cities provide; and 3) a selection of different cities would naturally lead to additional historical lessons. Circumstances matter. Like the Durants, I simply let the specifics I found lead me to universalities, for as I tell my students, historians do not begin with the hypothesis. Instead, we begin with the story.

To forget is to fail to recall, to cease noticing, or to disregard intentionally. *Forgotten Capitals* is about nine cities that fall into one of these three categories. In all cases, these cities are places that symbolized a region's political, economic, and cultural tensions at a particular moment in time. Significantly, none of the capitals are ghost towns or the sites of ancient ruins today. Being forgotten does not mean dead. Instead, these cities remain locally vital. They retain life and meaning. All that has changed is their national and international importance, and, therefore, most people's knowledge of them.

Forgotten Capitals is organized like an accordion, pulling and pushing between the broad and the specific. Some parts of each chapter showcase why details matter in the study of history, while other parts demonstrate why those details need to be put into a meaningful framework. To only use a broad brush risks losing too much nuance. To only focus on the particulars is to become lost in the forest. I hope that my accordion allows readers to appreciate why both aspects of historical inquiry are worthwhile.

Each chapter follows the same six-part structure:

1. **An Introduction:** I begin each chapter with a description of a particular event that took place in or near the forgotten capital. Like an amuse-bouche at a great restaurant, this section's goal is simply to set the scene and whet the appetite for more.

2. **A Little Historical Context:** Because history is a continuum, the past always influences the present. Each chapter's second section seeks to put the event described in the introduction into a broader historical context and account for the continuum. To provide the context, I discuss the relevant political, economic, social, cultural, religious, and environmental circumstances that surrounded the event. My aim here is to create meaning by providing the reader with a sufficient orientation to the situation.

3. **The City in a Particular Year:** In his book *Scattered Among the Peoples: the Jewish Diaspora in Twelve Portraits* (2003), Allan Levin explained the history of European Jews by focusing on their experiences in twelve cities in twelve different years. What emerges in this brilliantly-conceived work is a chronicle that melds individual stories and general patterns. Because I appreciated this work and his device so much, I have borrowed from it. The focal point of each chapter is a discussion of the capital city and its people at a particular moment in time. This allows me, like Levin, to highlight how and why the city is symbolic for a particular era.

4. **A Short Postscript:** A brief epilogue then follows, outlining the noteworthy events that occurred in the city in subsequent years. One of the goals of this section is to explain how and why the city lost its status as an important center of power, or why it has been ignored by so many.

5. **What the Capital Teaches:** After forty years of teaching American, European, and World History, I have been able to see some of the general patterns that have defined the human experience. The final section of *Forgotten Capitals* aspires to articulate the greater historical conclusions that can be drawn from the specifics presented in sections one and three. Why does the experience of this capital matter? What does it teach us about the past and about ourselves? Which of the Durants' conclusions still hold true?

6. **A Bibliography:** The bibliography presents a curated list of the most important books and articles I read and consulted while researching the chapter. Hopefully, this will prove more useful than a complete bibliography for those who want to learn more about a particular topic or who are curious about what influenced me. Listing every source, including websites that may no longer exist, simply threatened to overwhelm. I have also decided not to burden the reader with formal citations throughout the text. Instead, I am asking readers to trust that because I am a librarian and a teacher, I have used all of my sources honorably and with precision. My students would expect no less.

CHAPTER 1

JOLO
SULU SULTANATE

The British trading station on Balambangan Island was set back from the beach by 60 yards and surrounded by a protective wood stockade with nine guns and thick undergrowth. Inside the stockade, officers' quarters, barracks for Sepoy[2] guards, the fort's magazine, and an office formed a loose quadrangle. Spread some three miles along the beach in front of the station, there were warehouses, four residences, and segregated housing for Chinese traders. This island outpost, which was located some twelve miles off the northernmost point of Borneo, had existed peacefully for twelve years, but on the evening of February 25, 1775, men from Jolo, who were known as the Tausug,[3] surrounded the fort and prepared for a morning attack of revenge.

At dawn, a British sentry fired a gun to announce the change of watch and the start of another day. Some of the Sepoys went to bed, while others began their morning ablutions. Ten minutes later, a house near the beach was set afire; this was the signal for the Tausug to attack the fort. Their assault came with great speed and exceptional execution. Within minutes, those coming from the beach had successfully stormed the stockade, seized control of the nine guns, and fired upon the beach houses. Those who had spent the night hiding in the fort's surrounding thicket successfully killed the guards who were stationed at the magazine's door and captured the guns within. The officers, the Sepoys, and station chief John Herbert quickly realized the situation was hopeless and fled to the beach to board small vessels to take them to ships waiting offshore. As they sailed for safer waters, all they could see was thick smoke rising from the tropical island. Not only had the Sulu Sultanate protected its honor against the mighty British Empire on Balambangan, but it had acquired such a trove of weaponry, bullion, and opium in the process that Jolo would soon become the most powerful trading center in Southeast Asia.

---

[2] A "Sepoy " was a soldier from the Indian subcontinent serving in the British or another European army.
[3] The Tausug or "the people of the current" are still a major ethnic group in the Sulu Sea region today. Alternate spellings of the term include Taosug, Taosung, and Tausung.

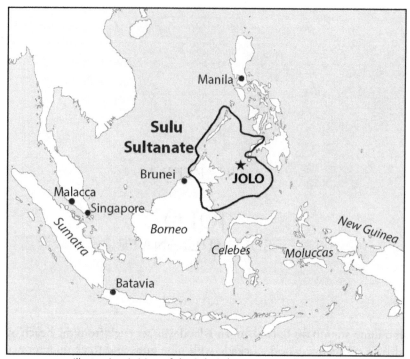

Illustration 1: Map of the Sulu Sultanate, c. 1775.

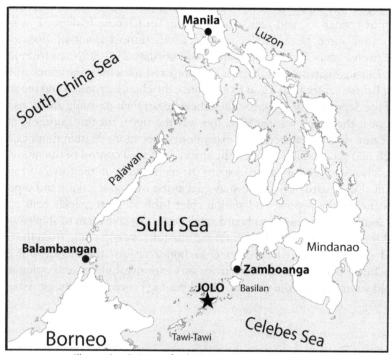

Illustration 2: Map of Sulu Sea Region, c. 1775.

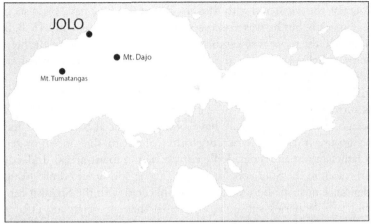

Illustration 3: Map of Jolo island, showing the location of Jolo town.

A Little Historical Context

The Sulu Sultanate was founded in the 1450s by Sharif ul-Hashim, who arrived on Jolo and married the daughter of a Malaysian prince, Rajah Baginda. Both men were Muslim refugees from Sumatra, and both needed each other to lay claim to legitimate political and spiritual authority. Their alliance set the pattern for how the maritime state would be governed for the next four centuries. Sulu's sultan may have stood at the apex of the society, but he did not reign

Illustration 4: Mosque on Jolo, c. 1840.

as an absolute monarch or as a mullah. Instead, the sultan regularly consulted with an assembly of Jolo's aristocracy, the *datus*, and with Muslim clerics. He may have been seen as one of God's representatives on earth, but he was also recognized to be fallible. Until 1578, Sulu's sultans also had to pay homage to the more well-established and powerful Sultan of Brunei. These traditions and understandings helped to make the Sulu court less elaborate in ritual and less formal in manner than others in the Malay world.

Although Islam had been introduced in the 14th century, conversion was slow and incomplete on the islands surrounding the Sulu Sea. Simple bamboo mosques may have dotted the islands of the archipelago, and sharia law may have been the official basis of the judicial system, but various ethnic groups practiced syncretic forms of Islam that incorporated other religious traditions. Polytheism remained decidedly entrenched in many areas. Indeed, the most visible change of conversion in the Sulu zone was that Tausug and other ethnic groups stopped eating pork. The religious landscape became more complicated with the Spanish capture of Manila in 1571, as Catholic missionaries subsequently began their proselytizing efforts throughout the Philippines.

As the Spanish pushed south, they increasingly came into conflict with Muslims ("the Moros"). The Spanish attacked the capital of the Sultanate of Brunei twice in the 1570s, and a Jesuit missionary with engineering expertise oversaw the construction of a major fortress at Zamboanga in 1635. This put the Spanish deep into the region Sulu's sultan and *datus* considered to be their territory. The Spanish subsequently attacked and briefly captured Jolo in 1638. As the

Illustration 5: This small fort near Zamboanga was typical of the structures the Spanish built in the Philippines in hopes of discouraging piracy.

seventeenth century progressed, however, the threat of a Chinese invasion of the Philippines and the ongoing consequences of the Eighty Years' War between the Dutch and the Spanish changed the political calculus in the Sulu region. The Spanish abandoned Zamboanga in 1669, and Moros and the Spanish began inching towards a mutually-beneficial accommodation. In 1736, Sultan Muhammad Alimud-Din I negotiated a commercial treaty with the Spanish and during the negotiations was accorded the honors of a foreign sovereign. Eight years later, he agreed to allow Jesuit missionaries to enter the sultanate and purchase land for the construction of a Catholic church. There were also agreements between Jolo and Manila to fight non-Muslim pirates from Borneo. Muslims in other parts of the Philippine archipelago did not reach such understandings with the Spanish colonizers.

Alimud-Din I's actions stirred considerable dissent amongst Jolo's *datus* and the Tausug of other classes. In 1748, Alimud-Din was deposed by his brother, Bantilan, and fled to Manila. While in Spanish hands, Alimud-Din converted to Catholicism and was baptized in 1750. Shortly thereafter, however, the Spanish learned that their friend in exile had been corresponding with numerous *datus*. They charged him with treason and quickly imprisoned him. When the British captured Manila in 1762 during the Seven Years' War, they found Alimud-Din in the dungeons of Manila's Fort Santiago. It was a discovery that once again changed the Sulu region's political and socio-economic patterns.

By the mid-eighteenth century, the British public was drinking tea in substantial quantities, usually with milk and sugar. In fact, tea had replaced ale as the preferred beverage with breakfast, and coffee and gin consumption dropped at other times of the day as a result of tea's ubiquitousness. A 1774 report stated, "Sugar is so generally in use, by the existence of tea, that even the poor wretches living in almshouses will not be without it." This popularity meant that the British East India Company coveted a trading center in southeast Asia that would facilitate its trade with China. It also sought a way to pay for the tea with a commodity that the Chinese wanted. By 1763, everything had fallen into place: the Seven Years War had come to an end, the British had determined that opium grown in India would sell well in China, and Alimud-Din had exchanged a minor, uninhabited island off the coast of Borneo, Balambangan, for British assistance in reclaiming his throne. Alimud-Din ruled for another decade, balancing the pro-British *datus* and pro-Spanish *datus* in the divided Sulu court.

In 1773, an aging Alimud-Din abdicated in favor of his son Mohammad Israel. Israel had largely grown up in Manila while his father was in prison. He was fluent in Spanish as a result of his education there, and had a sound understanding of Spanish customs and Catholic traditions. This helped to make him a strategic statesman as sultan, as he weighed British, Dutch, and Spanish interests in the region. What Israel soon concluded was that Alimud-Din's pro-British policy was ill-advised. Instead, Israel saw the British presence on Balambangan as a serious threat to Jolo's position as a trade center. The new sultan realized that the growing opium trade was quickly changing long-established business patterns, and that it was vital for Jolo to capitalize on opium traffic in order to retain its overall commercial position. To let Balambangan become the center of opium trade in southeast Asia was to risk the economic collapse of the sultanate.

In 1774, Israel's cousin, Teteng, was commissioned by Balambangan's station chief John Herbert to provide the necessary labor to harvest timber and construct houses on the island. When Teteng prepared to leave Balambangan before the job was completed, Herbert demanded that the aristocrat leave his slaves as collateral. Teteng saw this as an affront to his honor and protested, at which point Herbert disarmed Teteng and put him in stocks. After this humiliation in front of his entourage, Teteng vowed revenge. Upon his eventual return to Jolo, Teteng found Israel receptive and plans were made to remove the British from Sulu waters.

What Jolo gained from its conquest of Balambangan on February 25, 1775, in addition to the preservation of its trade position, was substantial: silver, ships, food, trade goods, and military stores, including 45 cannon, 228 rifles, 35 pistols, 45 swords, and 22,000 rounds of ammunition. Teteng offered these spoils and other items to Israel and the *datus*, who hailed Teteng for his exploits. Since the Tausug had not had access to large ordinance before the conquest of Balambangan, these gains were enough to shift the balance of power in the Sulu region, and Israel's sultanate became far more powerful than its traditional rivals on Mindanao.

Jolo c. 1775

Jolo is both an irregularly-shaped volcanic island, the second largest in a chain between Borneo and Mindanao, and the name of the island's principal port. The island is 37 miles long and is dominated by three peaks in its western half and two on its eastern half. The two highest of these, Mt. Tumatangas (2,661 feet) and Mt. Dajo (2,030 feet), give the island a dramatic profile when approached from the west. In the eighteenth century, these teak-forested peaks were separated from the coast by cultivated hills and plains, with the principal crops being tropical fruits, tapioca, coffee, cocoa, tobacco, sugar cane, taro, yams, and other vegetables, and livestock. Significantly, however, as a result of erratic rainfall and insufficient irrigable land, Jolo could not produce enough rice to feed its population. Instead, large quantities of rice were imported at considerable expense from the islands of Magindanao, Basilan, and Palawan.

To help offset these essential imports, Jolo's *datus* and merchants developed a complicated north-south and east-west trading system that was largely based upon food delicacies and luxury items for the Chinese market. First and foremost, there were tiny swallows' nests from Borneo, which were used in medicinal broths by the Chinese elite. Rare white nests were worth their weight in silver, but those with dark impurities still held sufficient value for them to be collected in large numbers. The resin in the bark of one of Borneo's giant trees[4] produced a purer camphor than was available elsewhere in Asia, and this was used by the Chinese as an anesthetic, an insect repellant, an itch reliever, and as an ingredient in perfumes. Other products were harvested throughout the Sulu region and brought to Jolo for resale and transport on Chinese junks. Sea cucumbers, which were in high demand in China, featured prominently in this trade. Due to the enormous variety in sea cucumber species, the Tausug were able to manipulate sale prices by limiting supplies and establishing a hierarchy based on color and difficulty of procurement. Prices quickly rose for the commodity. As today, shark fins and pearls were also valuable sea products, and mother-of-pearl became increasingly popular for use in furniture, cutlery, and jewelry in the late 18th and early 19th centuries. Because the Sulu region lacked sources of quality saltpeter, guns and gunpowder also quickly found a market in Jolo. And, given the number of vessels bound for China, opium also had a prominent place. Finally, because the Dutch barred Chinese junks from ports in Celebes and the Moluccas, Jolo became an important conduit between the Dutch East Indies and China. In exchange for the bird nests, sea slugs, mother of pearl, opium, sandalwood, and spices, junks sailed from China full of manufactured items, such as porcelain, lacquerware, textiles, and everyday metal goods, such as axe blades, pots and pans, cutlery, knives, and needles. Textiles were especially important to this trade because the tradition of local weaving on Jolo was quickly disappearing. Silk and cotton goods, particularly muslin and calico, were popular items for local customers in Jolo's markets as a result.

The profits made through Jolo's trade were exceptional, despite significant overhead costs. Chinese merchants regularly sold Sulu goods in China with a 100% profit, while their combined roundtrip imports and exports could earn them as much as a 300% profit. This was particularly impressive since these profit margins came after the sultan had taken his automatic 10% quota of all foreign commerce as port owner, after the Chinese had written off the debts *datus* often failed to honor, and after the exorbitant bribes Chinese bureaucrats expected in return for *Illustration 6: Harbor of Amoy, China, 1843. Amoy was a major port for the importation of Southeast Asian goods that passed through Jolo. Today, Amoy is the city of Xiamen.*

permission to unload arriving goods. There was simply that much money to be made in a trade that brought China and the islands of Southeast Asia together.

What generated these high profits and what made all of this trade possible was slavery. Slaves were the ones who risked life and limb, climbing Borneo's cliffs with rattan ropes to obtain bird nests and diving great depths for pearls and sea cucumbers. They were the ones who packed and hauled shipping barrels in Sulu Sea ports, who plowed fields and sowed rice, and who served as concubines. Perhaps more surprisingly, enslaved people also worked as bureaucrats, scribes, and merchants for the largely illiterate Tausug elite. One of the reasons for this breath of jobs was

---

[4] The tree is the *Dryobalanops camphora*, which can grow to 250 feet tall.

Illustration 7 and 8: Jolo harbor c. 1838, (top), and "A Visit to the Sultan of Jolo," c. 1838 (bottom).

that there were two types of slaves within the Sulu Sultanate: chattel slaves (men and women who had been kidnapped from other islands or the children of these captives), and debt slaves (people who owed money to the Tausug or people who had been heavily fined for committing a crime like adultery or theft). While some of the slavery in the Sultanate was akin to a seasonal obligation, like a *corvée*, it is also clear that societal power and social standing on Jolo was directly tied to the number of slaves held. Indeed, the elite's desire to improve their social standing, combined with the pressures of a rapidly expanding economy, meant that the number of slaves

7

sold in Jolo's slave markets increased substantially in the late 18th and early 19th centuries. In fact, while upwards of 3,000 people were annually kidnapped and brought to Jolo for sale in the late 18th century, there were as many as 6,000 people being abducted annually and sold on Jolo by 1845. Young women typically brought the highest prices at auction, depending on their health and ethnicity.

Much of this human trafficking was conducted by the Iranun people from southern Mindanao and the Samal people from the islands of Tawi-Tawi. Maritime raiding, kidnapping, and enslavement had existed for centuries in Southeast Asia, but until the 1760s these pursuits had been conducted on a small scale by independent operators, acting largely on their own initiative. By the time Israel had become sultan, however, the Iranun and Samal peoples had become specialist traders, who travelled with the monsoons to islands as distant as Luzon in the north, Sumatra in the south, New Guinea in the east, and the Malay Peninsula in the west to obtain slaves for Jolo's market. By 1800, there were at least 15,000 Iranun sea raiders operating in the region, and their coordinated efforts meant that some coastal areas saw a population decline of 40% as a result.

In January 1776, British East India Company captain Thomas Forrest visited Jolo. He commented at some length about the society, stating that both men and women "are fond of gaming," ride horses, "dress gaily" in white waistcoats, and annually share the "custom of bathing in the sea...decently covered." He also noted that the "Sooloos [sic] are fond of European music," that Sultan Israel and his niece could "dance a tolerable minuet," and that Jolo's "high priest" was a Turk who had "travelled a good deal in Europe," knew history, and was a very intelligent man." These observations help illustrate the ways in which Jolo's vigorous trade created memorable intercontinental cultural exchanges as well as economic ones. Not that these interactions were always positive: Forrest repeatedly condemned the *datus* as "haughty lords" whose "tyrannical manner" subjected "married women, unmarried women, and children" to slavery. He even took exception to the ways in which the *datus* treated the Chinese: "The Chinese must gain handsomely by their trade...else they would not put up with the rough usage they sometimes receive from the sturdy barons, the Datoos [sic]," Forrest wrote. Forrest also noted Sultan Israel's skill as leader as he maintained peace on the island that teamed with people from around the world. Later in 1776, for example, a gambling dispute broke out between a Tausug man and a Buginese man from Celebes. The situation quickly escalated with a shot being fired and a large crowd of "Sooloo" and about forty "Buggess" gathering in response, ready to fight. The Buginese drew their loaded blunderbusses as "the Sooloos stood opposite near them with uplifted lances....Had one blunderbuss gone off amongst the crowd, there would have been much bloodshed...but by the happy interposition of Sultan Israel... the affair went no further."

Unfortunately, Israel proved unable to reach a similar arrangement with the *datus* in his deeply divided court. On one side stood a pro-British faction, which was led by Israel's cousin, Alimud-Din II. This faction believed that the British could help the various Muslim sultanates in the southern Philippines resist Spain's long-standing efforts to convert Muslims, stop piracy, and control the Sulu Sea. On the other side stood a pro-Spanish faction led by Israel himself. This faction believed a peaceful accommodation could be found with the Spanish and that the real threat to Jolo was the way the British efforts in the region might disrupt established trading patterns. In 1774, the Spanish governor general in Manila responded to Israel's diplomatic overtures by sending Colonel Juan Cencelli and a fleet to Jolo to establish friendly relations with Israel, reconnoiter the British station on Balambangan, and harass Iranun pirates. Unfortunately for Israel, Cencelli disobeyed the orders he had been given, for he believed that Spain and the Sulu Sultanate were irreconcilable enemies. When Cencelli arrived at Jolo with his fleet, he purposefully offended the Tausug by not offering them the customary salutes. Israel and his faction were seriously weakened as a result of Cencelli's visit. Plotting against him began, and three years after the raid on Balambangan Island, Alimud-Din II loyalists struck by poisoning

Israel. Alimud-Din II became Jolo's new sultan in 1778. This succession proved to be an unlucky turn of events for the Sulu Sultanate, for Alimud-Din II and his successors lacked Israel's diplomatic sophistication and failed to adjust to rapidly changing circumstances. Israel's assassination precipitated Jolo's slow decline.

A Short Postscript

In the 1770s, French naturalist Pierre Sonnerat noted how Jolo's geographical position, standing almost as "a line of demarcation between the Philippines and the Moluccas," made it an important regional entrepot and a place where the European powers should curry favor. This geographic uniqueness ended in 1819, when Sir Thomas Stamford Raffles founded British Singapore. He secured legal rights to the sparsely-inhabited island by recognizing one of two claimants to the throne of a local sultanate: in exchange for the recognition and an annual monetary tribute, the Raffles and the English East India Company obtained the right to establish a new trading center for the region. What really distinguished Singapore from Jolo, Malacca, and Batavia, however, was that it was a tariff-free port. By putting a clear emphasis on free trade and by imposing laws consistently, Singapore quickly attracted settlers, including private Chinese traders and local merchants from the Dutch East Indies, who were eager to circumvent strict Dutch trade regulations. By 1824, over eleven thousand people resided in Singapore, slavery had been outlawed, and gambling and the opium trade were carefully regulated. Singapore officially became a British crown colony in 1867. By this point, it was a multicultural community—a place where Malays, Indians, Chinese, Arabs, and Europeans gathered to try to take advantage of expanding markets.

Partly as a result of Singapore's rise, Spain's ambitions for controlling the southern islands of

Illustration 9: Baltasar Giraudier, "Expedición a Joló," 1876. This etching depicts the Spanish conquest of Jolo with its technological and numerical superiority.

the Philippine archipelago grew. They looked to block British expansion in Southeast Asia and put an end to piracy in the region. In 1851, a Spanish flotilla of steam-powered ships easily destroyed a Tausug fleet of sail-powered prahus and occupied Jolo. The sultan was forced to sign a treaty which surrendered considerable sovereignty, but because the Spanish failed to establish a permanent garrison in Jolo, the treaty's terms were not effectively enforced. Therefore, it wasn't until 1876 that the Sulu Sultanate's demise finally came. That February, Spain sent a fleet of over 30 ships and 9,000 troops to attack Jolo. This mostly Filipino force quickly overwhelmed the Tausug as a result of their superior military technology. The Spanish then built a fort, encircled the city with a stone wall, and proceeded to destroy enemy strongholds on nearby islands. Officially, the Sulu Sultanate was no more.

Spain retained possession of the region until 1899, when the Americans occupied Jolo during the Spanish-American War. The treaty between the Americans and "His Highness the Sultan of Jolo" proclaimed American sovereignty and stipulated that the United States could "occupy and control such points in the Archipelago of Jolo as public interest seem to demand," but the treaty also protected Islam, upheld existing property ownership, and honored the "rights and dignities of his Highness the Sultan and his Datos." In addition, monthly salaries were paid to the sultan and important members of the aristocracy. These terms, as well as the fact that slavery was not outlawed, left much of Jolo's social order intact, but the Americans' arrival did not end local resistance to foreign rule. In fact, there were repeated rebellions, uprisings, skirmishes and battles, for as Mark Twain noted, the Sulus were "bitter against us because we have been trying for eight years to take their liberties away." One of the more notorious incidents in the ongoing conflict came in March 1906, when a group of 600 Muslim men, women, and children hiding in Mt. Dajo's crater were slaughtered on the premise that the Tausug were, to use the words of American Congressmen Charles H. Grosvenor, an "utterly lawless, treacherous, and bloodthirsty gang, never amenable to law or civilization." The indiscriminate killing of women and children

Illustration 10: "After the Battle at Mount Dajo on Jolo Island, Sulu province. March 7, 1906."

produced an outcry of American ministers and an investigation by other members of Congress. They condemned the mass murders and accused the army of a cover-up, but little changed in the Philippines. In fact, conflicts persisted between the Americans and the Tausug until World War II.

Philippine independence came July 4, 1946, but the island nation lacked a sense of cohesion and national identity. The split between its Catholic north and its Muslim south continued to fester as it had since the Spanish arrival in the sixteenth century. In fact, the disconnect was so great that in the late 1960s ethnographers were able to report that for rural Tausug, "identification with the Philippine nation and its legal system is almost non-existent." After President Ferdinand Marcos declared martial law, terminated an amnesty program, and demanded the surrender of firearms by all Filipinos in 1972, what had been a low-level insurgency became a full-scale rebellion, led by Nur Misuari's Moro National Liberation Front (MNLF). Marcos quickly sent troops to Jolo to suppress it. The resulting battle in February 1974 burned Jolo to the ground. The devastation was so great that 50 years later the city was still trying to recover. One symbol of this delayed recovery is that the island's public library didn't reopen until 2023.

Jolo's destruction and subsequent isolation created an atmosphere that easily attracted Islamic extremists. Beginning in the 1990s, an Al-Qaeda-offshoot called Abu Sayyaf began fighting for an independent state in the islands that had once been the Sulu Sultanate. They took control of Jolo, kidnapped tourists in Malaysia and held them for ransom, and were responsible for the deadliest terrorist attack in Philippine history: the bombing of a *MS Superferry 14* in February 2004 that killed 116 passengers. A war of attrition between the Philippine army and the terrorists followed, and with the passage of time and the arrest of key leaders, Abu Sayyaf struggled to attract new, ardent followers. In January 2019, the small cadre of remaining Abu Sayyaf members was able to set off two explosions during a mass in Jolo's Catholic cathedral, killing twenty people and injuring over a hundred, but by 2023 the governor of Sulu province was able to declare that Jolo was free of Abu Sayyaf militants and that the island was open for tourism. The fact that the Philippine army paired its anti-terrorism efforts with reopening schools, building roads, and providing supplies and services to remote areas helped to undercut support for Abu Sayyaf substantially. Villagers on Jolo began to fly the Philippine flag for the first time. This is an important symbol, but it remains to be seen if the peace will last in an archipelago full of factions and divided loyalties.

What Jolo Teaches

Jolo's experience as a capital city illustrates a number of important lessons for students of history. The first is that cultural continuity is a more powerful historical force than politics. Nations, empires, and their leaders come and go with the passage of time, but elements of culture such as religion, language, and artistic tradition are what truly endure. On Jolo, this can be seen in a number of ways. Jolo hasn't had a presiding Islamic government in 150 years, but the faith remains the dominant force on the island. A three-day festival each August commemorates Islam's arrival in the Sulu region, well-known narrative folk songs proclaim the Tausug bravery and independence against foreign intervention, and alcohol is not sold on the island because of the Quran's ban. The recognized heir to the Sulu Sultanate, Muedzul Lail Tan Kiram, has won international awards, and pursues a major international law suit against Malaysia over the status of northeastern Borneo, but locally his role is that of a revered father figure.[5] His Majesty is regularly called upon to serve in a variety of ceremonial capacities, such as officiating events and opening mosques, but he does not rule in the way of his forefathers. In this sense, Muedzul Lail Tan Kiram too has become more important as an enduring cultural symbol than as a political force.

The pattern of cultural survival without a state can be seen elsewhere in world history. Judaism, for example, survived its diasporas for millennia without a political entity to support it. Similarly, Tibetan Buddhism persists even though the Dalai Lama had to flee his Tibetan theocracy in 1959. Today, there may be as many as 20 million speakers of Kurmanji (Northern Kurdish) even though there is no internationally recognized state of Kurdistan and there are nine hundred thousand Euskara speakers in the world even though there is no Basque Republic. As with Jolo, these examples illustrate the ways in which cultures and customs outlast the political entities that originally bore them.

Second, the recent history of Jolo illustrates the way in which ideologically-based organizations frequently struggle to maintain their original cohesion and identity. This is because with the passage of time founding leaders die, factions develop, and tactics necessarily shift in changing circumstances. The values which were once held dear and which once enjoyed a broad consensus within the group are altered, if not distorted, in the wake of failed missions, daily hardships, and new opportunities. This splintering may take a generation, which is why resistance movements are often seen as having an intractable persistence, but in the long run radical ideologies struggle to sustain their mission. They become corrupted.

This can be seen in what has happened to Abu Sayyaf between its founding in 1991 by Afghan veteran Abdurajak Janjalani and its collapse by 2023. Originally meant to be a Southeast Asian offshoot of Al-Qaeda, Abu Sayyaf sought to establish a puritanical Islamic state in the southern Philippines by violent means. It was willing to work with other radical Muslim groups in the Philippines and Indonesia, but sought to undermine peace negotiations between Manila and more moderate Islamic organizations. After Janjalani died in 1998, Abu Sayyaf split into three distinct factions, all of which devolved into groups more devoted to crime and profit than the original political cause. In the first two decades of this century, the Abu Sayyaf cells used violence, including kidnapping and the bombing of civilian targets, to spread fear and force people to accede to their demands, but the cells' actions no longer represented a jihad. The founding ideology was lost, taken over by selfishness and greed. From Daniel Ortega's Nicaragua to Robert Mugabe's Zimbabwe, from Xi Jinping's China to Hugo Chavez's Venezuela, similar fates have befallen revolutionary movements around the globe.

---

[5] In 1974, the Philippines officially recognized the Sultanate of Sulu as the "legitimate claimant to the historical territories of the Republic of the Philippines" and helped install Muedzul-Lail Tan Kiram's father to the Sulu throne, but the Philippine government has not formally recognized the current sultan.

Curated Bibliography for Chapter 1

Abinales, Patricio N. and Donna J. Amoroso. *State and Society in the Philippines.* (2nd Ed.) Lanham, MD: Rowman & Littlefield, 2017.

Abshire, Jean E. *The History of Singapore.* Santa Barbara, CA: ABC-CLIO, 2011.

Abuza, Zachary, *Balik-Terrorism: The Return of the Abu Sayyaf.* Carlisle, PA: Strategic Studies Institute/Army War College, 2005.

Andaya, Barbara Watson and Leonard Y. Andaya, *An Early Modern History of Southeast Asia.* Cambridge, UK: Cambridge University Press, 2015.

Asreemoro. *Tausug and the Sulu Sultanate.* Kuala Lumpur, Malaysia: Saba Islamic Media, 2008.

Arce, Wilfredo F., Richard L. Stone and Nena B. Eslao. "Social Organization of the Muslim Peoples of Sulu." *Philippine Studies*, Vol. 11, No. 2 (April 1963). JSTOR.

Barrows, David P. *History of the Philippines.* Yonkers-on-Hudson, NY: World Book Company, 1926. HathiTrust.

Battle of Mt. Dajo Again Before House." *The Washington Post.* March 19, 1906, 1. ProQuest Historical Newspapers.

"Battle of Mt. Dajo Again Before House: Gen. Grosvenor Defends Action Of Troops In Killing Moros. Williams Replies Sharply Gen. Wood Cables Twice More And Secretary Taft Will Defend Him Before Committee." *New York Times.* March 20, 1906, 2. ProQuest Historical Newspapers.

Bourne, Edward Gaylord. *The Philippine Islands, 1493-1898, Volume 51, 1801-1840.* Emma Helen Blair (ed.). Cleveland, OH: The Arthur H. Clark Company, 1907. Project Gutenberg.

Bowring, Philip. *Empire of the Winds; The Global Role of Asia's Great Archipelago.* New York: I.B. Tauris, 2019.

Burbidge, F. W. *The Gardens of the Sun: A Naturalists Journal on the Mountains and in the Forests and Swamps of Borneo and the Sulu Archipelago.* London: John Murray, 1880. Project Gutenberg.

Burke, Jason. *Al-Qaeda: Casting the Shadow of Terror.* New York: I. B. Tauris, 2003.

Forrest, Thomas. *A Voyage of New Guinea and the Moluccas from Balambangan: Including an Account of Magindano, Sooloo and other Islands.* Dublin, Ireland: 1779.

Francia, Luis H. *History of the Philippines.* New York: Overlook Press, 2014.

Gommans, Jos and Ariel Lopez. *Philippine Confluence : Iberian, Chinese and Islamic Currents, C. 1500-1800.* Leiden: Leiden University Press, 2020.

Gray, John. "Killing Brings Its Own Rewards." *New Statesman*, Vol. 145, No. 5325 (2016). 65-68.

Greenway, H. D. S. "Guerrilla War Defies Solution In Philippines." *The Washington Post.* July 6, 1975. ProQuest Historical Newspapers.

Hodgson, Barbara. *Opium: A Portrait of the Heavenly Demon.* San Francisco: Chronicle Books, 1999.

Ingilan, Sajed S. "Tausug's Identity in Parang Sabil: a Critical Discourse Analysis," *CMU Journal of Science*, Vol. 22, No. 1 (January-December 2018). EBSCOhost.

Karnow, Stanley, *In Our Image: America's Empire in the Philippines.* New York: Ballantine Books, 1990.

Kiefer, Thomas M. "Institutionalized Friendship and Warfare Among the Tausug of Jolo." *Ethnology.* Vol. 7, No. 3 (July 1968). JSTOR.

Mahinay, Krizza Janica. "Writing Malaysia and the Moro Identity; An Analysis of the Moro National Liberation Front's Foreign Policy," *Insight Turkey.* Vol. 22, No. 1 (Winter 2020). Gale General OneFile.

Orosa, Sixto Y. *The Sulu Archipelago and Its People.* Yonkers-on-Hudson, New York: World Book Company, 1931.

"Parkhurst on Jolo Battle: Slaughter of Moros in Crater Ghastly to Look Upon. Prefers To Accept President's Message to Wood as an Official Rather than Personal Expression." *The Washington Post.* March 19, 1906, 1. ProQuest Historical Newspapers.

Parker, Matthew. *The Sugar Barons: Family, Corruption, Empire and War in the West Indies.* New York: Walker and Company, 2011.

Patail, Abdul Gani. *Putting to Rest: the Claim to Sabah by the Self-Proclaimed Sultanate of Sulu.* Kuala Lumpur, Malaysia: Institute Terjemahan and Buku Malaysia Berhad, 2013.

"Philippines Politics: Lasting Peace in the South Elusive after Jolo Bombing." *Economist Intelligence Unit: Country Views Wire.* January 30, 2019. Gale General OneFile.

Saberi, Helen. *Tea: A Global History.* London: Reaktion Books, 2010.

Saleeby, Najeeb M. *The History of Sulu.* Manila: Bureau of Public Printing, 1908. Project Gutenberg.

Sawyer, Frederic H. *The Inhabitants of the Philippines*. New York: Charles Scribner's Sons, 1900.

Scull, Nicolas C, Othman Alkhadher and Salman Alawadi. "Why People Join Terrorist Groups in Kuwait: A Qualitative Examination." *Political Psychology*. Vol. 41, No. 2 (April 2020). EBSCOhost.

Sinclair, Tengku Datu Henry W. *British Borneo: Annexation and Cessions, 1578-2012: the Formation of Brunei, Felicia, Labuan, Sarawak, Ellena, Elopura, Sabah, and Malaysia and the Claims of the Sultanate of Sulu.* Kota Kinabalu, Malaysia: Henry W. Sinclair, 2013.

Sonnerat, Pierre M. *Voyage aux Indes Orientales et à la Chine, fait par ordre du roi, depuisjusqu'en 1781.* Paris, L'auteur, 1782. Library of Congress. https://www.loc.gov/item/04029260/

Southeast Asian Port and Polity. Kathirithamby-Wells and John Villiers (eds.). Singapore: Singapore University Press, 1990.

Steinberg, David Joel Steinberg. *In Search of Southeast Asia: A Modern History.* Honolulu: University of Hawaii Press, 1987.

Sutherland, Heather. "The Sulu Zone Revisited." *Journal of Southeast Asian Studies*. 35 (1) (2004).

Sulu Studies 1. Gerard Rixham (ed.). Jolo, Sulu: Notre Dame of Jolo College. 1972.

Tagliacozzo, Eric. "A Necklace of Fins: Maritime Goods Trading in Maritime Southeast Asia, 1780-1860." *International Journal of Asian Studies*. 1.1 (2004).

"Treaty With Jolo's Sultan: Agreement to Assume Sovereignty, Made By Gen. Bates, Is Now Before the Senate. Chasing Aguinaldo Through The Clouds." *New York Times*. December 14, 1899, ProQuest Historical Newspapers.

Tremmel-Werner, Birgit. "Persistent Piracy in Philippines Water: Metropolitan Discourses about Chinese, Dutch, Japanese, and Moro Coastal Threats, 1570-1800." *Piracy in World History*. Stefan Eklöf Amirell, Bruce Buchan and Hans Hägerdal (eds.). Amsterdam: Amsterdam University Press, 2021. JSTOR.

Twain, Mark. *The Autobiography of Mark Twain*. Berkeley, CA: University of California Press, 2012.

Warren, James Francis. "The Port of Jolo and the Sulu Zone Slave Trade: An 1845 Report," *The Journal of Sophia Asian Studies*, 25, Murdoch University. https://resarchportal.murdoch.edu.au

Warren, James Francis. *The Sulu Zone 1768-1898: The Dynamics of External Trade, Slavery, and Ethnicity in the Transformation of a Southeast Asian Maritime State.* 2nd ed. Singapore: National University of Singapore, 2007.

Warren, Jim. "Balambangan and the Rise of the Sulu Sultanate, 1772-1775." *Journal of the Malaysian Branch of the Royal Asiatic Society*, Vol. 50, No. 1 (1977), JSTOR.

Williams, Lea E.. *Southeast Asia: A History*. New York: Oxford University Press, 1976.

Woo, Sau Pinn et al. "The Distribution and Diversity of Sea Cucumbers in the Coral Reefs of the South China Sea, Sulu Sea and Sulawesi Sea." *Deep Sea Research Part II: Topical Studies in Oceanography*. Volume 96, (November 2013). ScienceDirect.

Yabes, Criselda. "Creating Sulu: In Search of Policy Coalitions in the Conflict-Ridden Island." *Southeast Asian Studies*. Vol. 10, No. 2 (August 2021). DOI: 10.20495/seas.10.2_295

CHAPTER 2

QUETZALTENANGO
LOS ALTOS

On June 5, 1837, a British merchant working in Guatemala wrote a letter to a botany professor at the University of Glasgow. The purpose of George Ure Skinner's letter to William Jackson Hooker was to explain why he had not been able to collect the cacti specimens he had pledged to obtain. Skinner explained, "Dreadfully have we suffered and are suffering from the Cholera here—and all my plans have been completely upset, [for] it is impossible for me to comply with my promise." In an effort to compensate for the delay, Skinner described the 40 specimens of ferns he had been able to collect before cholera arrived in Guatemala, and he included drawings of a "splendid" orchid specimen and a "new species of fuchsia." Skinner enclosed two resplendent quetzals, the stunning bird from the cloud forest of the Guatemalan Highlands. Surely, the sacred bird of the ancient Maya, with its distinctive green, blue, and red plumage and 35-inch tail, might allay Hooker's frustration and not jeopardize the contract.

Skinner was not exaggerating about the public health situation in Guatemala. In fact, much of the world experienced a cholera pandemic in the 1830s as the bacterial disease spread to cities as disparate as Cairo and Canton, Montreal and Moscow, Paris and Perth. When New York, Havana, and Mexico City also succumbed, adding to the world's death toll, nervousness grew in Guatemala. Its Liberal government acted as best it could, even though no one in the 1830s understood how cholera was spread: it imposed quarantines, stockpiled medical supplies, closed the border with Mexico, improved sanitation, banned liquor sales, and prohibited burials inside churches. Fruit, chilis, peppers, coffee, and wild game were also proscribed in the belief that they made the body more susceptible to infection. Still, the disease came, with Guatemala's first case being reported on March 8, 1837. Even then, residents of Quetzaltenango, an important regional trading center in the Highlands, had been reassured by their doctors that the region's pure air, moderate temperatures, and clean streets would protect them from the disease. Because *vibrio cholerae* can live on food, clothing, and dead bodies for weeks, however, there were too many conduits for transmission. The city's first case was reported in June and by the end of July the disease had killed 161 Quetzaltecos. They became some of the 12,000 Guatemalans who died of cholera that year.

In February 1839, Skinner wrote another letter to Hooker, reporting that he had recently returned from Quetzaltenango and that he had collected a variety of specimens, including acorns, bulbs, cacti, ferns, fir cones, maize, and orchids during his journey. Interestingly, in his letter there is no mention of cholera, or that the city had recently become the capital of a self-declared independent state, or that the city's Indian elite had asked the Guatemalan army to reconquer it.

Illustration 11 and 12: These watercolors by unknown artists poke fun at the abundance of dubious remedies, protections, and advice that people adopted during the cholera epidemic of 1832.

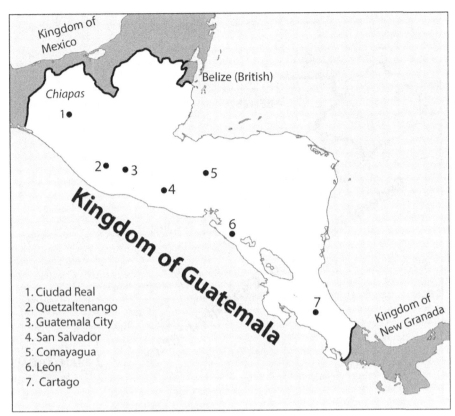

Illustration 13: Map of the Kingdom of Guatemala, c. 1800.

Illustration 14: Map of Guatemala in 1812.

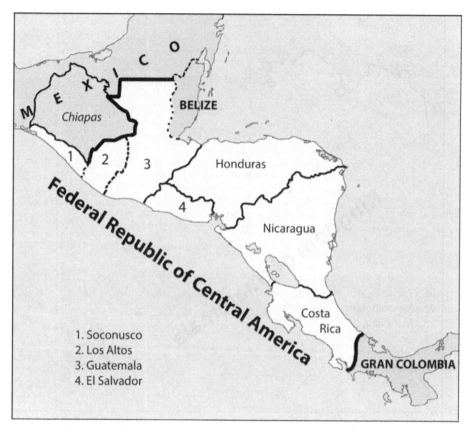

Illustration 15: Map of the Federal Republic of Central America, c. 1838.

1. Soconusco
2. Los Altos
3. Guatemala
4. El Salvador

Illustration 16: Map of Los Altos, c. 1838.

A Little Historical Context

The K'iche' (Quiché) are a Maya subgroup with a distinct language, who in the fifteenth century entered the fertile Highland valley where Quetzaltenango stands today. They quickly subjugated the local residents and named their major settlement Xelajú, meaning "under the ten [volcanic mountains that surround the city]." In 1524, a Spanish army of 400 men, led by Pedro de Alvarado and supported by as many as 20,000 Mexican allies, invaded the valley. Thanks to their technological superiority, as well as the inability of the K'iche' to secure alliances with other Maya groups, the Spanish quickly defeated the K'iche' in battle and then imposed their will upon the region. This included renaming Xelajú the "place of the quetzals" (Quetzaltenango), and placing the K'iche' in a forced labor system known as an *encomienda*. When Alvarado died in 1541, Guatemala's land grants were reorganized by the Crown. Spain also placed the people in its New World colonies into two separate legal entities: the *república de españoles* and the *república de indios*. Indians could only live in the communities or *pueblos* assigned to them, such as Quetzaltenango. These *pueblos* had their own municipal councils and legal systems, but they did not have all of the same rights and privileges that Spanish cities and towns did. By the late seventeenth century, however, the K'iche' elite proved able to use their hereditary governmental system, and other aspects of Spanish law, to assert their ownership of almost half the land in Quetzaltenango's valley. Once the K'iche' elite had acquired this wealth and status, they became a notable conservative political force.

In 1770, the Quetzaltenango district's population was 79% Indian and 21% Ladino.[6] Just thirty years later, non-Indians were near if not the majority in the region, despite the fact that Quetzaltenango had been designated as a *república de indios*. The reason for the demographic shift was largely due to Ladino migration to the Highlands and increased intermarriage. The amplified Ladino presence had two important consequences. First, it promoted the development of Quetzaltenango as an important commercial emporium—one that facilitated trade between the Pacific coast and the Gulf of Mexico and between Mexico and Guatemala City. The town had also become a military base, an industrial center, and a religious seat with a Franciscan convent. Its post office, consulate, courts, and tax collection office were important institutions for the region. Second, the Ladino migration created significant tensions between the conservative, indigenous K'iche' elite and the reform-minded, mixed race Ladinos, who wanted increased political representation, laissez-faire economic policies, mass education, and circumscribing the role of the Catholic Church. The ways in which these tensions played out, especially in Quetzaltenango, would determine the course of Guatemala's experience for much of the nineteenth century.

The spark that triggered the battle between Liberals and Conservatives in Guatemala came from Europe. In March 1808, Napoleon invaded Spain, deposed Ferdinand VII, and put his brother Joseph on the Spanish throne; this prompted a national uprising that was quickly supported by British troops. There was also a call for a national assembly, known as a Cortes, to write a constitution. This body met in the port of Cádiz in September 1810 and included representatives from Spain's colonies. Quetzaltenango's representative to the Cortes was Father José Cleto Montiel, who advocated for clerical reform, land redistribution, improving Indian-

---

[6] The term "Ladino" meant different things to different people in different places at different times in Guatemala's history. It also remains a term upon which historians struggle to find agreement. In Quetzaltenango, "Ladino" came to refer to all those who were not Maya, whether they were *Peninsulares* (those born in Spain) or Creoles (Spaniards born in the Americas) or *Mestizos* (those of Spanish and Indian heritage) or Mulattos (those of Spanish and African heritage). "Ladino" was a term that had social, legal, economic, and cultural implications, but by the eighteenth century it commonly stood for someone who was Spanish-speaking, but of mixed background. In other words, Ladinos were inherently an amorphous group.

Ladino interactions, an end to liquor taxes, and greater local autonomy and authority. Some of these ideas found their way into the final document, which was presented to the public in March 1812. It made Spain a constitutional monarchy, abolished the Inquisition, established an independent judiciary, protected a free press, promoted freer trade, and made all non-enslaved men equal before the law. Most importantly for places like Quetzaltenango, it ended the separate designations for the *república de españoles* and the *república de indios*, as well as the legal distinctions between cities, towns, and villages. Instead, all communities were to be governed by elected city councils. The Cádiz Constitution also abolished the Indian tribute of labor service that had been an important part of the Spanish colonial experience since the early 16th century.

In much of Latin America, the reforms of 1812, Ferdinand VII's rejection of them once he regained his throne, and Mexico's decade of war with Spain prompted heated calls for independence. Guatemala, however, remained surprisingly calm. It wasn't until September 1821 that it finally declared independence, doing so with a ceremony that honored the same rituals Spanish officials used at their inaugurations. There was a public reading of the act of independence, followed by the taking of a loyalty oath to the new state, and the tossing of newly-minted coins into the crowd; this ceremony was repeated in communities throughout Guatemala, including Quetzaltenango. But these oaths did not hold, for just three months later, Guatemala accepted annexation and joined the Mexican Empire under the rule of emperor Agustín de Iturbide. Iturbide had been a successful general and diplomat, but once on the throne proved unable to hold a fractious country that stretched from Oregon to Panama together. He abdicated his throne in March 1823. In July, five of the Central American states—Costa Rica, El Salvador, Guatemala, Honduras, and Nicaragua—responded to the changed circumstances in Mexico by agreeing to form a new nation, the United Provinces of Central America. This was a compromise decision, one that split the difference between the fear of being dominated by Mexico and the fear of being ill-prepared to stand alone economically or militarily. Only in Chiapas was the mood different: it decided to remain part of Mexico.[7]

Illustration 17: Gold coin issued by the Republica del Centro de America (the Federal Republic of Central America), 1835. Note the five mountain peaks, representing Costa Rica, El Salvador, Guatemala, Honduras, and Nicaragua. Los Altos wanted to be a sixth peak.

---

[7] The coastal region of Soconusco was once part of Chiapas, but in the 1830s many of its elite wished to join the Central American federation instead of Mexico. Soconusco's political status remained disputed until 1882.

With the call for a convention to write a new constitution, Quetzaltenango saw an opportunity to assert itself. It wanted to lead the Highlands—Los Altos—and become a separate state within the federation, thereby asserting its autonomy from Guatemala City. It argued that the new nation should be seen as a republic of cities, which would honor the important Spanish legal tradition of the *pueblo*, and would allow for more local voice in the determination of the rules for participation in the federation. Cities were, after all, the ones who sent representatives to the National Constituent Assembly, not the states. Initially, this assembly expressed a willingness to create as many as eight states within the federation, but this move was thwarted by conservatives and Quetzaltenango's bid for recognition failed. The Federal Republic of Central America was proclaimed on November 22, 1824, based upon a constitution that blended the ones drafted in Cádiz in 1812 and in Philadelphia in 1787. It called for a rather weak executive, an indirectly-elected Supreme Court, and a unicameral federal Congress with the number of representatives determined by a state's population. There was also an executive council, called the Senate, which could veto legislation unless overridden by three-quarters of the members of Congress. The constitution also moved the national capital from Guatemala City to San Salvador, outlawed slavery, proclaimed Catholicism as the state religion, limited clerics' participation in government, and guaranteed individual liberties, including freedom of the press. But the document did not bind the states firmly together, resolve fundamental conflicts between mercantilist Conservatives and laissez faire Liberals, or overcome the forces of localism and popular resistance. This meant that the Federal Republic spent much of the late 1820s and the 1830s in civil war.

Quetzaltenango c. 1838

The dream of creating the state of Los Altos within the Federal Republic of Central America did not die. In fact, by the late 1830s, Quetzaltenango's Liberal Ladinos were particularly vocal about the need, demanding that they be allowed to develop their commercial interests without Guatemalan interference. They specifically wanted to build roads to a port on the Pacific coast, thereby ending the export trade monopoly Guatemala City's merchants enjoyed. As long as Quetzaltenango was part of Guatemala and as long as it was subjected to its trade restrictions, the Highland city could not develop and prosper, Liberals argued. Significantly, the K'iche' leadership did not concur. They opposed the creation of Los Altos because they saw Liberal policies as a threat to their cultural identity and power. They preferred the status quo, specifically fearing that any change would also bring increased taxation.

Tensions between Quetzaltenango's Liberal Ladinos and Conservative K'iche' Maya swelled in 1837 with the arrival of the cholera pandemic. The municipal government, dominated by Ladinos, quickly closed tanneries and pottery workshops, cut down fruit trees, forbade the eating of pork, restricted Indian trade, prohibited liquor sales, and banned public mourning rituals including parades carrying the dead. Regulations often fell harder on Indians than Ladinos: while all twenty-five Indian butchers in the city had their shops closed, three Ladino ones remained open. While these actions proved quite insufficient in fighting the still-misunderstood disease, they did succeed in alienating Indians and angering other Conservatives. When the government sought to purify urban wells with chemicals, Catholic priests told their congregations that the Liberals had poisoned their water and urged them to ignore the government's public health regulations. Quetzaltenango's K'iche' population was receptive to this message, believing that the epidemic was yet another attempt by Ladinos and Spaniards to eradicate their culture. And this wasn't far from the truth, for many Ladinos saw the cultural assimilation of Indians as their long-term societal goal. Quetzaltenango's Ladinos also sought to portray cholera as a disease of the backward poor—people who needed Ladino leadership to manage the crises and help the Indian community embrace change and progress. The creation of an independent state would facilitate this, they argued.

On February 2, 1838, Liberal leaders in Quetzaltenango formally seceded from Guatemala and proclaimed Los Altos as the sixth state in the Federal Republic of Central America. The independence celebrations included fireworks, bullfights, parades, and the singing of hymns of gratitude. Liberals in surrounding municipalities, such as Mazatenango, Retalhuleu, Sololá, and Totonicapán, quickly declared their support for the new state as well, and all agreed to sponsor new elections to select a governing junta. This gave the independence movement more legitimacy since it utilized the tradition of the *pueblo* as the basis of the political authority to create the new government. Ironically, however, the union Quetzaltenango wanted to join was barely clinging to life. Conservative-led Nicaragua seceded from the Federal Republic in late April 1838. A month later, on May 30, the Federal Congress recognized the states to be "sovereign, free, and independent bodies," essentially letting the member states go their own way.

Illustration 18: Coat of Arms of Los Altos, carved in stone on the grave of heroes in the Cemetery of Quetzaltenango, 2014. The bird with the long tail is a male quetzal, an animal which has long had a cultural significance for the Maya. The mountain is the Santa María Volcano outside of Quetzaltenango.

Quetzaltenango's Liberal leaders did not hesitate: the very next day, Los Altos declared itself to be an independent country. Its leaders organized a provisional junta, led by a respected Liberal jurist, Marcelo Molina. As Molina once said, Los Altos was "invoked by those who wanted reform, and longed for by the peoples who, groaning among the cruel fluctuations of anarchy, awaited her like the rainbow of the storm." Fueled by this spirit, a Constituent Assembly had written a constitution by December and elected Molina as head of state. For the rest of 1838 and through all of 1839, Los Altos was free to make its own decisions.

Unfortunately, these decisions were not always good ones. As they assessed new taxes, implemented tariffs, and imposed labor demands in order to build roads and bridges to link Quetzaltenango to the Pacific, Molina and the Liberals bred considerable resentment within the K'iche' population. Suddenly, all of the fears the K'iche' Maya had about a Liberal Highland state seemed to be coming true: the Liberal Ladinos were determined to further their own political and economic interests at Maya expense. Therefore, the K'iche' appealed to Conservatives in Guatemala City for help, but instead soon found themselves an unexpected champion. Rafael Carrera was an illiterate, itinerant farmer living in southern Guatemala in the early 1830s, but by the end of the decade, he was the leader of an Indian army. When Los Altos' troops joined Liberal forces from El Salvador and helped to defeat Carrera in December 1838, Quetzaltenango's Ladino leaders failed to foresee the consequences. Instead, they plunged ahead, signing a friendship treaty on August 10, 1839 with the Liberal-dominated government of El Salvador. The ceremony in Quetzaltenango gave Los Altos its first formal diplomatic recognition, but the treaty renewed tensions with Carrera, who after a complicated string of events had become the de facto leader of Guatemala. While he had implicitly accepted Highland independence for a year and a half, the new alliance antagonized Carrera by putting him in the position of having to fight a war on two fronts. Consequently, Carrera issued Los Altos an ultimatum in December 1839, demanding the return of the weapons he had been forced to surrender a year earlier. When Los Altos refused, Carrera began preparing for war. He called upon the K'iche' and other Indian groups in Los Altos to begin an insurgency against the Quetzaltenango's Liberal government. Then, on January 25, 1840, Carrera invaded Los Altos with a thousand men. His victory was so complete that within less than forty-eight hours, the Liberals had sued for peace. On January 29, Carrera entered Quetzaltenango to be greeted by a joyous crowd, who saw him as a liberator. Carrera told the crowd that he was "not in thirst of blood or riches" or there for his "personal enhancement." Rather, Carrera's purpose was to "destroy the barbaric oppression in which those calling themselves Liberal patriots have held you." The clergy was once again to be held in esteem, labor service was to be eliminated and taxes were to be reduced to "no more than is absolutely necessary." Most importantly, Los Altos was once again a part of Guatemala.

A Short Postscript

The Los Altos region remains distinct, apart from the rest of Guatemala in many ways. Even the hope for an independent state did not quietly fade away, for there have been a long series of rebellions and uprisings against the government in Guatemala City. The first came in March 1840, when Liberals hoped to take advantage of Carrera's campaign in El Salvador; they again declared Los Altos to be a sovereign nation. Carrera quickly returned to the Highlands and captured the eighteen Liberal leaders who led the second independence movement. They were summarily executed on Quetzaltenango's main plaza in order to leave a more lasting impression of Guatemala's control. Ten years later, after Liberals surprisingly won the national elections for a new legislative assembly and Carrera resigned from office, Quetzaltenango's leaders took

23

advantage of the transition: they declared Los Altos' independence on August 26, 1848. Their reasoning was that Los Altos' reincorporation into Guatemala in 1840 had been illegal since it had been forced upon them by an authority they did not recognize as legitimate. El Salvador again recognized Los Altos as a sovereign nation, which encouraged Guatemala's Liberal provisional head of state, Juan Antonio Martínez, to admit that Highland needs had not been met in the past but would be in the future, if only Los Altos would rejoin with Guatemala. This did not placate Quetzaltenango's Liberals, and they refused Martínez's appeal. Behaving like a Conservative, Martínez responded to rejection by sending in troops to Los Altos in October to restore order. Capturing Quetzaltenango was not difficult, but controlling other parts of the region proved impossible as rebelliousness continued to fester. In fact, it wasn't until January 1850, after yet another declaration of independence, that Los Altos had been pacified and had accepted the authority of the Guatemalan government.

Los Altos may not have achieved independence, but it came to dominate Guatemalan politics for much of the 19th century anyway. In 1871, Liberal coffee planters, led by Justo Rufino Barrios, seized power of the national government. These plantation owners promoted the privatization of land, which ended K'iche' subsistence farming and transformed Guatemala into an export-oriented economy. The needs of the coffee plantations came to dominate Guatemalan

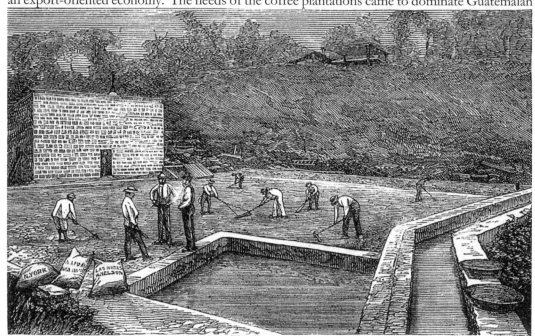

Illustration 19: "Work on a Coffee Plantation in Guatemala," 1877. The workers would have all been K'iche'.

policy. In 1877, in the aftermath of an Indian revolt, Ladino Liberals imposed a system of forced labor on the Maya in order to facilitate coffee production and its export; each *pueblo* became responsible for providing "the number of hands...asked for" by the owners for terms as long as a month." This infusion of forced labor meant that by 1880 coffee accounted for 92% of Guatemala's exports earnings. As the primary residence of the planting elite, Quetzaltenango benefited from this wealth. It grew substantially with the construction of new municipal buildings, grand boulevards, public gardens, schools, and penitentiaries. These institutions all spoke of Liberal accomplishments and possibilities for the future.

Unfortunately, that future was not a bright one for most of Los Altos' and Quetzaltenango's people. A major earthquake destroyed much of the capital on April 18, 1902, and, in 1930, heavy rains washed out the newly-constructed railroad to the Pacific that would have diversified the region's economic possibilities. Coffee remained king: between 1950 and 1964, the number of acres under cultivation rose 85%, and the amount of production rose 157%. This growth benefited the landed elite, but it did not make a material change in the lives of the Indian population. In fact, relations between Indians and Ladinos did not improve with the passage of time. By the mid-20th century, many Liberals were arguing that if Guatemala was to prosper, its Indian population should be forced to Westernize. As an editorial in a leading newspaper argued in 1945, "To strengthen the Indian culture is to condemn our country to eternal weakness, a perpetual cultural dualism." If Indians were not Westernized, then Guatemala's fate was to be "a kind of zoo for the entertainment of tourists." Such attitudes, as well as the CIA-sponsored *coup d'état* against Guatemala's democratically-elected president Jacobo Arbenz in June 1954, destabilized the country considerably. Guatemala experienced thirty-six years of civil war between 1960 and 1996 as the right-wing military battled leftist guerrillas. Successive governments met criticism with brutality, and Maya peasants were treated as insurgents even when they weren't. By the time a peace agreement was signed, *La Violencia* had destroyed 626 villages, taken 200,000 lives, and sent another 150,000 Guatemalans into exile. 83% of these victims were Maya. Today, Guatemala has the largest economy in Central America and a democracy, but almost half the population lives in poverty and two thirds of the population don't have faith in the integrity of national elections.

What Quetzaltenango Teaches

Quetzaltenango's history demonstrates the importance of three trends. The first is the power of localism, an affection or preference or loyalty for one's own region over that of a larger entity. This pattern might involve an allegiance to a city over a state or to a state over a nation. It can be seen in who roots for which teams in college football or the Premier League; in whether people first identify as being Americans or Californians, Chinese or Hong Kongese; and in the voting patterns of the United Kingdom's 2016 Brexit referendum, when Scotland voted quite differently than England. For Quetzaltenango, the power of localism became so intense that Los Altos declared its independence from Guatemala in 1838, 1840, 1844, 1848, and 1850. There were other significant protests in the region in 1786, 1820, 1821, and 1826 because of local concerns. Over a hundred years later, in 1957, Quetzaltenango refused a governmental decree to surrender all of its historical documents to the national archives. This too was an expression of local pride. These two centuries of dissent were driven by a complex and changing combination of economic, geographical, and social factors, but the striking through line is that the region continually maintained its desire to stand apart. Los Altos saw itself as being inherently different than the rest of Guatemala. Political entities from Catalan to Chechnya, from Greenland to Irian Jaya, from Tigray to Xinjiang, illustrate the same power of localism.

Secondly, there is often a correlation between the acquisition of wealth—whether its capital, property, or cryptocurrency—and political conservatism. This is inherent in the character of the capitalist system: those who have wealth want to keep it and those who have some usually want more. The K'iche' and other Indian elites in Guatemala demonstrate this phenomenon well, for once they had regained land ownership in the late seventeenth century, they became dependable allies of Guatemala's Conservatives. The K'iche' became determined to hold on to that which had once been taken away from them, and they remained deeply suspicious of Liberal land policies as a result. This was because it was vital for them to be able to perpetuate intergenerational wealth in order to preserve their community's identity. Conversely, those who lack wealth often seek change and support progressive politics as a result. Groups that have traditionally had difficulty passing wealth to heirs, such as American Blacks, often support income redistribution, reparations for past wrongs, and systemic change.

Third, diseases can be manipulated into powerful political weapons. This pattern can be seen throughout history, but one recent example involved the way in which Donald Trump used COVID-19 to rally his supporters. By denying the efficacy of vaccinations, by complaining about the overreach of government, and by feeding misinformation to the public, Trump was able to regain considerable national support in 2022 and 2023 in spite of his legal difficulties and encouragement of the January 6, 2021 Attack on the Capitol. This backing eventually propelled him to the Republican Party's nomination in 2024.[8] Similarly, the pattern of using disease to further political ends can be seen in the attempts to control venereal disease in India in the 19th century, sleeping sickness in colonial East Africa between 1880 and 1914, and tuberculosis amongst American Blacks in the first half of the 20th century. In all of these cases, disease became the means by which political goals—reelection, imperialism, or segregation—could be furthered and facilitated. In the case of Quetzaltenango, the 1837 cholera epidemic allowed Liberals to recast their long-simmering ethnic tensions with the K'iche' as a crisis that demanded immediate action. The Mayas quickly became a group whose traditions spread disease and whose habits put the health of the whole community at risk. Liberals portrayed them as intolerable obstacles to progress and modernity. By using the ways in which disease evokes fear, Quetzaltenango's Liberals were able to use the cholera outbreak to feed the call for an independent Los Altos.

---

[8] This book went to press just before the outcome of the 2024 American presidential election was known.

Curated Bibliography for Chapter 2

Anna, Timothy. "The Independence of Mexico and Central America." *Cambridge History of Latin America*. Vol. 3. Leslie Bethell (ed.). Cambridge, UK: Cambridge University Press, 1985.

Anna, Timothy. "The Rule of Agustin de Iturbide: A Reappraisal." *Journal of Latin American Studies*. Vol. 17, No. 1 (May 1985). JSTOR.

Bancroft, Hubert Howe. *Works of Hubert Howe Bancroft, History of Central America*. Vol. 8 (1801-1887). San Francisco, CA: The History Company, 1887.

Barua, Dhiman and William B. Greenough. *Cholera*. New York: Plenum Medical Book Co.,1992.

Carlsen, Robert S. *The War for the Heart and Soul of a Highland Maya Town*. Austin, TX: University of Texas, 2011.

Carey, David. *Our Elders Teach Us : Maya-Kaqchikel Historical Perspectives*. Tuscaloosa, AL: University of Alabama Press, 2001.

Chiozza, Giacomo and H. E. Goemans. *Leaders and International Conflict*. Cambridge, UK: Cambridge University Press, 2011.

Clegern, Wayne M. *Origins of Liberal Dictatorship in Guatemala, 1865-1873*. Niwot, CO: University of Colorado Press, 1994.

Coleman, William. *Cholera*. Philadelphia: Chelsea House, 2003.

Dym, Jordana. *From Sovereign Villages to Nation States: City, State and Federation in Central America, 1759-1839*. Albuquerque, NM: University of New Mexico Press, 2006.

Dym, Jordana. "'Our Pueblos, Fractions with No Central Unity': Municipal Sovereignty in Central America, 1808-1821." *Hispanic American Historical Review*. Vol. 86, No. 3 (August 2006). EBSCOhost.

Dym, Jordana. "Republic of Guatemala: Stitching Together a New Country." *New Countries: Capitalism, Revolutions, and Nations of the Americas, 1750-1870*. John Tutino (ed.). Durham, NC: Duke University Press, 2016. EBSCOhost.

El Salvador: A Country Study. Richard A. Haggerty (ed.). Washington, DC: Federal Research Division, Library of Congress. 1990.

Foster, Lynn V. *Brief History of Central America*. New York: Facts on File, 2000.

Gardner, Jeffery A. and Patricia Richards, "The Spatiality of Boundary Work." *Social Problems*. Vol. 64, No. 3 (August 2017). JSTOR.

Garrard, Virginia. *Protestantism in Guatemala: Living in the New Jerusalem*. Austin, TX: University of Texas Press, 1998.

Gonzalez, Alzate Jorge. "Pollack, Aaron (2008), Levantamiento K'iche' en Totonicapán, 1820: Los Lugares de las Políticas Subalternas." *Revista Liminar*. Vol. 8, No. 2 (Dec. 2010). EBSCOhost.

Grandin, Greg. "Archives in the Guatemalan Western Highlands." *Latin America Research Review*, Vol. 31, No. 1 (Winter 1996). Gale General OneFile.

Grandin, Greg and René Reeves. *The Blood of Guatemala: A History of Race and Nation*. Durham, NC: Duke University Press, 2000.

Gudmundson, Lowell and Héctor Lindo-Fuentes. *Central America, 1821-1871: Liberalism Before Reform*. Tuscaloosa, AL: University of Alabama Press, 1995.

Handy, Jim. "Democratizing What? Some Reflections on Nation, State, Ethnicity, Modernity, Commonality and Democracy in Guatemala." *Canadian Journal of Latin America and Caribbean Studies*. Vol. 27, No. 53 (2002). JSTOR.

Handy, Jim. *Gift of the Devil*. Boston, MA: South End Press, 1984.

Independence in Central America and Chiapas, 1770-1823. Aaron Pollock (ed.) Nancy T. Hancock (trans.). Norman, OK: Oklahoma University Press, 2009.

Jones, Oakah L. *Guatemala in the Spanish Colonial Period*. Norman, OK: Oklahoma University Press, 1994.

Komisaruk, Catherine. "All in a Day's Walk? The Gendered Geography of Native Migration in Colonial Chiapas and Guatemala." *Hispanic American Historical Review*. Vol. 100, No. 3 (August 2020). EBSCOhost.

Levine, Philippa. *Prostitution, Race and Politics : Policing Venereal Disease in the British Empire*. New York: Routledge, 2003. EBSCOhost.

McCreery, David. "Review: Invención criolla, sueño ladino, pesadilla indígena: Los Altos de Guatemala, de región a Estado, 1740-1850 by Arturo Taracena Arriola," *The American Historical Review,* Vol. 103, No. 4 (October 1998). JSTOR.

McCreery, David. *Rural Guatemala, 1760-1940.* Stanford, CA: Stanford University Press, 1994.

Miceli, Keith L. "Rafael Carrera: Defender and Promoter of Peasant Interests in Guatemala, 1837-1848." *The Americas.* Vol. 31, No. 1 (July 1974), JSTOR.

Molina, Marcelo. *Esposición A La Convención De Los Estados Centro-Americanos, Protestando Contra La Usurpación Del De Los Altos.* Mexico City, Mexico: Ignacio Cumplido, 1841.

Pollack, Aaron. "Las Cortes de Cádiz en Totonicapan: una Alianza Insólita en un Año Insólito (1813)." *Studia Historica Contemporánea.* Vol. 27 (2009). EBSCOhost.

Roberts, Samuel Kelton Jr. *Infectious Fear: Politics, Disease, and the Health Effects of Segregation. Studies in Social Medicine.* Chapel Hill: The University of North Carolina Press, 2009.

Rough Guide to Guatemala. Unknown: Rough Guides, 2019.

Santoro, Miléna and Erick D. Langer. *Hemispheric Indigeneities: Native Identity and Agency in Mesoamerica, the Andes, and Canada.* Lincoln, NE: University of Nebraska Press, 2018. EBSCOhost.

Sarazua, Juan Carlos. "Política y Etnicidad, y Servicio Militar. Dos Experiencias paralelas en MesoAmérica, Chiapas y Guatemala, 1808-1871." *Revista de Historia de América.* Vol. 152 (2016). EBSCOhost.

Sarazua Perez, Juan Carlos. "Oficinas, Empleados y Recaudación: El Papel de la Hacienda Pública en la Organización Territorial de Guatemala, 1826-1850." *Revista de Historia.* Issue 69 (2014). Gale OneFile: Informe Académico.

Schlesinger, Stephen C. *Bitter Fruit: the Untold Story of the American Coup in Guatemala.* Garden City, NY: Doubleday, 1982.

Skinner, George Ure. "Letter from George Ure Skinner to Sir William Jackson Hooker." February 9, 1839. Directors' Correspondence, 68/120. Royal Botanic Gardens, Kew. JSTOR.

Stefoff, Rebecca. *Independence and Revolution in Mexico, 1810-1940.* New York: Facts on File, 1993.

Taracena Arriola, Arturo, Juan Pablo Pira, and Celia Marcos. "La Construcción Nacional de Territorio de Guatemala, 1825-1934 (1)." *Revista de Historia.* Issue 45 (2002). EBSCOhost.

Taracena Arriola, Arturo. *Invención criolla, sueño ladino, pesadilla indígena : Los Altos de Guatemala, de región a Estado, 1740-1871.* Guatemala City, Guatemala: Biblioteca Básica de Historia de Guatemala /Fundación Soros Guatemala, 2011.

Tietz, Jeff. "Quetzaltenango." *Triquarterly.* Vol. 115 (Spring 2003), EBSCOhost.

Sanford, Victoria. *Buried Secrets: Truth and Human Rights in Guatemala.* New York: Palgrave Macmillan, 2003.

Schwartzkopf, Stacey. "Rural Castas, State Projects and Ethnic Transformations in Western Guatemala, 1800-1821." *Ethnohistory.* Vol. 60, No. 4 (Fall 2013). EBSCOhost.

Steinberg, Michael K., Matthew J. Taylor, Michelle Moran-Taylor. "Coffee and Mayan Cultural Commodification in Guatemala." *Geographical Review.* 104, No. 3 (July 1, 2014). EBSCOhost.

"World Bank in Guatemala," World Bank Group, April 3, 2024.
    https://www.worldbank.org/en/country/guatemala/overview#1

"United Provinces of Central America Rises and Falls; 1823-1840." *Global Events: Milestone Events Throughout History,* Vol. 3. Jennifer Stock (ed.). 2014. Gale World History in Context.

Urban Analysis: Quetzaltenango. Guatemala City, Guatemala: Unknown, 1964.

Visoni-Alonzo, Gilmar. The Carrera Revolt and 'Hybrid Warfare' in Nineteenth-Century Central America. London, UK: Palgrave Macmillan, 2017.

Webel, Mari K. *The Politics of Disease Control: Sleeping Sickness in Eastern Africa, 1890–1920.* Athens, OH: Ohio University Press, 2019. EBSCOhost.

Woodward, Ralph Lee, Jr. "Arce, Manual José (1787-1847)." *Encyclopedia of Latin American History and Culture,* Vol. 1. New York: Charles Scribner's Sons, 2005. Gale World History in Context.

Woodward, R. L. Jr. "Central America from Independence to 1867." *Cambridge History of Latin America.* Vol. 3. Leslie Bethell (ed.). Cambridge, UK: Cambridge University Press, 1985.

Woodward, Ralph Lee, Jr. "Central America, United Provinces of, Constitution of 1824," *Encyclopedia of Latin American History and Culture,* Vol. 2. New York: Charles Scribner's Sons, 2008. Gale World History in Context.

Woodward, Ralph Lee, Jr. *Rafael Carrera and the Emergence of the Republic of Guatemala, 1821-1871.* Athens, GA: University of Georgia, 1993.

"World Peace Foundation Pamphlet Series," Vol. VII. Boston, MA: World Peace Foundation, 1917.

CHAPTER 3

FILLMORE CITY
UTAH TERRITORY

On January 6, 1856, Mormon leader Parley P. Pratt wrote a plaintive letter to his wife Belinda from the hopeful town of Fillmore City, complaining that he had not received any mail and that "all is loneliness the whole week" as a result. On the same day, Pratt's legislative colleague, Albert Carrington, also wrote to his family from Utah's new territorial capital. He too noted the absence of mail and the sense of isolation it produced, but Carrington devoted most of his letter to his concerns about the reports of wood stealing and of an outbreak of measles in Salt Lake City. Then he added something of a surprise: he confides to his beloved that he has been too busy to "call upon the girls" to see "whether there are any here [in Fillmore] whom I might fancy

as wives… [for] I would like to take wives as fast and as many as might be righteous." The surprise isn't really that the nineteenth century Mormon legislator was a polygamist; many of his colleagues also practiced plural marriage in accordance with the teachings of the Church of Jesus Christ of Latter Day Saints at the time. Rather, the surprise comes in the matter-of-fact way Carrington tells his two current wives and four surviving children about the extent of both his personal desire and his commitment to follow the Church's teachings. It is even more revealing that Carrington looks to gain his wives' support for new arrivals to the family; as he wrote a few weeks before, "You are doubtless wide awake in this matter, and I know that if I even found a girl whom I might fancy that I consider your judgment on women better than mine, and I should prefer to have you all see her before I made a final agreement."

Illustration 20: Albert Carrington, c. 1872.

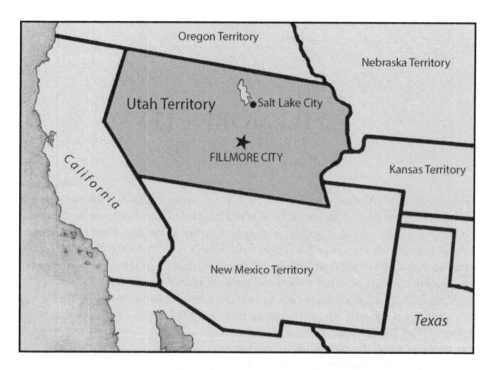

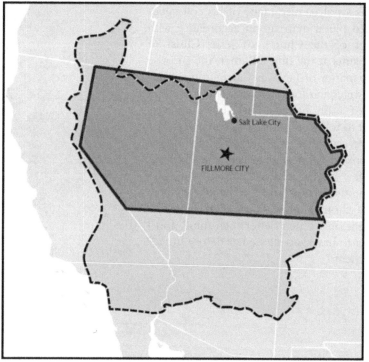

Illustrations 21 and 22: Map of the Utah Territory in 1854 (top), and map comparing the boundaries of the proposed state of Deseret with the Utah Territory in 1854 (bottom).

A Little Historical Context

One day in spring 1820, as a fourteen-year-old boy named Joseph Smith prayed alone in the woods of upstate New York, God and Jesus jointly appeared before him. Unable to find fulfillment with the Baptists, Methodists, Presbyterians, or the other competing denominations in the region, Smith asked "the Personages who stood above me in the light, which of all the sects was right...and which I should join." The Lord answered that "they were all wrong" and that Smith should not join any of them. This experience led Smith to set about building what one noted journalist recently described as an "almost achingly American" religion or what presidential candidate and Utah Senator Mitt Romney described as "a quintessentially American faith." Ten years later, after a series of visionary encounters with the Angel Moroni, Smith published *The Book of Mormon: Another Testament of Jesus Christ*. This book is seen by members of the Church of Christ of Latter Day Saints (LDS) as a work of Scripture, for it details "God's dealings with ancient inhabitants of the Americas and contains the fullness of the everlasting gospel." With it, Smith became recognized as a prophet and began to attract both followers and critics. Vicious persecution of the Mormons also became commonplace, as they emigrated from Kirkland, Ohio to Far West, Missouri and then to Nauvoo, Illinois. At one point, Smith was tarred and feathered by a hateful crowd, but survived.

Non-Mormons or "Gentiles" found the Saints threatening for a variety of religious and non-religious reasons. As they gathered in large numbers to establish their communal, utopian Zion, Mormons altered societal patterns around them, both politically and economically. When they voted, they often did so as a block, according to the wishes of a remarkably charismatic leader. This changed the outcome of local elections, and gave the Mormons what many considered to be an undue influence. Indeed, it was one thing to found a new religious community in the early nineteenth century, but it was something else altogether to have that community be a theocracy. Similarly, adherence to Smith's 1831 revelation that church members should surrender their property for the benefit of the church and its members, changed commercial patterns. Gentiles had to trade with Mormons on the church's terms, instead of with individual customers. Mormons were also targets because they were often seen as not really being Christians. Not only did Mormons have their own sacred texts, but they also rejected Trinitarianism—the belief most Christians have that God the Father, Jesus, and the Holy Spirit are united in one divine essence. (For Mormons, God, Jesus, and the Holy Spirit are "three separate beings who are one in purpose.") They also proclaimed a superiority to those of other faiths and celebrated their own holidays, such as Smith's birthday. But more than anything else, it was Smith's endorsement of polygamy that brought the Saints scorn. As Elizabeth Ferris, the wife of the US Secretary for Utah, once vividly wrote, "We are unquestionably in the midst of a society of fanatics, who are controlled by a gang of licentious villains." The potent combination of Gentile outrage, resentment, and fear culminated in Smith's assassination at the hands of an enraged mob in Carthage, Illinois on June 27, 1844.

Brigham Young, who converted to Smith's faith in 1832, led most of the Saints to Utah, beginning in 1847. He, and the other Apostles in the church's governing Quorum of Twelve, then set about reconstituting Smith's authoritarian theocracy in the valley between the Wasatch Mountains and the Great Salt Lake. Because the Mormons arrived collectively in Utah and did so with a system of governance already in place through the church, the political organization of the region by the Saints provoked considerable concern in Washington. This suspicion was amplified in January 1849, when the LDS leadership petitioned Congress for territorial recognition of the state of Deseret. The petition included a list of nominees to govern Deseret, all of whom were leaders in the Mormon church. Brigham Young, for

Illustrations 23 and 24: Rendering of Joseph Smith, 1845 (left), and Brigham Young daguerreotype, 1853 (right). According to the LDS church in Salt Lake City, no portraits or photographs of Joseph Smith were created during his lifetime.

example, would be the governor; Heber C. Kimball (the church's second most important figure), the chief justice; Parley P. Pratt an associate judge; and Albert Carrington the assessor and tax collector. This group of officials was never elected in a democratic fashion: instead, eligible voters only had the choice of ratifying a predetermined slate or not. When not one ballot was cast against the slate, it became clear that democracy did not really exist in the region. Similarly, the proceedings of Deseret's constitutional convention were manipulated so as to not be truly democratic.

Congress could have perhaps overlooked these irregularities and granted Deseret status were it not for three intertwining factors: the size of the area requested, the issue of American slavery, and the moral objections to polygamy. The outcome of the Mexican-American War in 1848 left the United States with over half a million square miles of new territory, and, although the Civil War was still twelve years away, Americans had become sharply divided over the possibility of slavery's expansion. Men like Illinois Senator Stephen A. Douglas hoped that the idea of popular sovereignty—letting a territory or state's citizens, rather than national legislators, settle a question—could resolve the conflict; this led to Congress deciding to fold the Deseret issue into its Compromise of 1850: Utah and New Mexico were given territorial status with popular sovereignty, California was admitted as a free state, the Fugitive Slave Act made it illegal to help runaway slaves trying to escape, and slave trading (but not slavery) was outlawed in the nation's capital. President Millard Fillmore then appointed Brigham Young as Utah's first territorial governor, thereby keeping the Mormons, non-Mormons and Native Americans in the region under Young's authority. This upset the critics of polygamy, who noted that if popular sovereignty applied to slavery, then it could also be applied to polygamy, and that was unacceptable. This was why the Republican Party's platform in 1856 called for an end to "those twin relics of barbarism—polygamy and slavery."

Despite the forbidding realities of the climate and geology of the Great Basin, as well as the threat of federal action against polygamy, Young believed that Mormon settlements could legitimately be established throughout the region. He envisioned it becoming a hub of thriving communities, for as he told his followers in early 1849, "As the Saints gather here and get strong enough to possess the land, God will temper the climate…and we will build towns and cities by the hundreds….This will become the great highway of nations." Another Apostle of the church, Jedediah Grant, held that the hardships of the region cultivated virtue, thereby attracting good settlers. As he once said,

> I want the Territory filled up in the north and the south, in the east and in the west, and to see the valleys flourish and blossom as a rose. I like to see hardy men come forth from the other side of the ocean; I like to see them pouring in by the tens of thousands….[And] I am glad that our crops failed…[for] it teaches the people a lesson, it keeps the corrupt at bay, for they know that they would have to starve or import their rations should they come to injure us in the Territory of Utah.

There were, of course, already people who called the Great Basin home, having learned how to make the harsh environment work for them. Before the Spanish explorers arrived in 1776 and American explorers arrived in the early 1840s, the Ute, Gosiute, Shoshone, South Paiute, Navajo, Mono and Washoe people all lived in the lands that became the Utah Territory.

In order to facilitate the settlement he sought, Young believed that the capital should be located near the geographical center of the Utah Territory, instead of remaining in Salt Lake City. A "fair division of time and travel" and "convenience of the people" mattered. Therefore, on October 4, 1851, the territorial legislature passed a resolution authorizing the creation of a commission to select a site for the new capital, which was to be named Fillmore City in honor of Millard Fillmore—a president sympathetic to the Mormons, and a man who strongly believed in the right of Americans to follow their own conscience in matters of faith. On October 21, Young and his fellow commissioners set off for the Pahvant Valley, some 150 miles south of Salt Lake. They were joined there by a group of new emigrants led by Anson Call. On October 28, Young walked with Heber C. Kimball and Joseph Lee Robinson along Chalk Creek, a stream "fourteen feet wide by one foot deep with a swift current and pebbly bed" that was lined with cottonwoods and willows. When they came to a grove of cedars upstream, Young said, "this is a sightly spot, a lovely place," and

Illustration 25: President Millard Fillmore.

Kimball and Robinson quickly agreed. Then, "putting his cane determinedly down" Young designated the northeast corner of the public square upon which the new capitol building would be constructed. The next day, the formal survey began, with the land divided into square blocks of 1¼ acres each, and Anson Call's ninety colonists from thirty families began to construct housing and a fort near the future site of the territorial capitol. As in other new settlements, these colonists were specifically selected in order to provide the community with a balance of specialized skills, such as blacksmithing and weaving, carpentry and masonry. Samuel Pierce Hoyt, for example, was chosen to go to Fillmore because he was a carpenter and ironmonger.

This activity quickly attracted the attention of local Indians, who were members of the Pahvant band of the Ute tribe. They were led by a young chief named Kanosh, who spoke English, and visited the encampment on its first night. Kanosh, who was eventually baptized and became a Mormon elder, believed in peaceful relations with the newcomers. He wanted their technology, and he was interested in learning more about their farming techniques, for as he told Brigham Young at their first meeting, Kanosh's people had grown pumpkins, beans, corn, and potatoes in the region for generations. Because Fillmore benefited significantly from Kanosh's peaceful orientation, the chief was quite surprised by the sound of firing rifles on July 4, 1852. Kanosh quickly gathered 60 of his warriors and brought them to town, worried that war had begun. When Anson Call presented the Kanosh and Pahvants with bread and explained the reason for the celebration, accounts hold that the Indians removed their war paint and happily joined in the festivities, which included shooting, jumping and racing contests. The Indians were also asked to partake of the community meal, a roasted ox, and they appreciated the gesture of friendship this represented. While some of the accounts of this event have an apocryphal, First Thanksgiving undertone to them, it is also clear that the early interactions between the Mormon settlers and the Pahvants were more friendly and positive than happened in other parts of Utah, let alone elsewhere in the West.

In the Territory's official report to Washington about the selection of the Fillmore City site, there was little mention of the indigenous population, but the region was hailed for its "rich and picturesquely diversified landscape" with tall cedars and fertile soils, "bounded by mountain ranges, here lifting high their lone peaks and serrated crests...defined in the pure sky of this altitude." It was on this basis that the federal government awarded Utah $20,000 to build a new capitol building. Fillmore's reality, however, was quite different. As one early colonizer noted as he looked over the valley's uninviting sagebrush and rocky soil, "this is a hard commencement."

Illustration 26: Sagebrush landscape south of modern Fillmore with the Pahvant Mountain Range in the background. Successfully capturing snow melt proved vital for farming in the valley.

But commence they did. Within four months, thirty adobe houses had been erected in such a way that their rear exterior walls also served as part of the fortress' defenses. Wood pickets completed the enclosure. A schoolhouse, which doubled as a meeting hall and church for the community, opened in December 1851 and there was a large public corral for livestock. Henry Davies later inaugurated the region's first saw mill to facilitate further construction. Fifty more emigrants arrived to join the community in January 1852, and a post office followed soon after their arrival. Christian Peter Beauregard opened a blacksmithy and planned Fillmore's first irrigation system. As progress continued apace, Fillmore began to feel like an established frontier town: within three years of its foundation, a two-story adobe church stood within the grounds of the fort, and both a brick kiln and a gristmill were in full operation. Most symbolically, the red sandstone walls of the territorial statehouse's south wing had reached their second level, giving Fillmore's residents "high hopes of having the legislature meet here [in] another year."

The capitol's architect was Truman O. Angell, who had been trained as a carpenter, but lacked formal architectural training. He joined the LDS church in upstate New York as a young man in late 1832, took a leading role in the construction of the Mormon temple in Kirkland, Ohio, and served as the project foreman for the temple in Nauvoo, Illinois. By the time he arrived in Utah in 1848, Angell knew more about architecture than any other Mormon, but he was a builder, not an innovator or designer. Therefore, Angell turned to others for his inspiration. His plan for the capitol—four rectangular wings joined together under a dome in the form of a Greek cross—was stylistically eclectic. It drew heavily from the Greek Revival movement that dominated American architecture in the first half of the nineteenth century, but did so without precision. The columns and triangular

Illustration 27: Turman O. Angell

pediments that Americans had come to associate with democracy and power were present, but the colossal edifice above largely abandoned these elements, replacing them with a smooth melon dome that has repeatedly (but rather unhelpfully) been described as "Moorish." In fact, the

Illustration 28: Drawing of Plan for Utah Capitol Building, Fillmore, by Truman O. Angell, c. 1852.

shape of Angell's planned dome looks a bit like Filippo Brunelleschi's famous one for Florence's cathedral, but Angell's was more bulbous and heavy. Angell planned to adorn the top of this dome with a cupola. A seagull, just about to take off from a beehive, would serve as the capitol's finial. This was a tribute to Mormon industriousness and perseverance, and honored the famous story of the seagulls that arrived in Salt Lake City in 1848 to devour swarms of crickets in time to save the early settlers' crops. For the Saints, the "Miracle of the Gulls" was a divine intervention, and Angell's finial on the capitol symbolized the connection Mormons sought between their church and their state.

Fillmore City c. 1855

On October 20, 1855, workers put the finishing touch on the capitol's south wing. The news was enough that Brigham Young and other officials decided to meet in Fillmore City for the forthcoming legislative session in December. Those coming from Salt Lake found the roads good and the weather cooperative and reached Fillmore in four and a half days. Those who didn't stay in one of Fillmore's two inns boarded with families in town. Councilor Lorin Farr, for example, paid $5 a week for the privilege, which was 25¢ more than boarders typically paid elsewhere in Utah. Either Farr enjoyed better accommodations and meals—perhaps he stayed in one of the town's newly-constructed brick houses—or Fillmore's residents were being rather entrepreneurial. Albert Carrington had no complaints, however, for he found that his host's "table was excellent, his wife kind and very agreeable, my sleeping arrangements warm and comfortable."

Utah's fifth legislative session, with a House of Representatives and a Legislative Council, opened on December 10 in a large, light-filled room on the second floor of Angell's South Wing. There were 26 representatives and 13 councilors, plus a group of non-voting officials, such as the chaplain and the sergeant-at-arms. The proceedings were conducted with a close adherence to procedure, even though *Robert's Rules of Order* had yet to be published. This began with quorum counts, credential checks, and motions to elect officers for the term, including the Speaker of the House and President of the Council. Then, because of British parliamentary traditions, there had to be a formal vote to extend a "Freedom of the House" to Governor Young, Utah's secretary and treasurer Almon Babbitt, and important judges, so that they could have legitimate access to the proceedings. Then the two houses had to vote to meet in joint session, which was done to expedite the anticipated work.

The first substantive agenda item was Utah's application to join the Union "as a free and independent state," which was "to be cheerfully submitted to the warm hearted [Stephen A.] Douglas Democrats, believing them competent to do the subject ample justice." This appeal necessitated a bill to call for a constitutional convention, but these major issues were soon followed by a litany of very particular bills relating to grazing rights, water rights, and industry. Aaron Johnson and Urich Curtis "and 122 others," for example, wanted "the right to take one third of the water of Spanish Fork Creek for irrigating"; W. W. Phelps and Hugh McKinney wanted to be granted "herd ground & Ranch north of Kansas prairie," and "Sidney Roberts et. al." sought "the right of turning water out of Big Cottonwood to propel machinery for making paper." Other bills concerned taxes, city charters, county boundaries, judicial boundaries, the penitentiary, the militia, and funding for the future University of Utah. In mid-January 1856, legislators' attention turned to petitions to Congress for increased funding to pay for specific needs. These "memorials to Congress" sought money to complete the State House in Fillmore, to improve roads and mail services, and to secure the right of way for a telegraph line from Missouri to Utah.

In each case, a bill had to be introduced and read. Then it was referred to a committee for discussion. If approved in committee, the bill came back to the House or Council, where it was read for a second time and debated. At this point, amendments could be added. Once the amendments were set, the bill was read for the third time and voted upon. In the case of the Spanish Fork Creek irrigation bill, this process took nine days. It could be mind-numbing work, for as Albert Carrington told his wives after sixteen days of meetings, "the Assembly have not yet passed any acts of general interest." It was, however, important work: the close adherence to protocol was necessary because the legislature was creating Western law where little existed before. This was particularly true of property rights, for the federal government had been slow to negotiate treaties with the region's Indian communities and had sent incompetent appointees to fill judicial offices. Consequently, the settlers' ownership of the land was legally uncertain and the courts were ill-equipped to offer a resolution. The legislature attempted to compensate for these limitations by granting numerous herding grants to prominent individuals within the Territory, but that was a tedious job.

Despite the protestations of councilors like Lorenzo Snow that all was work in Fillmore with no time "to get away from public business" there were, in fact, memorable recreational events. December 1, 1855, witnessed the adjournment of the court, which led its officials and bystanders to celebrate in unexpected ways, given church teachings. Representative Hosea Stout recorded that, despite Fillmore's ban on liquor sales, "[we had] a good oyster supper, [accompanied by] brandy and cherry brandy to the tune of some ten or twelve bottles....All got gloriously drunk and it went till midnight." Christmas night witnessed "the grandest ball ever given in the State House" with attendees arriving on their sleighs, "for the beautiful snow was mantling the ground, making this a typical Christmas tide," according to one authoritative account. Similarly, at New Year's 1856, Chaplain Parley P. Pratt reported that the cotillion dance that lasted until midnight and attracted "some eighty men...and still more women." And because a theatrical association had been formed in fall 1855 in anticipation of the legislators' arrival, there were plays to attend. In Fillmore, the choice for the male legislators seemed to be between events with illicit alcohol or permissible events in the company of women.

This intemperate behavior of the legislators affirmed the growing unease the church's top leaders had developed about the moral integrity of their Zion. The sabbath was no longer being strictly kept, Saints were selfishly putting their own needs above those of the community, and too many people were abandoning the faith entirely, leaving for California. This was especially true after the crop failure and famine of 1855. One of the first statements officially expressing concern came in July 1855, when Apostle Jedediah Grant declared that "The Church needs trimming up" and like a tree, some branches "had better be cut off." In the Fillmore State House on December 31, 1855, Council president and church Apostle Heber C. Kimball echoed this sentiment, warning a joint session, "Every house that is not a House of God should be removed destructively." Therefore, we must "spy [upon]...the enemies in our midst, upset their nastiness, upset their wicked combinations, and cast out their nuisances." The rhetoric grew until July 1856, when Apostle Grant demanded a great reformation of the church. He declared, "I would like to see the work of the reformation commence, and continue until every man had to walk to the line, then we have something like union." The experience of the Mormon reformation "proved to be deep and pungent" to borrow the words of diarist Joseph Lee Robinson, as confessors were assigned to visit every Mormon house in order to obtain acknowledgements of sinful thoughts and misdeeds. These failings were then publicly announced before the congregation on Sundays, but after an appropriate repentance, church members were often rebaptized as a symbol of their newfound purity and renewed commitment as faithful Mormons. In Fillmore, Brigham Young spoke on September 21, 1856, declaring that he "would no longer dwell among a people filled with contention, covetousness, pride and iniquity." For Young, there had to be a separation of the righteous from the ungodly, and he asked the people of Fillmore to commit themselves to his cause. All did so, as a religious fervor swept the Territory before the next legislative session began in December 1856.

On December 8, the House and Council met, but neither had a quorum, either in the morning or the afternoon. This situation led those present to organize themselves temporarily so that they could pass just one bill: to adjourn to Salt Lake City's Social Hall and reconvene there on December 15. It proved to be the last bill passed in Fillmore.

The reasons for the return to Salt Lake City were complex. Brigham Young had not been feeling well that month, and he did not want to undertake the journey to Fillmore. Because his influence was so pervasive and all-encompassing in the Territory, meaningful legislative work could not realistically proceed unless Young was present. Second, the federal government had not approved any new funding for the capitol's construction and the costs for the one completed wing were already 66% more than the $20,000 originally allocated. Many legislators must have believed that the building would never be completed, so it was silly to continue to meet in Fillmore—especially when there were "suitable accommodations" in Salt Lake. But most of all, the legislators put their own needs and wishes ahead of the goal of locating the capital near the geographical center of Territory. As Councilor Albert Carrington wrote December 30, 1855, "Legislating in Fillmore is not half so pleasant as it used to be in [Salt Lake] City, where I could be at home every night." Representative Hosea Stout concurred, saying on January 1, "Hail the new year, but O the dull times in Fillmore City. My long tarry here is sinking me *ennui* and recalling vivid remembrance of 'Sweet Home.'" Indeed, the only advantage Carrington could see to the new capital was that in Fillmore, "we have but little to distract our thoughts and attention from the business before us." This was not enough. Nor was symbolism of moving the capital from Salt Lake City in order to show greater independence from federal appointees. In the end, Salt Lake would always be the focus of the Territory because it was the epicenter of the Mormon Church. Utah's capital had to be there too.

A Short Postscript

It didn't take long for Fillmore City's residents to figure out that their community had lost its status as Utah's territorial capital. Certainly, the situation was clear by December 1858, when a few members of the legislature met in the south wing for a procedural vote to once again adjourn to Salt Lake City. More than a few families left for California the following spring as a result of this realization, joining those who had already moved in 1857 and 1858, but the majority of Fillmore's residents remained. These loyalists continued to farm and raise livestock while looking to make the town worthy of its status as the county seat. Fillmore was formally incorporated in 1867, which allowed it to build a new stone schoolhouse with tax dollars, instead of with volunteer labor. The arrival of a telegraph line in January 1867 increased Fillmore's communication with the outside world. In 1869, the town put a dam on Chalk Creek in order to control water and irrigation more precisely, and the community joined Brigham Young's Zion's Co-Operative Mercantile Institution (ZCMI) in order to pool resources and obtain better prices for their agricultural goods. By 1872, Fillmore had a courthouse, a steam saw mill, a tavern selling alcohol, a new Mormon church, and a grand, twenty-four-room hotel with stately verandas for its guests. In other words, Fillmore may not have been Utah's capital, but it progressed nonetheless.

One of the people who witnessed this progress was James Starley. He was born in Sussex, England and joined the Latter Day Saints in January 1854, after meeting a Mormon missionary. In December 1854, Starley boarded the *Clara Wheeler* in Liverpool with his wife, Caroline; his two daughters, Jane and Julia; and more than 400 other recent converts. Their voyage across the Atlantic to New Orleans was rough, but not just because of the weather. A measles outbreak took the lives of at least fifteen children and two adults during the 48-day journey. Then, on a paddlewheel up the Mississippi River to St. Louis, Caroline and Julia died within two days of one another and were buried in Arkansas. Starley proceeded to St. Louis, where he made arrangements for twelve-year-old Jane's care and witnessed her re-baptism and confirmation. He then "engaged passage" on a boat up the Missouri River to Atchison, Kansas, where he joined a wagon train of other emigrants for the overland trip to Utah. The arduousness of the journey can be measured in footwear: Starley had to buy a new pair of boots in Kansas for $5.00 and a second pair in Laramie, Wyoming for $8.00, as the snow began to fall. He arrived in Salt Lake on November 19, 1855. A year and a half later, Starley married another woman from Sussex and moved to Fillmore, where Brigham Young had assigned him to live for ten years and build a plant nursery. Starley chose to remain in Fillmore after his term of service and in 1870 was growing everything from pecans and apricots to asparagus and gooseberries, from sugar cane and beans to beets and roses. His daily journal documents everyday life in late nineteenth century Fillmore for a dutiful Mormon citizen, for Starley noted when he served on juries, paid his tithings, took the sacrament, and heard Young and other church leaders speak whenever they passed through. Starley also noted how he worked for the town for a day and a half to pay off his annual water tax, helped build the foundation for the new schoolhouse, and sold calves and yearlings to the ZCMI in the fall. He was a jack-of-all-trades, a man who could shingle roofs, repair chimneys, make cupboards, and harvest grain. If his neighbors were half as industrious as Starley was, it's not surprising that Fillmore survived. Today, many of the town's prominent families are the direct descendants of the original settlers, and this gives Fillmore

Illustration 29: The South Wing of the Territorial Statehouse, seen from the east side. Representatives met in the room that occupies the whole second floor.

Illustration 30: The South Wing of the Territorial Statehouse, seen from the west side.

considerable unity and civic pride.

The south wing of the capitol survived too. Between 1858 and 1880, it served as a civic center, religious meeting house, and theater. Between 1881 and 1895, the former capital hosted a Presbyterian-run school, but when that school closed, the building was left vacant for many years. Fillmore seemed to no longer need it. In the mid-1920s, however, the Daughters of Utah Pioneers identified it as a historic structure worth saving. The restored building opened as a museum in 1930, and it officially became a part of the Utah state park system in 1957.

What Fillmore City Teaches

Fillmore City's capital experience, as brief as it was, reminds us of two historical truths. The first is that a forceful clash of values within a society can irreparably divide it. This was true in Germany during the Protestant Reformation, was true in Antebellum America because of slavery, and is true today because of the Populism of Donald Trump. Notably, the Mormon experience with polygamy in nineteenth century Utah also illustrates the point, for the practice of plural marriage divided the Mormon community deeply. After Joseph Smith was assassinated in 1844, most Mormons moved to Utah with Brigham Young, but others remained in Nauvoo and eventually established the Reorganized Church of Jesus Christ of Latter Day Saints. The

RLDS rejected Young's leadership, renounced polygamy, accepted Trinitarianism, and disavowed several other controversial doctrines. They also held that the prophet's oldest son, Joseph Smith III, was the only legitimate successor. This sectarian division still exists today.

Those descendants of Mormons who made the trek to Utah were also internally divided by the concept of plural marriage. Some were supporters like Eliza R. Snow, who once told a group of women in Salt Lake City:

> Our enemies pretend that in Utah, woman is held in a state of vassalage—that she does not act from choice, but by coercion—that we would even prefer life elsewhere, were it possible for us to make our escape. What nonsense! We all know that if we wished, we could leave at any time—either to go singly or we could rise *en masse*, and there is no power here that could or would ever wish to prevent us.

Others were quite vocal about their opposition to polygamy, but accepted it because they saw it as a test of their faith. And still others refused to consent to it, regardless of the church's teaching. One such woman was a tough-looking Fillmore resident named Mary Johnston Huntsman. She is said to have thrown a cup of coffee in Brigham Young's face when he suggested Mary's husband take a second wife. Another was Young's last wife, Ann Eliza Webb, who refused to live with Young's other wives and in August 1873 "had her household furniture carted down to an auctioneer's and took up her residence in the Walker House," a non-Mormon owned hotel. Then she sued Young for an astonishing $220,000, claiming neglect, abuse, and fraud, and began a national speaking tour to condemn the evil of polygamy in Utah.

The tensions over polygamy simmered for decades, but 1890 the church renounced the practice, thereby healing some of the national and local divides. This change paved the way for Utah to be admitted as a state in 1896, even as divisions continued to fester. Members of a splinter sect, the Fundamentalist Church of Christ of Latter-Day Saints (FLDS), continued to practice polygamy until 2006, when its leader was arrested for numerous felonies. A Gallup poll at the time showed that 25% of Americans believed most Mormons endorsed plural marriage; this shows a significant lack of understanding about the Saints and emphasizes the continuing division between Mormons and other Americans. Tellingly, Mormons understand this: in 2011, 68% of those Mormons polled agreed that the American people do not see Mormonism as a part of mainstream American life. Indeed, in the United States today, the Saints remain Other, despite their Norman Rockwell-like emphasis on community, family, and faith.

Second, Fillmore City illustrates how loyalty is indispensable for long-term institutional success. It does not particularly matter if that loyalty is sincerely felt or strategically employed. What does matter is that individuals act in such a way that a government's, or a business', or a school's, or a church's interests are consistently and ethically bolstered over time. Such actions help ensure multi-generational continuity for the institution. This pattern is nicely illustrated through an examination of the membership of the December 1855-1856 Legislative Council. Of its thirteen members, nine joined the church within the first six years of its organization and two of them were baptized within its first six months. One was Joseph Smith's first cousin. All were men who professed their LDS allegiance early and remained loyal to it, even in the face of turmoil and hardship. Once in Utah, these men came to hold leadership positions, not only in the legislature, but also within the church itself. They were so important, in fact, that four of the thirteen councilors were also Apostles in the church's governing Quorum of Twelve:

Thirteen Councilors, 1855-56	Who Were Early Converts	Who Were Also Apostles
Albert Carrington	Lorin Farr	Orson Pratt
Lorin Farr	Benjamin F. Johnson	George A. Smith
Leonard E. Harrington	Heber C. Kimball	Lorenzo Snow
Benjamin F. Johnson	Isaac Morley	Wilford Woodruff
Heber C. Kimball	Orson Pratt	
Isaac Morley	George A. Smith	
Orson Pratt	Lorenzo Snow	
John A. Ray	John Stoker	
George A. Smith	Wilford Woodruff	
Lorenzo Snow		
John Stoker		
Daniel H. Wells		
Wilford Woodruff		

Figure 1: Leadership and Seniority in the Utah Territorial Legislature, 1855-1856. Isaac Morley and Orson Pratt joined the Church within its first six months and George A. Smith was the first cousin of Joseph Smith.

These men possessed an unwavering loyalty to the Mormon church. They were certain that they were doing God's work, and they were determined to build a vital religious community in the Great Basin Desert. Above all else, it was their persistence, their pattern of longevity and commitment, that facilitated Utah's essential connection between the LDS church and the territorial government in the nineteenth century.

Curated Bibliography for Chapter 3

Acts, Resolutions, and Memorials Passed at Several Annual Sessions at the Legislative Assembly of the Territory of Utah. Great Salt Lake City: Joseph Cain, 1855.

Albert Carrington Papers. MS 549, Box 1, F4. Special Collections, J. Willard Marriott Library, University of Utah.

Albert Carrington Papers. MS 549, Box 3A, F1, F2. Special Collections, J. Willard Marriott Library, University of Utah.

Alvord Trevor. "Certainty to Distrust: Conversion in Early Mormonism." *The John Whitmer Historical Association Journal.* Vol. 30 (2010). JSTOR.

Andrew, Laurel B. *The Early Temples of the Mormons: The Architecture of the Millennial Kingdom in the American West.* Albany, NY: State University of New York Press, 1978.

Arrington, Leonard J. *Brigham Young: American Moses.* New York: Alfred A. Knopf, 1985.

Arrington, Leonard J. *Great Basin Kingdom: An Economic History of the Latter-Day Saints, 1830-1900.* Urbana, IL: University of Illinois Press, 2005.

"Brigham's Divorce Suit." *New York Times.* August 3, 1873, 5. ProQuest Historical Newspapers.

"Brigham Young: What His Seventeenth Wife Says of Him--His Mean Treatment of Her--The Prophet Afraid of One of His Spouses." *Chicago Daily Tribune.* August 11, 1873, 8. ProQuest Historical Newspapers.

Brigham Young: The Man and His Work. Salt Lake City, UT: Deseret News Press, 1936.

Campbell, Eugene E. *Establishing Zion: The Mormon Church in the American West, 1847-1869.* Salt Lake City, UT: Signature Books, 1988.

Coppins, McKay. "The Most American Religion." *The Atlantic.* Vol. 327, No. 1 (January 2021). EBSCOhost.

Cooley, Everett L. "Report of an Expedition to Locate Utah's First Capitol." *Utah Historical Quarterly.* Vol. XXIII (1955).

Crawley, Peter. "The Constitution of the State of Deseret," *Brigham Young University Studies,* Vol. 29, No. 4 (FALL 1989). JSTOR.

Day, Stella H., Sebrina C. Ekins, and Josephine B. Walker. *100 Years of History of Millard County.* Unknown: Daughters of Utah Pioneers, 1951.

De Bow, J. D. B. *Statistical View of the United States, Embracing Its Territory, Population….* Washington, DC: B. Tucker, 1854. https://catalog.hathitrust.org

Dougherty, Matthew W. "None Can Deliver: Imagining Lamanites and Feeling Mormon, 1837-1847." *Journal of Mormon History.* Vol. 43, No.3 (July 2017). JSTOR.

Ferris, B.G. *Mrs. Mormons at Home with Some Incidents of Travel from Missouri to California, 1852-1853 in a Series of Letters.* New York: Dix & Edwards, 1856.

Fontana, David and Aziz Huq. "Institutional Loyalties in Constitutional Law." *Public Law and Legal Theory Working Papers.* 634 (2017). https://chicagounbound.uchicago.edu

Furniss, Norman F. *The Mormon Conflict, 1850-1859.* New Haven, CT: Yale University Press, 1966.

Givens, Terryl. *Mormonism: What Everyone Needs to Know.* New York: Oxford University Press, 2020.

Hamilton, C. Mark. *Nineteenth-Century Mormon Architecture & City Planning.* New York: Oxford University Press, 1995.

Hine, Robert V., John Mack Faragher, and Jon T. Coleman. *The American West : A New Interpretive History.* New Haven, CT: Yale University Press, 2017.

James Starley Papers, MS 91, F. 1, Special Collections, J. Willard Marriott Library, University of Utah.

"Journal of James Starley." *Utah Historical Quarterly.* Volume 9, No. 1-4 (1941). https://issuu.com/

Joseph Lee Robinson Journal. Manuscript ACCN 2162. Special Collections, J. Willard Marriott Library, University of Utah.

Journals of the House of Representatives…[and] the Legislative Assembly of the Territory of Utah. Great Salt Lake City: George Hales, 1853.

Kimball, Stanley B. *Heber C. Kimball: Mormon Patriarch and Pioneer.* Urbana, IL: University of Illinois, 1986.

Kingdom of the West: the Mormons and the American Frontier. Vol.16: The Whites Want Every Thing: Indian-Mormon Relations, 1847-1877. Will Bagley (ed.). Norman, OK: University of Oklahoma Press and The Arthur H. Clark Company, 2019.

Long, Amy Oaks, David J. Farr, and Susan Easton Black. *Lorin Farr*. Orem, UT: Millennial Press, 2007.

Lyman, Edward Leo and Linda Kings Newell. *A History of Millard County*. Salt Lake City, UT: Utah State Historical Commission and Millard County Commission, 1999.

Lyman, Edward Leo. "Reviewed Works: Forgotten Kingdom: the Mormon Theocracy in the American West 1847-1896 by David L. Bigler." *Journal of Mormon History*. Vol. 26, No. 1 (Spring 2000). JSTOR

Message from the President of the United States Transmitting Information in Reference to the Condition of Affairs in the Territory of Utah. 32nd Congress, 1st Session, January 9, 1852. Special Collections, J. Willard Marriott Library, University of Utah.

"Mormons in America – Certain in Their Beliefs, Uncertain of Their Place in Society." *Pew Research Center*. January 12, 2011. https://www.pewresearch.org/

Mormonism: A Historical Encyclopedia. Paul Reeve and Ardis E. Parshall (eds.) Santa Barbara, CA: ABC-CLIO, 2010.

On the Mormon Frontier: The Diary of Hosea Stout, 1844-1861. Juanita Brooks (ed.). Salt Lake City, UT: University of Utah Press and the Utah State Historical Society, 1964.

On the Potter's Wheel: The Diaries of Heber C. Kimball. Stanley B. Kimball (ed.). Salt Lake City, UT: Signature Books, 1987.

Oxford history of the American West, The. Clyde A. Milner, Carol A. O'Connor, and Martha A. Sandweiss (eds.). New York: Oxford University Press, 1994.

Parley P. Pratt Papers. MS 14, Box 1, FL 3, F 11. Special Collections, J. Willard Marriott Library, University of Utah.

"Polygamy Among the Mormons: The Second Lecture of Mrs. Ann Eliza Young." *New York Times*. December, 20 1873, 4. ProQuest Historical Newspapers.

Powell, Allan Kent. *Utah History Encyclopedia*. Salt Lake City, UT: University of Utah Press, 1994.

Pratt, Orson. *Masterful Discourses and Writings of Orson Pratt*. Salt Lake City, UT: Book Craft, Inc., 1962.

Reiter, Joan Swallow. *The Women*. Alexandria, VA: Time-Life Books, 1978.

Remini, Robert V. *Joseph Smith*. New York: Viking, 2002.

Sessions, Gene A. *Mormon Thunder: A Documentary History of Jedediah Morgan Grant*. Urbana, IL: University of Illinois, 1982.

"Seventeenth Wife, The: The Prophet's Perfidy and Parsimony Exposed--A Discarded Woman's Suit For $20,000, " *Chicago Daily Tribune*, August 4, 1873, 8. ProQuest Historical Newspapers.

Smith, George A. "The 1847 Mormon Pioneer Trek: A View from Unpublished Journal of Albert Carrington." *Overland Journal*. Vol. 27, No.1 (Spring 2009).

Smith, Eliza R. Snow. *Biography and Family Record of Lorenzo Snow*. Salt Lake City, UT: Deseret News Company, 1884.

Snow, Eliza R. "13 January 1870: Public Meeting; Salt Lake City Adobe Tabernacle, Salt Lake City, Utah Territory," *The Discourses of Eliza R. Snow*. Salt Lake City: The Church Historian's Press, 2021. https://www.churchhistorianspress.org

"Territorial Statehouse," *Territorial Statehouse State Park Museum, Utah State Parks and Recreation*. August 2009. https://stateparks.utah.gov

Volney King Papers. MS 631, Box 1, F1. Special Collections, J. Willard Marriott Library, University of Utah.

Volney King Papers. MS 631, Box 2, F1. Special Collections, J. Willard Marriott Library, University of Utah.

CHAPTER 4

RABAUL
GERMAN NEW GUINEA

On a breezy afternoon in late 1913, hundreds of Europeans, Melanesians, and Polynesians gathered to honor the death of a remarkable woman, "Queen Emma." She was a thrice-married Samoan-American businesswoman of royal birth, who had moved to the Bismarck Archipelago in 1878 to escape oppressive social conventions and seek her fortune as a trader. Savvy, free-spirited, and eventually quite rich, Emma Coe Forsayth Farrell Kolbe was German New Guinea's dominant personality in the late Victorian and Edwardian period.

Queen Emma's home was Gunantambu, which was located some eighteen miles south of the new colonial capital, Rabaul, and near the modern town of Kokopo. While her main house may not have had electricity, refrigeration, or a septic system, it was still considered the most lavish home in the South Pacific. Standing on a promontory overlooking Blanche Bay and flanked by bungalows for members of her Samoan family, the single-story house was a center of social life for decades. Arriving guests would walk across lawns and through gardens on a broad path until they reached the two large ornamental pillars that stood at the base of a twenty-foot-wide cement staircase. Ascending the forty steps, guests would come to the white-painted house lifted off the ground by sturdy cement piers. Its lunette-shaped entrance and deep verandah welcomed. Inside, the house was furnished with thick carpets, bold tapestries, and heavy furniture from around the world. Perhaps the most unusual piece of décor was a large Catholic altar from a never-built church, which Emma had converted into a sideboard bar. Well stocked with cognac and other expensive liquors, Emma enjoyed playing the role of bartender, while her large staff prepared 28-course dinners served on gold-leaf china. When she really wanted to make a statement about her exalted position and wealth, Queen Emma would wear white satin dresses with long trains and don her diamond tiara.

Queen Emma died on July 21, 1913 in Monte Carlo, where her third husband had gone to gamble and had fallen ill. Sixty-two-year-old Emma went to care for him, but the couple got into an automobile accident while driving along the Riviera and never recovered. She died two days after he did and was cremated. Her remains were then returned to New Guinea. The elaborate funeral, held near her Gunantambu estate, was planned by her oldest son, James Myndersee Coe Forsayth, and Heinrich Rudolph Wahlen, the businessman to whom Emma had adroitly sold her land and company in 1910 on the hunch that Europe was approaching war. The two men rode to the cemetery in the only automobile in New Guinea, followed by a long procession that included the colony's governor, most of the colony's European community, and hundreds of indigenous people from the Tolai tribe. A Wesleyan Methodist minister officiated the ceremony, even

Illustration 31: Queen Emma in San Francisco in 1896.

45

though Emma had often had an adversarial relationship with the clergy. A champagne reception followed afterwards, which featured magnums of Emma's favorite beverage. For everyone present, it must have felt like the end of the era that it was.

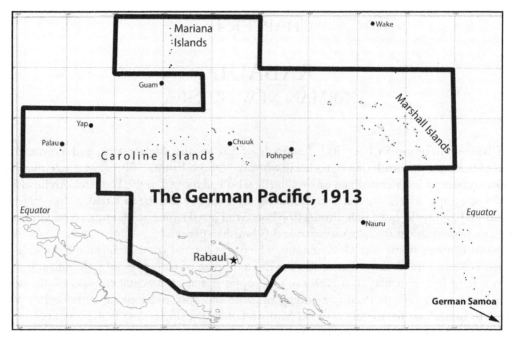

Illustration 32: Map of the German colonial possessions in the Pacific in 1913.

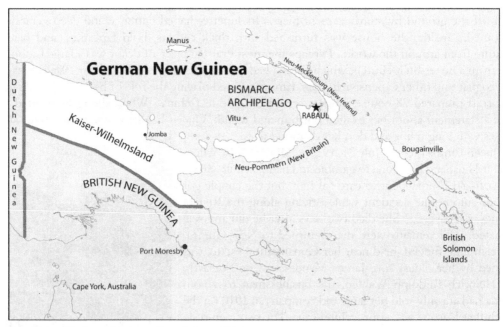

Illustration 33: Map of German New Guinea, 1913.

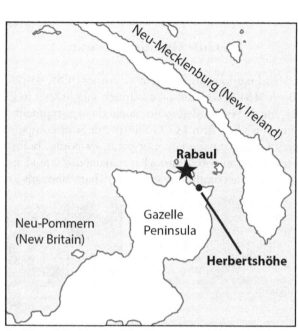

Illustration 34: Map of the islands of Neu-Pommern and Neu-Mecklenburg in 1913.

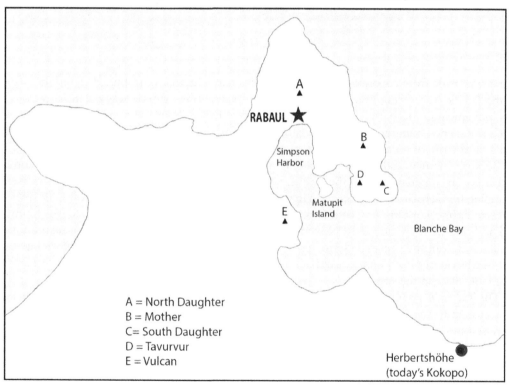

Illustration 35: Map of the Gazelle Peninsula and the area around Rabaul.

A Little Historical Context:

Queen Emma financed her luxurious life in a remote corner of the world through her extensive coconut plantations. By the 1840s, coconut oil was much sought after in Europe for its industrial use in soap and candles, but the oil tended to go rancid during shipment. Working in Samoa in the late 1860s, the German trading firm J.C. Godeffroy & Sons compensated for this problem by developing a process for drying the coconut meat, or copra, before shipment. Once in Europe, the oil was extracted from copra, and what remained was sold as winter fodder for pigs and cows. This process made the commodity valuable. That value only grew in the 1880s, when

Illustration 36 and 37: Pile of coconuts in New Britain, early 1900s (left), and drying copra in the Dutch East Indies, c. 1920, (right).

margarine made from coconut oil became an inexpensive alternative to butter. Soon the islands of the Pacific were being transformed into copra plantations. Emma was on the forefront of this movement in Melanesia, having seen what Godeffroy & Sons did in her native Samoa. By 1895, she owned hundreds of thousands of acres of the best land in German New Guinea and had a third more of it under cultivation than her nearest competitor.

Because Germany did not become a unified country until 1871, the Germans were latecomers to European imperialism. In the 1880s, when Godeffroy & Sons and other traders began appealing for German naval protection in the face of increased British assertiveness in the region, German Chancellor Otto von Bismarck abandoned his long opposition to colonial development and authorized annexations. In November 1884, 200 German marines landed near the future capital of Rabaul and declared German sovereignty over the islands of the Bismarck Archipelago and northeastern New Guinea. As Kaiser Wilhelm II later said, Germany too was to have its profitable place in the sun.

The German government gave the responsibility for governing and developing the new protectorate to the Neu Guinea Kompagnie (NGK). According to its charter, the company exercised the Kaiser's authority in all matters except foreign relations and the administration of justice. This position befit the ego of NGK's micromanaging and authoritarian chairman Adolph von Hansemann, but these advantages did not translate into profits. Instead, a litany of mistakes occurred. The company chose to base its operations in malaria-infested Kaiser-Wilhelmsland, which was difficult to traverse and was occupied by indigenous groups who were generally quite hostile to the German arrival. Attacks on NGK personnel and property began in 1886 and continued persistently. To make its problems worse, the company tried to plant crops ill-suited to the region's environmental conditions, such as cotton and tobacco, and it remained committed to a plantation economic model based upon difficult-to-obtain indentured labor. By 1890, just five years into the contract, it was clear that the NGK could not both fulfill its administrative responsibilities to govern the colony and hope to make a profit for its shareholders. Debate raged in the Reichstag for a decade over how to resolve the situation, but in 1899 a settlement was finally reached and the Neu Guinea Kompagnie transferred its colonial administrative responsibilities back to the German government.

With this new freedom, the NGK was able to devote its attention to the development of copra and profit. This resulted in an enormous amount of human suffering. The company's German employees—many of whom had enlisted to pay off personal debts—soon found themselves suffering from depression as they became demoralized by low wages, poor housing, relentless paperwork, threat of disease, boredom, and isolation. Alcohol provided an escape for too many. Contracted indentured laborers, whether Chinese, Javanese, or Melanesian, endured far worse, as their mortality rates show. In late 1891, for example, 313 Chinese "coolies" arrived at the Jomba settlement in Kaiser-Wilhelmsland; eight weeks later, less than a third were sufficiently fit to do any type of work, and by Christmas 83 had died. At Astrolabe, another mainland settlement nearby, 40.3% of the workers perished between 1887 and 1903. The estimated annual death rate between those same years for all indentured workers in German New Guinea is 28%, but one German naval report posited that the mortality rate for 1903 alone was 60%. Laborers in the Dutch and British portions of the island of New Guinea certainly faced terrible working conditions, but the suffering and death in Kaiser-Wilhelmsland was on an altogether different scale. One reason for this was that workers rarely had enough to eat. The government-mandated minimum ration for contracted laborers remained at malnutritional levels to the end of German occupation.

When it took over administrative responsibilities from the Neu Guinea Kompagnie in 1899, the colonial government was in a remarkably precarious position. The first governor, Rudolf von Bennigsen, theoretically oversaw Kaiser-Wilhelmsland; Neu-Pommern (New Britain), Neu-Mecklenburg (New Ireland), Bougainville, and many smaller islands in the Bismarck Archipelago; Nauru; the Marshall Islands; and, thanks to the recent purchase from Spain, the Caroline Islands and the Mariana Islands, except for Guam. This was an area larger than the continental United States. The problem of distance was compounded by a lack of infrastructure. A letter from Berlin to Rabaul, for example, took at least 42 days to arrive and was dependent upon making the desired shipping connections in Naples and Hong Kong. A telegram from the Marshall Islands couldn't be received in Berlin until twenty days after it was sent. Far more isolated than German Southwest Africa (Namibia) or German East Africa (Tanzania), New Guinea was the only German colony without a government printing press. A lack of personnel also proved to be an issue: as late as 1911 there were only eleven colonial administrators on the payroll to supervise all of Germany's Pacific holdings except Samoa. Most significantly, there was the colonial government's dependence on the goodwill of the indigenous population.

Illustration 38: Postage stamp from German New Guinea, 1901. The ship is the Kaiser's yacht, "SMS Hohenzollern."

Around Rabaul, on the Gazelle Peninsula, these people came to be known as the Tolai. Prior to the German arrival, the Tolai lived in a decentralized, prosperous, matrilineal society with an elaborate trade system between coastal and interior groups. The region's fertile soil, purposefully cultivated in accordance with a seasonal cycle, produced a bounty that allowed the Tolai to live considerably beyond the

Illustration 39: "Tolai chief with two brothers, 1889.

subsistence level. The society's use of shell money (*tambu*) allowed for the accumulation of wealth in terms that were recognizable by nineteenth century Europeans. Land ownership was also of central importance to the Tolai because all land parcels were associated with a clan's founding ancestor. With the arrival of Queen Emma and other planters, misunderstandings over land use and ownership frequently arose. This may best be illustrated when in March 1890 Queen Emma wanted to build a road from her warehouses to the nearest port. The Tolai objected, subsequently attacked, and killed several people. The government sent out a punitive expedition to search for the killers, but could not get the Tolai to surrender the perpetrators. Even the destruction of hundreds of Tolai homes could not get the Tolai to budge. Instead, the Tolai attacked again, armed with rifles, spears, and axes. Only when the Tolai decided to sue for peace in order to restore the trade *they* desired was order reestablished on the Gazelle Peninsula. This episode, as well as how few Germans there were to address the situation and how long it took to inform Berlin, demonstrates the fragility of the new government.

With the passage of a few years, however, the colonial government's surprisingly youthful officials gained experience and improved their effectiveness. This change can be seen in the German response to a severe typhoon that struck the Micronesian island of Pohnpei on April 20, 1905. The winds may have reached 138 mph, which would have classified it as a catastrophic Category 4 storm by today's standards. The resulting damage was so complete that every house on the island was destroyed. Churches, government buildings, businesses, and warehouses were blown off their stone foundations and mature coconut palm trees were leveled by pieces of corrugated iron flying around the island. Hillsides were stripped of vegetation during the storm and subsequent landslides added to the devastation. Eighteen people died. In the aftermath of the disaster, fears grew that many more Pohnpeians would die because of food shortages. Not only had many of the island's breadfruit trees fallen, but the yam vines that climbed up the breadfruit trees were also uprooted. Fifty percent of Ponhpei's coconut palms were toppled by the typhoon, as were almost all of its banana trees. All of the island's staples had been decimated. Additionally, domesticated pigs drowned or died after being hit by falling debris, and the loss of so many canoes made fishing difficult. As the official report to the colonial office in Berlin noted, "the economic prospects of [Pohnpei] seem desperate. Trade is destroyed for years." The situation was even worse on some of the outlying atolls, where the raging seawater removed protective sandbars and flooded islets. On tiny Pingelap, for example, 113 people died of starvation or disease by 1906. In the wake of this humanitarian crisis, the German colonial government took two steps to help alleviate the immediate problems: they provided cash and significant amounts of canned food and rice to Pohnpei's residents, and they evacuated people from the ruined atolls. Not coincidentally, these steps also supported their long-term colonial objectives. By requiring Pohnpeians to surrender guns and ammunition in exchange for the cash or food, the goal of local pacification was considerably advanced; by offering resettlement, colonial officials gained additional labor where they wanted it. In other words, the German response to the typhoon was both supportive and calculating. This fit well with a dynamic new governor's overall approach to colonial administration.

Rabaul c. 1913:

Rabaul gazes upon a stunning, if threatening, setting. About 1400 years ago, a volcanic explosion created a new caldera at the north end of New Britain's Gazelle Peninsula. When seawater breached the caldera's southern rim, it formed one of the world's finest anchorages, now called Simpson Harbor. Rising above the port are three magnificent volcanos that predate the creation of the caldera. They are known as North Daughter, South Daughter and The Mother, which is the tallest at 2100 feet. In addition, two more recent and still-active volcanos, Mt. Tavurvur and Mt. Vulcan, guard the harbor's entrance as restless sentinels.

Illustration 40: Rabaul, three volcanos, and Simpson Harbor, 2007. The volcanos from left to right are Mother, South Daughter, and Tavurvur, which is erupting.

Rabaul, which means "mangroves" in the language of the Tolai, was built by the Germans to take advantage of the well-protected, deep-water port. It replaced the previous capital of Herbertshöhe (today's Kokopo). Work began in 1904 with the draining of a swamp and the construction of a long wharf that could accommodate large merchant and naval ships on each side. To facilitate the movement of goods between the pier and the town, a narrow-gauge tram line was soon added. Bremen's Norddeutscher Lloyd shipping firm, which had won the exclusive right to handle all of New Guinea's exports in exchange for providing inter-island service for the colony, had its main office next to the wharf. It was decorated with a gingerbread lattice entrance and verandah that seemed rather incongruous next to the functional maritime activity around it. Such was life in Rabaul, for the town exhibited ambition and avarice, wrapped in the veneer of the quaint.

The town was laid out on a sensible grid pattern with broad avenues lined with mature shade trees to provide relief from the tropical heat and to give Rabaul an established feel. One American traveler worried that this was a purposefully misleading design:

> Visitors and travelers…revelled in the grand impressions gained of this charming town, and did not hesitate to put in print the imaginations that the whole of German New Guinea, to possess such a splendid capital, must be thickly populated with Germans and developed in an extensive and extraordinary manner.

Others were more generous. Even as early as 1910, one reporter maintained, "I have never seen so young a settlement…with such good stores, private houses, and hotels." A British visitor elaborated a few years later:

> [Rabaul is] a beautiful little town built on low-lying land with the steep ridge of hills for a background. The well-laid-out streets are lined with rows of trees and frequently there are also rows down the middle. In one, the acacias were in bloom and showed masses of scarlet and yellow flowers. In another are magnificent casuarinas, with mysterious music in their slender rustling branches. The wooden bungalows, standing on high piles, usually have only two or three rooms, but these are large and airy with many windows and doors. They are surrounded by wide verandas, opening here and there into spacious porches which are furnished as sitting-rooms and adored with plants, creepers and flowers; and here one chiefly lives.
>   Everywhere is bright green grass, with flowering trees and shrubs, especially vivid-hued crotons. There are few fences, the properties being separated from one another by low green hedges. One hardly realizes that Rabaul is within four and a half degrees of the Equator, the welcome green and shade give such a delightfully cool effect.

In other words, Rabaul's lush fertility and volcanic surroundings corresponded with a European's image of a tropical paradise.

Illustration 41: tree-lined street in Rabaul, early 1900s.

Illustration 42: Customs House in Rabaul, c. 1935

Behind this impression, the situation was more complex. While Rabaul offered amenities that were far superior to those available at Port Moresby in British New Guinea, and had the ability to impress, the capital was really still a frontier town. Indeed, one German visitor in 1911 described the settlement as "little more than a collection of huts." There were only 266 White[9] residents, most of whom were German and male. These Europeans lived in racially segregated neighborhoods, just as each other ethnic group in Rabaul did. According to a zoning plan from 1913, many of the town's civic institutions were racially segregated as well: there was a European hospital and a native hospital, a European school and a native school, a European jail and a native jail. The town's leisure club, with its fashionable tennis courts, was for Whites only, and Rabaul's cemetery sections were delineated by ethnicity. The community's two churches, one Catholic and one Wesleyan Methodist, were among the few institutions that welcomed regardless of race. Another was Rabaul's botanical garden, which got its start as an experimental agricultural station in 1905. By 1912, the garden was staffed by well-paid experts, employed as many as fifty Melanesian laborers, and was conducting experiments with different fertilizers and tropical plants. In 1913, the garden was expanded to include a demonstration area, where the Tolai received plants and were taught how best to grow them. As one reporter noted in 1913, the botanical garden was "greatly visited by passengers on steamers…[for] the garden contains some 10,140 plants and trees. A more complete collection of tropical flora would be hard to find in any South Sea port."

---

[9] Following the recommendation of the National Association of Black Journalists in 2020, I have capitalized all ethnicities and racial categories in the text.

In the segregated outpost, there were 79 Malays, who lived in their own district and worked as police officers, clerks, overseers, and servants. The capital was also home to 109 Japanese, who were generally skilled tradesmen, and 452 Chinese, who were predominantly merchants. Rabaul's lively Chinatown had six main retail stores, as well as restaurants, laundries, and shops for butchers, tailors, carpenters, and mechanics. One of Rabaul's prominent Chinese residents was Ah Tam, who came to New Guinea in the 1880s as a cook. By 1903, he had married a Tolai woman, developed his own shipbuilding business on nearby Matupit Island, and opened a boarding house and restaurant there. He was known for offering his guests mineral baths and medical treatments during their stay. In 1904, Ah Tam gained permission to open a brothel, on the condition that his three Japanese employees submit to weekly medical examinations. When the capital formally moved to Rabaul in 1910, Ah Tam relocated his brothel to Chinatown; by late 1913, he was employing as many as thirty women to serve a Chinese, Japanese, and European clientele. The 27 Micronesians and 2,447 Melanesians, who lived in the area around the town

Illustration 43: The Chinese District of Rabaul, c. 1935.

and who formed the vast majority of Rabaul's population, were not welcome. Ah Tam's prominence and financial success granted him an exemption from the usual segregation rules in Rabaul; instead of living in Chinatown, he owned a waterfront house with full views of North Daughter, South Daughter and The Mother and lived next door to the army captain. They would have spoken with one another in pidgin English, which was the multicultural community's lingua franca.

Ah Tam's brothel was not Rabaul's only establishment in Chinatown built on vice. Its gambling hall, for example, was so popular that it was open twenty-four hours a day. There were also opium dens, which were fueled by both a legal and an illicit trade, and numerous bars that encouraged the patriotic singing of traditional German drinking songs. Indigenous police and soldiers helped maintain order in the thriving, occasionally bawdy port that served as a coal refueling station and popular port of call for the German navy. Well-trained "in their khaki uniforms" they "look a quite smart set of men," one reporter noted in 1910.

On Namanula Ridge above the town stood the stately governor's residence. In 1913, New Guinea's governor was a principled, energetic man named Albert Hahl. He had been born in 1868 into a Protestant family in predominantly Catholic Bavaria, where his father operated a brewery. Hahl did well in school and after completing his secondary education, he studied law and economics at the University of Würzburg. In 1893, he earned his Doctor of Law. He began his career working in Bavaria's Interior

Illustration 44: Entrance to the Governor's House, Rabaul, 1935.

Ministry, but soon took a position with the Foreign Office in Berlin. He had originally hoped to be posted to German East Africa, but in January 1896 Hahl was offered a promotion that would change his life: he was appointed to be an imperial judge in New Guinea. Hahl jumped at the chance to have such responsibility at twenty-seven and quickly left for the Pacific. In 1899, when Germany purchased the Caroline Islands from Spain and Micronesia was incorporated into New Guinea's colonial administration, Hahl was tapped to become the vice-governor and oversee the official transfer of sovereignty. Because Hahl managed to succeed where the Spanish had failed, bringing peace to Pohnpei, Chuuk, and other parts of Micronesia, Kaiser Wilhelm II appointed Hahl to be governor of New Guinea in November 1902. He served for eleven years, during which time he struggled to reconcile the vastly different expectations of Berlin officials, the plantation owners, and the Pacific Islanders.

At Hahl's appointment ceremony in Berlin, Wilhelm II and his Foreign Office staff made it clear that they wanted New Guinea to be developed with speed and efficiency. Hahl was subsequently criticized for not being able to do so. He responded that unlike Germany's colonies in Africa, New Guinea did not have sufficient personnel to explore or pacify the interiors of the major islands. Germans had yet, for example, to venture up the mighty Sepik River, so the development of inhospitable Kaiser-Wilhelmsland would take time. When Berlin added the expectation in 1906 that the colonies had to be budgetarily self-sufficient, Hahl was being asked to do more with less. He resisted, realizing that the new expectation would necessitate additional taxes and create more resentment. Because Berlin had other priorities, it didn't particularly care about the local consequences. The Kaiser and the Foreign Office simply wanted quick, inexpensive exploitation. They reduced Hahl's imperial subsidy by almost a half between 1906 and 1911.

The plantation owners and managers largely shared in Berlin's quick-greed materialism. The only reason they were in New Guinea was to make money, and they wanted to do that as swiftly as possible. To meet this goal, the planters demanded more land and more free labor. They believed that as representatives of an advanced civilization, they had a natural right to utilize any land they wanted. The planters also called for the forced conscription of New Guineans in order to produce as much copra as possible; they argued that because all German men were conscripted into the army for at least two years, the Melanesians should likewise be conscripted to work. Hahl saw through the reasoning and noted that the planters simply "set themselves up and maintain themselves as little autocrats." He resisted many planter demands, but by 1914 German planters had acquired 39% of the arable land on the Gazelle Peninsula anyway. Colonial governors may have had considerable autonomy, but they also needed to be mindful of their fellow expatriates, lest too many complaints reach Berlin. In an effort to placate the planters,

Hahl agreed in April 1904 to the establishment of a Government Council to provide the governor with advice on colonial policy.

The indigenous response to colonialism was almost as diverse as the thousands of islands that composed the German Pacific empire. Some, like the Tolai, were more cooperative because they decided that the commercial advantages of the German presence outweighed the political and cultural disadvantages. Conversely, conflict in the Vitu Islands perpetuated for years. Some tribes allied themselves with Christian missionaries for their own secular benefits, while others purposefully led German explorers into the lands of their traditional enemies. On Manus, the people saw the Germans as foreigners who should be killed, not obeyed. There were instances, such as on Pohnpei in 1910 and 1911, when the indigenous response to colonial rule was so intense that suppressing the revolt required five naval ships, 300 German marines, and 170 Melanesian troops. Because German influence was largely limited to the coastal areas, however, the vast majority of Melanesians had no contact with the Germans whatsoever.

In his effort to balance these conflicting demands, Hahl developed his own vision for the Pacific. This involved commercial development, immigration from Asia, and protection for the indigenous population. He specifically hoped that New Guinea and the Bismarck Archipelago would become akin to British Malaya, where Chinese, Filipino, Indian, and Malay immigrants would work to export raw materials for the German industrial economy. The New Guineans would be allowed to develop on land "permanently reserved for the natives...which they themselves considered desirable." In this approach, Hahl was certainly not immune to the racial prejudices and paternalism that characterized most Europeans during the age of imperialism, but this governor was not cut from the same cloth as some of his counterparts in Africa. He did not, for example, support genocide. Hahl saw indigenous violence as an inevitable component of colonialism. It was an act of war that

Illustration 45: "Albert Hahl (1868-1945).

was the natural outcome of conflicting interests. As a result of this orientation, Hahl did not treat Pacific Islanders as criminals, and he worked to end violence as quickly as possible. In his mind, retribution was certainly necessary at times, but such actions had to be measured. They also needed to be coupled with conciliatory gestures so that the cycle of violence would not be perpetuated. He also understood that German legal concepts and assumptions differed from those of the indigenous tribes. This awareness is why he learned the Tolai's language within three months of his arrival on the Gazelle Peninsula, why he was willing to dress in a grass skirt on occasion, and why he participated in the kava drinking rituals. Because he could see issues from multiple perspectives as a result of his judicial experience, Hahl also ensured that planters did not interfere with sacred sites.

Hahl was particularly worried about indigenous depopulation. To combat the problem, he imposed a ban on women serving as indentured laborers, forbade recruiting men from areas that were in danger of population decline, and disallowed land purchases by planters on islands where land was scarce. As he wrote in 1901, "If we want to preserve a healthy and growing native population, fit to work, we have to [ensure]...that they have sufficient land on which they can live and propagate according to their own customs." This is why Hahl denied certain European land claims, established large land reserves for the Melanesians, and encouraged them to cultivate gardens that could sell produce to Europeans. Hahl also persuaded a few tribal chiefs to "establish coconut plantations so that they could participate in the copra trade economy themselves. In conjunction with these policies, Hahl also thought about the environment more holistically. When exotic bird hunters threatened to exterminate certain species, Hahl increased the rates for hunting licenses, raised export fees, limited the size of hunting parties, and established well-defined hunting seasons.

To help enforce these policies, Hahl appointed indigenous intermediary agents, known as *luluais*. Their job was to maintain order, adjudicate disputes, impose fines, and enforce German policies. This blending of judicial and police duties was not always effective and the system rarely penetrated beyond the coastal areas, but it did help facilitate the realization of two long-term German goals: road building and moving New Guineans to a cash economy. In 1906, Hahl introduced a head tax on every able-bodied man, which had to be paid in cash. Those who were unable to do so were required to work off the tax by building roads for the government. The *luluai* was responsible for collecting the tax or enforcing the hard labor penalty. The *luluai's* reward for fulfilling these duties was ten percent of the tax revenue, which gave village leaders plenty of incentive to act on behalf of the colonial government. The *luluai* system was what made at least parts of New Guinea governable.

In April 1914, Hahl left Rabaul aboard a mail steamer for Germany to take a job as the director of the Neu Guinea Kompagnie. He was accompanied by his wife and their two daughters. In his eleven years as governor, Hahl had watched Rabaul emerge out of a mangrove forest to become the symbol of German accomplishment in the Pacific. He had imposed himself on the local population, but had done so with compassion, as one of the last pages in his memoir details:

> It appeared as if the long years of struggle to persuade the coastal and island people to adapt to the new order which had overwhelmed their world had achieved their objective: blood feuds and head-hunting [cannibalism] had been stopped. The villages and clans deferred to the authorities appointed from among their own number and had learned to put to economic use their hereditary lands, now guaranteed to them in perpetuity.

The final page of the memoir discusses details in the colonial budget and documents the work Hahl wanted to undertake in Kaiser-Wilhelmsland. It is a pragmatic reflection. What fascinates, however, is that Hahl's words end on an altogether different note: "The *Komet* escorted our mail steamer for a short distance. The tall mountains of the peninsula of craters held our gaze until they sank into the darkness of approaching night."

Hahl was a practical romantic, and Rabaul reflected the governor's ethos well.

A Short Postscript:

In the opening weeks of World War I, the Australians captured Rabaul. After the war, the German colonies in the Pacific became part of the League of Nations Mandates, which were administered by Australia, Japan, New Zealand, and the United States. This political change did

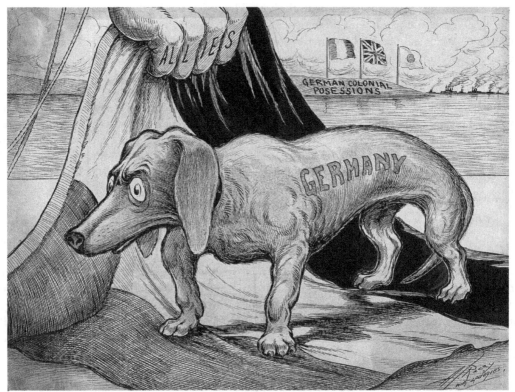

Illustration 46: Political cartoon, c. 1914. The German flag is being pulled by the Allies from under a dachshund, thereby representing the seizure of German colonies in the Pacific by the Allies during the First World War.

not result in meaningful social change for Pacific Islanders in Melanesia.[10]   In Rabaul, for example, Australian authorities maintained German administrative systems and relationships with the Tolai so as to continue the flow of copra production.

On the early afternoon of May 28, 1937, Rabaul experienced a notable earthquake, or *gurias* as the Tolai called the familiar earth trembling. Aftershocks continued for the next twenty-four hours, until Mt. Vulcan erupted in the late afternoon of May 29, sending white ash and pumice miles into the air. That evening, lightning burst within the volcanic cloud as rain poured down. An American copra freighter, the *Golden Bear*, managed to take 750 people aboard and radio for additional help before dashing past Mt. Vulcan and into Blanche Bay as light dawned on May 30. One ship that responded to the distress call was the *Montoro*, but it could not reach Rabaul. As one eyewitness recalled, the "thunderous roars from the bowels of the earth," the "spurts of flame" and the "clouds of ashes…so thick that they obscured the sky" made entering Simpson Harbor impossible. Another summarized: "Talk about all Hell breaking loose! Nothing in Dante's description of the Inferno came anywhere near equaling that awesome sight." Fortunately, many of Rabaul's residents had spent the night trekking over a pass between The Mother and North Daughter to reach a beach on the Blanche Bay coast. The *Montoro*'s lifeboats and Tolai canoes were able to evacuate over 5000 Asians, Melanesians, and Whites on May 30. This rescue came just in the nick of time because that afternoon Mt. Tavurvur began hurling

---

[10] The situation was a bit different in Micronesia, where Japanese authorities looked to make islands like Yap and Chuuk a central part of their growing Pacific empire. This included encouraging Japanese emigration, new economic development, and establishing military bases.

Illustration 47: Erupting volcano near Rabaul, 1937.

black ash into the sky. As had happened in 1878, Simpson Harbor again witnessed a double eruption as its two sentinels dueled. By the time the *gurias* and falling ash finally stopped, Mt. Vulcan had grown over 600 feet in height and 505 Tolai and two Europeans had died as a result of being buried, asphyxiated, or drowned.

Rabaul survived the calamity, but given its geological surroundings many questioned the wisdom of retaining it as the capital of New Guinea. Commissioned studies reached differing conclusions and no final decision was made before the outbreak of World War II. During the war, the Japanese used Rabaul's exceptional harbor as their primary base in the South Pacific and transformed the area into a stronghold. The Allied attempt to retake Rabaul proved to be the longest battle of the war. After 1945, Port Moresby became New Guinea's capital, but Rabaul remained an important port. That status ended in September 1994, when Mt. Vulcan and Mt. Tavurvur once again erupted simultaneously. This joint explosion left five dead and resulted in as much as two feet of white ash falling on Rabaul. The city looked like it had experienced a blizzard. Subsequent rains turned the ash into something resembling cement, causing the collapse of many buildings. In fact, most buildings within five miles of Mt. Tavurvur sustained serious structural damage and virtually every building in the southern part of Rabaul collapsed under the ash's weight. 50,000 people were displaced. Except for a few hearty souls, the city was abandoned.

Illustration 48: Rabaul's ruined post office in October 1994.

Illustration 49: Turanguna Street, October 1994. Note how the paw prints have been fossilized in the hardened ash.

What Rabaul Teaches

Rabaul and German New Guinea remind us of two valuable lessons. The first is that historical periods are not experienced the same way by everyone. Even individuals, neighborhoods, tribes, or nations in close proximity do not necessarily share in the same historical phenomena. Rather, a person's history and a place's history is singular. It is something that is uniquely experienced by individuals or groups. As anthropologist Clifford Gertz argued in the 1960s and 1970s, there is no uniformity in the human experience. For Gertz, we are all shaped by our particular circumstances and the culture in which we live.

Imperialism in German New Guinea showcases this reality because of its diversity. Its largest landmasses—Kaiser-Wilhelmsland, Neu-Pommern and Neu-Mecklenburg and Bougainville— were largely composed of almost impenetrable rainforests and rugged mountains that allowed its people to develop hundreds of different languages and live in hundreds of different societies, each with distinctive rituals and customs. In Micronesia, there may have been more cultural unity and easier access, but the vast distances of the Pacific meant any given island's experience could be much different than that of its closest neighbors. The vagaries of weather alone, from typhoons to droughts, illustrate the point.

What this diversity specifically meant in the late nineteenth and early twentieth centuries is that imperialism was not universally experienced the same way. This was especially true on the peripheries of empire, for imperialism wasn't a wholly negative experience for all Pacific Islanders. While there is no denying the vast suffering produced by the forced labor systems or the horrific death rates associated with German colonialism in Kaiser-Wilhelmsland, it is also important to remember that certain indigenous peoples benefited from colonialism. Many

60

Melanesian and Micronesian chiefs and other leaders, for example, wanted to become *luluai* and help enforce colonial law. They sought this office because, by becoming intermediaries between the Germans and a tribe, these men could increase their *mana*—a supernatural essence that allowed a possessor to shape the world around him. By associating themselves with colonial authorities, planters, traders, or missionaries, tribal leaders reinforced indigenous social patterns and gained greater access to European material resources. This enhanced their *mana* significantly. Indigenous women supported German rule as well because of the peace it brought between long-warring tribes. It is also important to remember that there were those imperialist administrators who felt something other than contempt for non-Europeans. Albert Hahl is a notable example of this. To cast every late nineteenth century European in the tropics in the same light is also to betray the essential individuality of the human experience. Such subtleties underscore the complexities of colonialism, rather than detract from its gruesome realities and legacies.

Secondly, Rabaul symbolizes the fragility of human endeavor in the face of nature. The Germans, Australians, and New Guineans after them worked hard to build a capital that befit the image of a tropical Eden. The volcanic eruptions of 1937 and 1994 leveled those efforts in a flash. As with Roman Pompeii, the 2004 Indian Ocean tsunami, Hurricane Katrina, and other natural disasters, humans may construct a complex web of infrastructure in hopes of creating a better community, but Mother Nature will always have the final say as to how long those dreams will stand. As Ecclesiastes 2:11 reminds us, "Then I looked on all the works that my hands had wrought, and on the labor that I had labored to do: and behold, all was vanity and vexation of spirit, and there was no profit under the sun."

Curated Bibliography for Chapter 4

"750 Rescued by Ship in Volcanic Disaster." *New York Times.* July 12, 1937. 2. ProQuest Historical Newspapers.

"5000 Made Homeless by Volcano and Tidal Wave." *Chicago Daily Tribune.* June 2, 1937. 10. ProQuest Historical Newspapers.

Bennett, Judith A. "Pacific Coconut: Comestible, Comfort, and Commodity." *Journal of Pacific History.* Vol. 53, No. 4 (December 2018). EBSCOhost.

Blythe, Jennifer Mary. "The War with Peter: Commercial Development in the Vitu Islands, German New Guinea," *Journal of Colonialism & Colonial History.* Vol. 20, No. 1 (Spring 2019). ProQuest Central.

Buschmann, Rainer. *Anthropology's Global Histories: The Ethnographic Frontier in German New Guinea, 1870-1935.* Honolulu, Hawai'i: University of Hawai'i Press, 2009.

Cahill, Peter. "Chinese in Rabaul, 1921-1942: Normal Practices or Containing the Yellow Peril?" *Journal of Pacific History.* Vol. 31, No. 1 (June, 1996). JSTOR.

Coffee Frank. *Forty Years in the Pacific: The Lure of the Great Ocean.* New York: Oceanic Publishing Co., 1920.

Conroy, John D. "The Chinese in Colonial Rabaul: An Informal History." *Crawford School Research Paper.* No. 14-07. Canberra, Australia: Australian National University, 2014.

Conroy, John D. *The Informal Economy in Development: Evidence from German, British and Australian New Guinea.* Canberra, Australia: Australian National University, 2020.

Davies, Margrit. *Public Health and Colonialism: The Case of German New Guinea, 1884-1914.* Wiesbaden, Germany: Harrassowitz Verlag, 2002.

Drossier, Holger. "Copra World: Coconuts, Plantations, and Cooperatives in German Samoa." *Journal of Pacific History.* Vol. 53, No. 4 (December 2018). EBSCOhost.

Epstein, A. L. *In the Midst of Life: Affect and Ideation in the World of the Tolai.* Berkeley, CA: University of California Press, 1992. EBSCOebooks.

Epstein, A. L. *Matupit: Land, Politics, and Change Among the Tolai of New Britain.* Berkeley, CA: University of California Press, 1969.

Epstein, A. L. "The Tolai of the Gazelle Peninsula." *Journal of the Polynesian Society.* Vol. 70, No. 4 (December 1961). JSTOR.

Firth, Stewart. "Albert Hahl: Governor of German New Guinea." *Papua New Guinea Portraits: The Expatriate Experience.* James Griffin (ed.). Canberra, Australia: Australian National University, 1978.

Firth, Stewart. *New Guinea Under the Germans.* Melbourne, Australia: Melbourne University Press, 1983.

Firth, Stewart. "The Transformation of the Labour Trade in German New Guinea, 1899-1914." *Journal of Pacific History.* Vol. 11, No. 1 (1976). JSTOR.

Gamble, Bruce. *Fortress Rabaul: The Battle for the Southwest Pacific, January 1942-April 1943.* Minneapolis, MN: Zenith Press, 2010. EBSCOebooks.

Geertz, Clifford. *The Interpretation of Cultures: Selected Essays.* New York: Basic Books, 2017.

Hahl, Albert. *Governor in New Guinea.* Peter G. Sack and Dymphna Clark (eds. and trans.). Canberra, Australia: Australian National University, 1980.

Hempenstall, Peter. "The Neglected Empire: The Superstructure of the Colonial State in German Melanesia." *Germans in the Tropics: Essays in German Colonial History.* Arthur J. Knoll and Lewis H. Gann (eds.). New York: Greenwood Press, 1987.

Hempenstall, Peter J. *Pacific Islanders Under German Rule: A Study in the Meaning of Colonial Resistance.* Canberra, Australia: Australian National University, 2016.

Hezel, Francis. *Strangers in Their Own Land: A Century of Colonial Rule in the Caroline and Marshall Islands.* Honolulu, HI: University of Hawai'i Press, 1995.

Hiery, Hermann. *The Neglected War: The German South Pacific and the Influence of World War I.* Honolulu, HI: University of Hawai'i Press, 1995.

Hiromitsu, Iwamoto. "The Origin and Development of Japanese Settlement in Papua and New Guinea, 1890-1914." *Japan and the Pacific, 1540-1920.* Mark Caprio and Matsuda Koichirō (eds.). Abingdon, UK: Routledge, 2016.

Johnson, Charles. "Huge Empire Lost to Germany: Fighting in Asia and Africa Has Wrested…" *New York Times.* August 1, 1915. SM7. ProQuest Historical Newspapers.

Johnson, Edward Lee. "Education in Micronesia: The Challenge of History." Thesis. University of

Hawai'i, 1971.

Johnson, R. Wally. "Calderas, Ignimbrites and the 1937 Eruption at Rabaul: 1914-1940," *Fire Mountains of the Islands: A History of Volcanic Eruptions and Disaster Management in Papua New Guinea and the Solomon Islands.* Canberra, Australia: Australian National University, 2013. JSTOR.

Levy, Josh. "Ideal Coconut Country: Commodified Coconuts and the Scientific Plantation in Pohnpei, Micronesia." *Journal of Pacific History.* Vol. 53, No. 4 (December 2018). EBSCOhost.

Lowell, Thomas. "They Saw a Volcano Born!" *Los Angeles Times.* October 3, 1937. J7. ProQuest Historical Newspapers.

Marcus, G. E. "Manifestations of Mana: Political Power and Divine Inspiration in Polynesia." *Choice.* 52.5 (January 2015). ProQuest Central.

Moran, Michael. *Beyond the Coral Sea: Travels in the Old Empires of the South-west Pacific.* London UK: Flamingo/HarperCollins, 2004.

Moses, J. A. "The German Empire in Melanesia, 1884-1914: A German Self-Analysis." *The History of Melanesia.* K.S. Inglis (ed.). Canberra: Australian National University/University of Papua and New Guinea, 1969.

"Mud Blocks a Harbor in Undersea Quake." *New York Times.* June 2, 1937. 25. ProQuest Historical Newspapers.

Neumann, Klaus. *Not the Way It Really Was: Constructing the Tolai Past.* Honolulu, Hawai'i: University of Hawai'i Press, 1992.

Ohff, Hans-Jürgen. *Disastrous Ventures: German and British Enterprises in East New Guinea Up to 1914.* Melbourne, Australia: Plenum Publishing, 2015.

Oram, Nigel. "Reviewed Works: Governor in New Guinea by Albert Hahl." *The Journal of the Polynesian Society.* Vol. 91, No. 1 (March 1982). JSTOR.

Overall, Lilian. *A Woman's Impression of Germany New Guinea.* New York: Dodd, Mead and Company, 1923.

Neumann, Klaus. "Nostalgia for Rabaul." *Oceania.* Vol. 67, Nl. 3 (March 1997). JSTOR.

"Papua New Guinea, Zoning Plan of Rabaul - Bebauungsplan von Rabaul, 1:5 000, 1913," Open Research Repository, Australian National University, http://hdl.handle.net/1885/219805.

Robson, Robert William. *Queen Emma: the Samoan-American Girl Who Founded an Empire in 19th Century New Guinea.* San Francisco, CA: Tri-Ocean Books, 1965.

Sack, Peter. "The End of the Hahl Era in German New Guinea: Voluntary Career Change or Removal from Office?" *The Journal of Pacific History.* Vol. 25, No. 2 (December 1990). JSTOR.

Sack, Peter. *Phantom History, the Rule of Law and the Colonial State: The Case of German New Guinea.* Canberra, Australia: Australian National University, 2001.

Smith, Woodruff D. *German Colonial Empire.* Chapel Hill, NC: University of North Carolina Press, 1978.

Spennemann, Dirk H. R. "Government Publishing in the German Pacific, 1885-1914." *Journal of Pacific History.* Vol. 52, No. 1 (March 2017), EBSCOhost.

Spennemann, Dirk H. R. "Trial and Error: The Introduction of Plants and Animals to German Micronesia, 1885-1914." *Journal of Pacific History.* Vol. 54, No. 4 (December 2019). EBSCOhost.

Spennemann, Dirk H. R. *Typhoons in Micronesia: A History of Tropical Cyclones and their Effects until 1914.* Saipan, Micronesia: Division of Historic Preservation, 2004.

Steen, Andreas. "Germany and the Chinese Coolie: Labor, Resistance, and the Struggle for Equality, 1884-1914." *German Colonialism Revisited: Africa, Asia, and Oceanic Experiences.* Nina Berman, Klaus Mühlhahn, and Patrice Nganang (eds.). Ann Arbor, MI: University of Michigan Press, 2014.

Stephenson, Charles. *Germany's Asia-Pacific Empire: Colonization and Naval Policy, 1885-1914.* Woodbridge, UK: The Boydell Press, 2009.

Swadling, Pamela. *Plumes from Paradise: Trade Cycles in Outer Southeast Asia and their Impact on New Guinea and Nearby Islands until 1920.* Boroko, Papua New Guinea, 1996.

Van der Grijp, Paul. *Manifestations of Mana: Political Power and Divine Inspiration in Polynesia.* Zürich, Switzerland: Lit Verlag, 2014.

"Volcano Destroys Island Town, Five Hundred Reported Killed." *Los Angeles Times.* July 9, 1937. 1. ProQuest Historical Newspapers.

Walther, Daniel J. "Radicalizing Sex: Same-Sex Relations, German Colonial Authority and *Deutschtum.*" *Journal of the History of Sexuality.* Vol. 17, No. 1 (2008). EBSCOhost.

Walther, Daniel J. *Sex and Control: Venereal Disease, Colonial Physicians and Indigenous Agency in German Colonialism, 1884-1914.* New York: Berghahn Books, 2015.

CHAPTER 5

ENGELS
VOLGA GERMAN ASSR

On September 6, 1929, leftist German theater producer Erwin Piscator premiered the controversial play *The Merchant of Berlin*, which was set in 1923 as inflation overwhelmed Weimar Germany's economy. The production was unusual because it featured innovative stagecraft and championed what Piscator defined as purposeful political theater. The communist sought to emphasize the era's economic, cultural, political, and social tensions through a set design that called for film screens to be mounted behind three small stages. These three platforms, which interacted with one another through a complex system of elevators and conveyor belts, represented the proletariat, the middle class, and the Junkers, Prussia's landed aristocracy and military class. By projecting documentary film footage onto the screens and behind the actors, Piscator was able to portray the proletariat as tragic figures, the Junkers as grotesque figures, and the middle class as combining the tragic and the grotesque in a decidedly problematic manner. The play's plot centers upon a nearly-broke Jewish man, who speculates at an opportune moment and becomes wealthy enough to own his own shop. In the third act, the audience learns that this man, Simon Kaftan, has gained his affluence by selling arms to a secret right-wing group bent on using violence to further its political agenda. When this group instigates a riot, Kaftan's store is looted and then gutted by fire. The act ends with street cleaners sweeping up debris, worthless paper money, soldiers' helmets, and a soldier's body, while singing the words, "trash, away with it." With this scene, Piscator vividly condemns all who do not stand with the proletariat and challenges his audience to engage in civil disobedience to confront the status quo.

The production angered a large swath of Berlin's political spectrum, from Nazi Brownshirts, who began patrolling outside the theater, to the bourgeois press, which condemned Piscator for turning the German stage "into a madhouse and carnival where the lowest vulgarity is peddled." They derided the play as "a revue of puerile screeching hate" that was "an effrontery without parallel." The production closed after just six weeks, but Piscator was unapologetic; as he said the following April, "Never was it more essential than now to take sides: the side of the proletariat. More than ever the theatre must nail its flag fanatically to the mast of politics: the politics of the proletariat." For Piscator, it wasn't enough for theater to have a political message; rather, theater needed to be an agitating political force that could educate the proletariat in order to bring about revolutionary political change.

In spring 1931, Piscator arrived in Moscow, becoming a part of the growing exodus of communist artists from Weimar Germany. He was soon elected to the Presidium of the International Association of Revolutionary Theaters (MORT), and in 1933 he became the organization's president. Unwilling to simply be a figurehead of a self-serving organization, Piscator decided to use the group's

Illustration 50: Erwin Piscator in Berlin, 1929.

resources and contacts to build a great antifascist theater that would stand as a symbol of proletarian resistance to Nazi rule. It would feature exceptional directors, playwrights, and actors, including Bertolt Brecht and Friedrich Wolf, who could inspire and lead. Surprisingly, the home for this theater was neither Moscow nor Leningrad. Instead, the chosen site was Engels, the capital of the newly-recognized Volga German Autonomous Soviet Socialist Republic.

Illustration 51: Map of key cities in Western Russia and Eastern Europe in 1936.

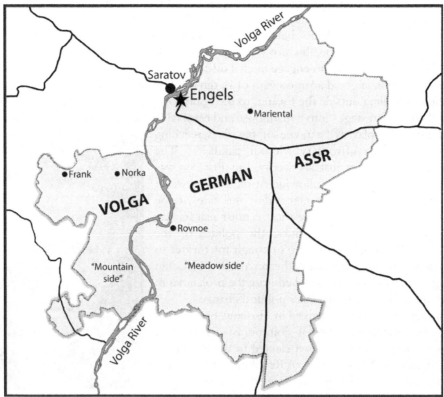

Illustration 52: Map of the Volga German ASSR in 1936.

A Little Historical Context

In July 1763, Catherine the Great issued a manifesto to promote foreign immigration to border areas within her empire. The decree promised Christian immigrants the freedom to worship as they wished, the right to self-government, and a permanent exemption from military service. Settlers were also offered their choice of land, interest-free loans for ten years, an exemption from all taxes for thirty years, and the right to import their possessions duty free. There were to be no restrictions on the immigrants' vocations and all were to have legal standing as Russian subjects. The Russian government even agreed to cover relocation expenses, such as food and transportation, and allowed immigrants the right to purchase serfs. While the Russian government did not specifically recruit Germans, these generous terms particularly appealed to them as a result of the ways in which their countryside had been ruined by the Seven Years' War. By 1774, over 30,000 Germans had resettled in Russia, mostly along the banks of the Middle Volga, near the established town of Saratov.

Illustration 53: Lutheran Church in the village of Norka, January 1881. Note the Western architectural style with columns, a pediment, and tower with Romanesque arches. This is clearly not an onion-domed Orthodox Church.

It was an unfamiliar land, especially because farming in this part of Russia was far more difficult than in Germany. Not only was the annual rainfall on the Volga about half of that in the driest areas of Germany, but rain typically didn't come in the spring as crops grew. Instead, strong winds from Central Asia prevailed, drying out the soil to create a semi-arid environment that was also prone to late frosts. Scorchingly hot in the summer and bitterly cold in the winter, the environment on the Volga steppe was similar to that of the western parts of Kansas and Nebraska. Adapting to this harsh environment, the German immigrants settled into more than a hundred small villages on both sides of Russia's great river. The western bank was settled first, thanks to its better soil and the availability of timber; it became known as the Mountain Side. Its villages had log houses with thatched roofs and were centered around the community's chosen church, whether Catholic, Lutheran, or Mennonite. Across

Illustration 54: Colorized photograph of camels with Meadow Side farmer and plow.

Illustration 55: Wattled granary and farm buildings, Volga region, c.1885.

the two-mile-wide Volga was the flatter Meadow Side. Here, the village church looked down on wattled sod houses that were lined with clay and then whitewashed. On both sides of the river, the fields were mainly sown with high-protein durum wheat, which was largely exported as the region's primary cash crop. Farmers also grew rye, millet, oats, and barley, sunflowers, sugar beets, and tobacco for local use, but because the Volga farmers did not practice crop rotation or use chemical fertilizers, the soil was easily exhausted. Camels were often used as draft animals, confirming the fact that the colonists were in the wild borderland steppe between Europe and Asia.

Neither the Mountain or Meadow Volga Germans ever developed what might be identified as a national consciousness. Instead, they remained quite isolated from one another, as well as from Orthodox Christian Russians in the region and from the capital of Engels, with each German village acting autonomously. They built their own schools, churches, and houses with little to no assistance from the outside world. One of the reasons for this independence was that the immigrants continued to think of themselves as Bavarians, Hessians, or Swabians, instead of as Germans who shared a common identity. As the generations passed, this regional identification did not fade, even as these people also developed a strong attachment to their adopted land and maintained a notable loyalty to the Russian monarchy that had allowed them to escape war-torn Germany. By the early twentieth century, there were efforts to promote a sense of pan-Germanism, but it was an uphill battle. The German Association in the city of Saratov, for example, sponsored a series of lectures, balls, and gymnastic performances in an effort to generate *Volkstrum*, but the events typically attracted only 150-200 people in years immediately preceding World War I. Since there were over 500,000 ethnic Germans in the region by 1914, it is clear that there was more than physical distance that separated the farmers and Saratov. Engels experienced more success in promoting pan-Germanism, supporting a German theater, a 600-person German choir, several churches, a museum, a university, a publishing house, numerous German language schools, and an impressive system of nursery schools, but these institutions were largely patronized by more recent immigrants than the Volga Germans. Indeed, many historians argue rural Volga Germans formed a distinct population. They were people who simply saw themselves as dutiful Russian subjects who had little in common with ethnic Germans in the Ukraine or with those Germans in Russia who sought political autonomy.

With the outbreak of World War I, the Volga Germans were drafted into the tsar's army, becoming part of the 300,000 men of German heritage who fought against Kaiser Wilhelm II. This service did not prevent the rise of xenophobic, anti-German sentiments as the war progressed: Saratov and surrounding towns witnessed vandals loot and destroy hundreds of shops and flats in May 1915; it became illegal to speak German in public; and the tsarist government ordered the confiscation of all land owned by German Russians early in 1918. The Volga Germans welcomed the news of the February Revolution that deposed Nicholas II because the change of government nullified this order. They were less sanguine about the October Revolution that put the Bolsheviks in power eight months later, and many Volga Germans fought against the Bolsheviks during the Russian Civil War. Lenin responded to this situation by trying to win German support at home and abroad. In October 1918, he announced the recognition of a semi-autonomous region governed by the Volga German Workers' Commune. Lenin hoped that by promoting Volga German self-rule, he could not only stop them from supporting the pro-tsarist Whites, but also provide the proletariat in Germany with an inspiration for what could happen after a Bolshevik-led revolution. The Volga Germans could model what a post-revolutionary Germany might look like. This propaganda campaign continued after the Civil War with the creation of the Volga German Autonomous Soviet Socialist Republic on January 6, 1924. The government's capital was the town that would become known as Engels.[11]

Engels c. 1936

When Erwin Piscator arrived in Engels in January 1936, he found a river community of about 60,000 people[12] that did not possess a strong German milieu. In fact, only 12% of Engels' population was of German heritage. Instead, Engels was a predominantly Russian and Ukrainian community that was being held hostage by central planners in Moscow. In July 1932, the Council of People's Commissars had recommended that all municipal construction in Engels be halted; they wanted to wait until a decision could be made regarding the feasibility of constructing a dam on the Volga—a dam that would necessitate the relocation of the Volga German ASSR's capital. This delay meant that although the town faced a significant housing shortage, had no sewage system, and provided running water to only a tenth of its residents, there had been no municipal construction for more than three years. Engels' five buses struggled to provide service over the town's largely unpaved streets, just as its electrical grid suffered from frequent interruptions in service. Most residents lived in one-story wooden buildings with sharply-pitched roofs and two windows facing the main facade. These windows were framed with shutters, decorated panels, and elaboratively-carved platbands or lintels. Wealthier residents lived in two-story stone or brick houses that came in an eclectic range of architectural styles. Their streets had streetlights, but much of the town did not. Everyone, however, faced the frequent problem of malaria. There were several factories in town, including a brick and tile operation, a tractor repair plant, a new bakery, and a glue works, but the giant meat-packing center authorized by the Soviet government in 1929 had yet to begin operations. Railroads connected Engels to Astrakhan near the Caspian Sea and to Uralsk and Tashkent in modern Kazakhstan, but because a bridge had yet to be built across the Volga in this region, there was no rail connection to Saratov. All this meant that when Piscator arrived, Engels would have felt to him more like an oversized village than a true capital city.

Illustration 56: Bone Grinding and Glue Plant in Engels, c. 1930.

---

[11] In 1934, the town of Pokrovsk was renamed Engels after Friedrich Engels (1820-1895), Karl Marx's collaborator and patron. This change was as a part of a campaign to rename Russian cities after communist leaders. Other examples include Stalingrad (formerly Tsaritsyn, now Volgograd) and Leningrad (formerly Petrograd, now St. Petersburg.)

[12] No official census was taken in Russia in the 1930s, so this figure is an estimate; what is known is that the census in 1926 lists the population of Pokrovsk (Engels) as 34,345; the community's population in 1941 was 73,200.

Engels was also near the center of a region that had recently known considerable hardship. In 1920, the Bolshevik government announced a new round of mandatory grain requisitions with a goal of collecting 42% of the Volga German summer grain harvest. Military food brigades were sent to collect the crops and punish those who refused to cooperate. When the harvest largely

Illustration 57: Anti-Kulak Poster. The text says, "We will not let any priest and kulak into our collective farm!" The Volga Germans were accused of being prosperous peasants or kulaks.

failed due to drought, the government's seizures compounded the problems of the drought and left an insufficient amount of seed grain for the following year. This created an outright catastrophe as the drought continued and the Volga River dropped to its lowest level in decades. By summer 1921, people were eating dogs, cats, and rats, and by February 1922 some people were reported to have resorted to cannibalism, digging up dead bodies for food. Only when food supplies from international relief organizations began to enter Russia was the crisis mitigated. Even then, it is estimated that 70,000 Volga Germans fled the region and 48,000 Volga Germans died. The 1930s witnessed more suffering, thanks to Stalin's policy of forced land collectivization and his goal of eliminating prosperous peasants (or kulaks) as a class. The Volga Germans were particular targets for these initiatives: by March 1930, 60% of the farms in the Volga German ASSR had been collectivized (as compared to 25% within Russia itself), and more than 25,000 people had been deported as enemies of the state, often to labor camps in Siberia. When another drought struck the region in 1933-1934, famine again followed, but this time Stalin refused to accept any

international relief. Consequently, more than 100,000 people migrated to other parts of the Soviet Union in an attempt to escape starvation and 55,000 Volga Germans died. Russian chauvinists, including a party official from Chelyabinsk, saw this calamity as a "great benefit" since "the losses from starvation have mainly affected the alien races" and opened up lands for Russian settlement. Indeed, for most in Moscow, including Stalin, Russians mattered more in the multicultural Soviet Union than anyone else.

The government based in Engels mirrored the paranoia of the Stalinist state as a whole with its overlapping and competing jurisdictions, the omnipresence of the secret police, and a frequent reshuffling of personnel. In fact, there was little continuity in the ASSR's leadership as a result of Stalin's methods, as the career of Adam Andreevich Welsch makes clear. He was born into a poor family in the Volga German village of Rovnoe in 1893 and grew up working as a shepherd and laborer. During World War I, he served in the tsarist army, fighting against the Ottoman Empire in the Caucuses. Hospital records show that he was wounded three times. After the war, he became a member of the secret police in his hometown and began quickly moving up the ranks. By 1921, Welsch was chairman of Rovnoe's city council, and he had become the people's commissar of agriculture for the German Volga ASSR by 1930. After a stint in Moscow studying Marxist-Leninism, fortifying his ideological credentials and establishing more political connections, Welsch returned to the Volga to lead the supposedly autonomous republic. Between December 1934 and August 1937, Welsch chaired the Volga German Council of People's Commissars and its Central Executive Committee, which was the regional committee of the Communist Party of the Soviet Union. During his time in these offices, he followed Stalin's lead by arbitrarily arresting and executing perceived opponents of the state. Then, as Stalin's second round of purges gained in momentum, the tables turned and Welsch became a target. He was charged with treason and subsequently shot in Saratov on January 21, 1938. Being an official in Stalinist Russia was a game of roulette.

It was against this complex background that Erwin Piscator sought to build his didactic, high-quality theater for the masses. His goal was to create an institution that would symbolize proletarian resistance to Nazi rule and honor the cultural legacy of the Weimar Republic. He hoped to attract antifascist actors and directors of the highest caliber to join a well-financed, state-supported program that could educate the people and serve as an inspirational refuge for leftist exiles. The opening season's program was to begin with Maxim Gorky's 1910 play *Vassa Zheleznova*, which tells the story of a materialistic matriarch whose family is destroyed by bourgeois ambition and greed. Other scheduled works included Friedrich Wolf's *Professor Mamlock* (about a Jewish doctor being refused the right to work in 1933 in the immediate wake of Hitler's becoming Germany's chancellor), and Bertolt Brecht's *Round Heads and Pointed Heads* (about a fictitious country whose leaders disguise class antagonisms by pitting people with round heads against those with pointed heads). In spring 1936, the company's twenty resident actors went to Moscow to receive additional training, and by August rehearsals were underway in Engels' existing German language theater.

There were several hurdles to achieving what turned out to be a quixotic dream. The first was language. The Volga Germans spoke more than sixteen dialects, none of which matched those used in Germany today. In fact, their language was closer to that spoken during the Reformation than it was to modern German. In addition, most of the Volga Germans did not speak any Russian. This situation stemmed from the isolation of the original colonists, as well as from the natural blending that occurred as the generations passed and people from different villages intermarried. By the 1930s, it was impossible to trace what the Volga Germans spoke in villages like Frank, Norka, Mariental, or Rovnoe back to established regional dialects in Germany like Bavarian, Hessian, or Pomeranian. There had simply been too much linguistic divergence, as the following few examples show:

English	Volga German	Modern German
beets	Rieve	Rüben
bicycle	Tretwage	Fahrrad
cows/cattle	Kih	Vieh
infection	Rotlaf	Infektion

But the linguistic issue wasn't simply limited to pronunciations or vocabulary. It also involved definitions:

Word	Volga Meaning	Modern Meaning
blecht	shy	bleeds
doll	mentally slow	unusual, great
Fledermaus	miller moth	bat
Gaul	horse	nag

All of this made the Volga Germans almost unintelligible to Piscator and the other Weimar émigrés. While the unanticipated awkwardness of not being able to communicate with ease could have provided the fodder for a memorable comedy, Piscator was only interested in devoting his theater to serious political work. He had a mission to accomplish, a dream to fulfill, and he was not going to let a language barrier stand in his way. Piscator's solution was to supplement his Volga German troupe with Ukrainian Germans and to provide specialized language training in modern German for the Volga German actors.

Another hurdle for Piscator was the extent to which the Volga Germans were isolated from the world around them. They had yet to develop a Marxist class consciousness, and they knew little of Nazi ideology or Hitler's rise to power. These factors meant that the plays that Piscator wanted to produce were not ones that were likely to appeal to Meadow Side farmers. In addition, urban residents had grown weary of the cultural propaganda known as agitprop. They were in

Illustration 58: Soviet agitprop poster, 1920. The text says, "Labor Will Be the Masters of the World."

Illustration 59: Soviet agitprop poster. The text says, "The Red Ploughman," 1920.

the mood for something lighter and more subtle, especially after the years of hardship. Other impediments included Piscator's failure to entice Bertolt Brecht to become the Engels' theater dramaturg, the refusal of key émigrés directors to move to Engels, and Stalin's dissolution of the venture's sponsoring agency, the International Association of Revolutionary Theaters (MORT).

In the end, only one production ever reached the Engels stage, Friedrich Wolf's anti-fascist play *The Trojan Horse*. In January 1937, the theater was denounced as an anti-Soviet, bourgeois enterprise and many of the people associated with it were arrested. This too was a part of Stalin's second round of purges as the dictator became increasingly paranoid about spying German émigrés. Piscator only escaped persecution because while he was on a promotional trip to Paris, he received a tip telling him not to return to the USSR. It was a tip that saved his life.

A Short Postscript

As early as 1934, the Soviet Union's secret police, the NKVD, began compiling lists of individuals of German ancestry living within the USSR. When Hitler launched Operation Barbarossa on June 22, 1941, these lists were used to facilitate the deportation of hundreds of

Illustration 60: Official Soviet photograph of Lavrentiy Beria, the head of the NKVD from 1938-1946.

thousands of ethnic Germans from western Russia to Siberia and Kazakhstan. The operation was put in motion after Lavrentiy Beria, head of the NKVD, and Vyacheslav Molotov, the Chairman of the Council of People's Commissars, traveled to Engels later in June to assess the viability of the operation and the degree of urgency. Their recommendation to Stalin was that the entire German population of the ASSR needed to be removed as soon as the harvest was complete. Those in urban areas could be removed earlier. Hence, in early July, the NKVD occupied Engels, cut off all communication with the outside world, and began arresting civic leaders. Then, on August 27, Beria issued the resettlement order and three days later the government announced the news. The decree proclaimed that "tens of thousands of saboteurs and spies" had extensively infiltrated the Volga German community and "were awaiting a signal from Germany" to act. It was necessary to remove them in order to protect them and to prevent sabotage. All were subject to the decree, including communist party members and the families of soldiers fighting in the Red Army, except for those German women who had married Russian men. According to Beria's decree, the deportees were granted sufficient time to put their affairs in order and to prepare for the move; they specifically had the right to bring personal property and possessions with them, provided that these items could be easily moved. For items that could not be, such as farm equipment and livestock, the value of the property was to be assessed and promissory notes issued in compensation.

In actuality, little of this happened. Most deportees only had a few hours' notice to prepare, were only allowed to bring what they could personally carry, and did not receive governmental promissory notes. Indeed, the operation proceeded with vicious efficiency. In less than three weeks, between September 3 and September 20, NKVD agents loaded 438,280 Volga Germans onto trucks, took them to the nearest railway station, and squeezed them into unsanitary boxcars heading east. Displaced Russians and Ukrainians quickly moved into the abandoned houses, relieved to find farming equipment and cultivated lands at their disposal. Ethnic Germans from other parts of the Soviet Union were also subjected to deportation, bringing the total number of

Illustration 61 and 62: People waiting for deportation in 1941 (left) and the eviction card for the family of Conrad Schreiber from the village of Norka (right). Conrad was executed in Norka police station by the NKVD in 1937, but the rest of the family survived the forced evacuation and eventually emigrated to Germany and the United States.

Soviet Germans uprooted to 840,000; of these, at least 228,000 or 27% died as a result of their experiences during their expulsion. Those Soviet Germans who did survive the journey to Siberia or Kazakhstan were subjected to forced labor, mostly felling timber for railroad construction. This work applied to all men between 15 and 55 and all women between 16 and 45, unless pregnant or nursing. Soviet Germans were certainly not the only ethnic minority group the government subjected to resettlement during the war—Chechens, Finns, Greeks, Kalmyks, Koreans, Tartars and others were as well—but the Germans were the only ones who experienced forced labor in large numbers.

When the war ended, the Volga Germans were not permitted to return to their farms. Instead, the Volga German Autonomous Soviet Socialist Republic ceased to exist as a political entity, its territories absorbed by surrounding administrative districts. Stalin's message in this decision was clear: peace would not bring forgiveness. In 1954, Khrushchev denounced Stalin's policy of forced deportation during the war, closed the special settlements and labor camps, and allowed certain groups, including the Chechens and Kalmyks, to return to their original homes. This rehabilitation did not apply to Germans. Hence, most chose to remain working in Siberia or Kazakhstan. Even in 1964, when the Volga Germans were specifically absolved of Nazi collaboration by the Presidium of the Supreme Soviet, they could not return to their homes because doing so would require the resettlement of 500,000 Russians in the Volga area. As the Chair of the Presidium Anastas Mikoyan said, "not everything done in history is correctable."

Between 1971-1980, 64,000 Soviet Germans, most of them with origins in the Volga region, migrated to West Germany. In the late 1980s, emigration soared, culminating in 500,000 applications in 1990. By 2010, there were only 7,579 people of German descent in the area that was once the Volga German Autonomous Soviet Socialist Republic. Most had become Russian speakers. In other words, with the disbursement of the Volga Germans and their subsequent assimilation into other societies, the world lost one of its ethnic groups.

Today, Engels is a city of about 250,000 people with an industrial base specializing in the production of electrical machinery, trains and railway cars, plastics, synthetic detergents, and paper. Agriculture accounts for only 20% of the city's export production. Most of Engels' residents live in rather depressing apartment blocks surrounding the city, but Engels' historic core offers a variety of public parks, restored buildings, river beaches, museums, and squares that appeal. Near the city's largest park, there is a regional operetta theater that seeks to blend popular entertainment with didactic themes. The major production for 2023 was *Zorro*, a two-act musical that used the "language of dance" to "awaken the most tender feelings in the viewer" and to prove that "good and justice triumphs against evil." In 2024, the Saratovskiy Oblastnoy Teatr Operetty staged *From the Heroes of Bygone Times*, a one act which commemorates The Great Patriotic War (World War II) and the defeat of fascism. Using "excerpts from genuine letters from frontline soldiers" the musical is "full of sincerity, human warmth, and…the harsh, searing truth that young people should know." Erwin Piscator would be pleased to know that educational theater for the masses perseveres in Engels.

What Engels Teaches

In addition to the frank truth that "not everything in history is correctable," Engels symbolizes two historical lessons. The first is that there is more than just a physical distance that separates most capitals from the lands they govern. Indeed, there is often a profound dissonance in understanding between a national, regional, or city government and everyday people. That the government in Engels had little connection with most Volga Germans was a product of its being dominated either by Russians or by refugees from Nazi Germany. These people did not know much about the experience of the Volga Germans in the countryside, nor did they particularly care. Power and influence originated elsewhere, not in the hands of isolated farmers who spoke an odd language. This type of discord is still found around the world today: according to a 2021 survey conducted in twenty-eight countries, most individuals see their government as being far less ethical and far less effective than other institutions they rely upon, such as businesses, NGOs, and media. This shows that people around the world remain alienated from the governments that are supposed to serve them. As with Engels, the consequences of this resentment and bitterness are often tragic.

Secondly, nomenclature matters. The change of the capital's name from Pokrovsk to Engels in 1931 reflected a particular political milieu and reveals how a new nation wanted to remember and interpret its past. A parallel might be found in American history, for how we designate the conflict between 1861 and 1865 dives to the very core of its meaning: "The Civil War," "The War Between the States", and "The War of Northern Aggression" each have very different political connotations. Similarly, it mattered to the Soviet Union's leadership that St. Petersburg be renamed Leningrad and that Tsaritsyn become Stalingrad. This is why there were thousands of city name changes in during the first two decades of the Soviet Union's existence; about the only thing that made Engels' name change unusual was that it honored someone who had been deceased for more than three decades instead of a current leader in the USSR. Furthermore, it's worth noting that while "Engels" may still be the official designation for the former capital of the Volga German ASSR, most of the people living in the city today use its old name, "Pokrovsk." This reveals how ephemeral ideologically-based nomenclature can be and how persistent tradition is. Names may change, but attitudes often don't.

Curated Bibliography for Chapter 5

Alexopoulos, Golfo. *Stalin's Outcasts: Aliens, Citizens, and the Soviet State, 1926-1936*. Ithaca, NY: Cornell University Press, 2003.

Akhmetova, Maria V. "'A Town with Two Names': A Historical Oikonym in Modern Context (the Case of The Town of Pokrovsk/Engels." *Voprosy Onomastiki*. Vol. 18, No. 1 (2021).

Aumüller, Matthias. "Viktor Irmunskij and German Mundartforschung." *Studies in Eastern European Thought*. Vol. 60, No, 4 (December 2008). ProQuest.

Blank, Stephen. *The Sorcerer as Apprentice: Stalin as Commissar of Nationalities, 1917-1924*. Westport, CT: Greenwood Press, 1994.

Bursa, G.R.F. "Political Changes of Names in Soviet Towns." *The Slavonic and East European Review*. Vol. 62, No.2 (April 1985). JSTOR.

Centre-Local Relations in the Stalinist State. E.A. Rees (ed.). New York: Palgrave Macmillan, 2002.

Conquest, Robert. *The Harvest of Sorrow: Soviet Collectivization and the Terror-Famine*. New York: Oxford University Press, 1986.

"Edelman Trust Barometer, 2021: A Global Report." Edelman: Chicago, IL: 2021. https://www.edelman.com

End to Silence, An: Uncensored Opinion in the Soviet Union from Roy Medvedev's Underground Magazine Political Diary. Stephen F. Cohen (ed.) and George Saunders (trans.). New York: W. W. Norton, 1982.

Falaleeva, Lyudmila A. "'Little Cogs of the Huge State Machine': Formation and Development of Nursery Care System in 1920s-1930s (on the Materials of the Republic of Germans in the Volga Region). *Journal of Volgograd State University: History, Area Studies and International Relations*. Vol. 22, No. 2 (2017).

Fitzpatrick, Sheila. *Stalin's Peasants: Resistance and Survival in the Russian Village after Collectivization*. New York: Oxford University Press, 1984.

Fleischhauer, Ingeborg and Benjamin Pinkus. *The Soviet Germans: Past and Present*. London: C. Hurst & Company, 1986.

Hartley, Janet M. *A History of Russia's Greatest River*. New Haven, CT: Yale University Press, 2021.

Keller, Conrad. *The German Colonies in South Russia, 1804-1904*. Anthony Becher (trans.). Lincoln, NE: American Historical Society of Germans From Russia, 1980.

Keller, Conrad. *The German Colonies in South Russia, 1804-1904*. Anthony Becher (trans.). Vol. 2. Lincoln, NE: American Historical Society of Germans From Russia, 1983.

Kloberdanz, Timothy J. and Rosalinda Kloberdanz. *Thunder on the Steppe: Volga German Folklife in Changing Russia*. Lincoln, NE: American Historical Society of Germans from Russia, 1993.

Long, James W. *From Privileged to Dispossessed: The Volga Germans 1860-1917*. Lincoln, NE: University of Nebraska Press, 1988.

Long, James W. "The Volga Germans and the Famine of 1921." *The Russian Review*. Vol. 51, No. 4 (October 1992). JSTOR.

Loup, Alfred Joseph III, "The Theatrical Productions of Erwin Piscator in Weimar Germany: 1920-1931." Dissertation. Baton Rouge, LA: Louisiana State University, 1972.

Mally, Lynn. "Exporting Soviet Culture: The Case of Agitprop Theater." *Slavic Review*, Vol. 62, No. 2 (Summer, 2003). JSTOR.

Martin, Terry. *The Affirmative Action Empire: Nations and Nationalism in the Soviet Union, 1923-1939*. Ithaca, NY: Cornell University Press, 2001.

Manz, Stefan. *Constructing a German Diaspora: the 'Greater German Empire' 1871-1914*. New York: Routledge, 2014.

Mehring, Walter. "Der Kaufmann von Berlin." *Volksbühne am Rosa Luxemburg Platz*. No Date. https://volksbuehne.adk.de/praxis/en/der_kaufmann_von_berlin/index.html

Mukhina, Irina. *The Germans of the Soviet Union*. London: Routledge, 2007.

Nationalities Question in the Post-Soviet States, The. Graham Smith (ed.). New York: Longman, 1996.

Newman, E. M. *Seeing Russia*. New York: Funk & Wagnalls Company, 1928.

Palmier, Jean-Michel. *Weimar in Exile: The Antifascist Emigration in Europe and America*. London Verso, 2006.

Patenaude, Bertrand M. *The Big Show in Bololand: The American Relief Expedition to Soviet Russia in the Famine of 1921*. Stanford, CA: Stanford University Press, 2002.

Piscator, Erwin. *The Political Theatre*. Hugh Rorrison (trans.). London: Eyre Methuen, 1980.

Priestland, David. *Stalinism and the Politics of Mobilization: Ideas, Power, and Terror in Inter-war Russia.* New York: Oxford University Press, 2007.

Pohl, J. Otto. *Ethnic Cleansing in the USSR, 1937-1949.* Westport, CT: Greenwood Press, 1999.

Pohl, J. Otto. "Soviet Apartheid: Stalin's Ethnic Deportations, Special Settlement Restrictions, and the Labor Army: the Case of the Ethnic Germans in the USSR." *Human Rights Review.* Vol. 13, No. 2 (June 2012). ProQuest.

Pohl, J. Otto. "Volk auf dem Weg: Transnational Migration of the Russian-Germans from 1763 to the Present Day." *Studies in Ethnicity and Nationalism.* Vol. 9, No. 2 (2009). ProQuest.

Raleigh, Donald J. *Revolution on the Volga: 1917 in Saratov.* Ithaca, NY: Cornell University Press, 1986.

"Republic of Volga Germans." https://lexikon.wolgadeutsche.net

Richardson, Michael, D. *Revolutionary Theater and the Classical Heritage.* Bern, Switzerland: Peter Lang, 2007.

Ro'i, Yaacov. "The Transformation of Historiography on the 'Punished Peoples'." *History and Memory.* Vol. 21, No. 2 (Fall 2009). ProQuest.

"Russian Federation: The Head of the Region Valery Radaev Inspected New Rolling Stock." MENA *Report.* July 17, 2021. ProQuest.

Scott, Hamish. "The Seven Years War and Europe's "Ancien Régime." *War in History.* Vol. 18, No. 4 (November 2011). JSTOR.

Sysoeva, E. A. and V. A. Samogorov. "Architecture of Residential Wooden Houses in the Cities of Samara Province in the Second Half of the XIX-Early XX Centuries." *IOP Conference Series: Science and Engineering,* 775 (2020).

Sheehy, Ann. *The Crimea Tatars and Volga Germans: Soviet Treatment of Two National Minorities.* London: Minority Rights Group, 1971.

Soviet Federation, Nationalism and Economic Decentralization. Alastair McAuley (ed.). New York: St. Martin's Press, 1991.

"Soviet Government to Grant Autonomy to German Colony." *The Washington Post.* March 12, 1924, 4. ProQuest Historical Newspapers.

Soviet Union, The: A Documentary History. Vol. 2 (1939-1991). Edward Aoton and Tom Stableford (eds.) Exeter, UK: University of Exeter Press, 2007.

Soviet Union 1935. New York: International Publishers, 1935.

Stalin, Joseph. "Speech on Agrarian Policy, December 27, 1929." Hanover College https://history.hanover.edu/courses/excerpts/111stalin.html

"Thousands of Red Soldiers are of German Ancestry." *The Washington Post.* July 21, 1941, 7. ProQuest Historical Newspapers.

Twentieth-Century German Dramatists, 1919-1992. Wolfgang D. Elfe and James Harlem (eds.). Detroit, MI: Gale Research, 1992.

Van Eijl, Carrie and Klaus J. Bale. *The Encyclopedia of European Migration and Minorities: From the Seventeenth Century to the Present.* Cambridge, UK: Cambridge University Press, 2011.

Villiers, Marq de. *Down the Volga: A Journey Through Mother Russia in a Time of Troubles.* New York: Viking, 1992.

Willett, John. *The Theater of Erwin Piscator.* London: Eyre Methuen, 1978.

Yankovyak-Rutkovska, Maria. "About 'Arbuse': One of the First 'Rusisms' in the Language of Russian Germans." *Journal of Linguistics.* Vol. 65, No. 1 (2014). ProQuest.

CHAPTER 6

XINJING
MANCHUKUO

Two days after joining the Manchuria Motion Picture Corporation, eighteen year-old Yamaguchi Yoshiko found herself in a train compartment, dressed in pajamas and snuggling a middle-aged Japanese actor she didn't know. She had been suddenly and quite unexpectedly cast as the leading actress in a rather silly 1938 comedy involving a newlywed couple traveling to Beijing in a couchette. But Yoshiko had not been cast in *Honeymoon Express* because of her physique, personality, or previous film experience. Instead, she won the role because she sprang from a unique background that could be exploited to further political ends.

Yoshiko was born in Mukden, China[13] in 1920 to Japanese immigrants. Her father taught Chinese to Japanese citizens working for the South Manchurian Railway (SMR) and raised Yoshiko to be bilingual. He also had her attend Chinese girls schools in order to help her attain a cultural fluency that spanned different cultures. This proved fortuitous, for in 1933, Yoshiko gave a music recital in the best hotel in Mukden that was attended by representatives of the Fengtian Radio Broadcasting Company. These men were looking for girls who could read music, speak Mandarin, and understand Japanese. Yoshiko fit the bill perfectly and was soon recruited to sing patriotic songs for Japan's newly-created puppet state of Manchukuo. These consisted of rearranged Chinese folk tunes and new works that promoted friendship between the region's five ethnic groups: Manchurians, Han Chinese, Mongolians, Koreans, and Japanese.

As a singer for the Fengtian Radio Broadcasting Company and as an actress working for the Manchuria Motion Picture Corporation, Yoshiko adopted a stage name—one specifically designed to appeal to Chinese audiences. She became Li Xianglan.[14] Industry-generated publicity hailed her as "a unique presence that dazzles" thanks to her "modern exotic charm" and ability to speak three languages with "remarkable dexterity." "Bursting upon the scene like a comet across the sky," Li Xianglan's "striking brilliance" had enhanced Manchurian film "beyond imagination." But the real basis of the actress' appeal for government officials was that she could fit so well with the 1938 guidelines issued by Japan's Censorship Division. All Japanese films were meant to "re-educate the masses" by celebrating "the family system and…the national spirit of self-sacrifice." They should suppress "the tendency toward individualism inspired by European and American films," reinforce "traditional values," and imbue "respect for fathers and elder brothers." This meant that Yoshiko was soon cast in melodramas in which she played

---

[13] Proper nouns, especially changing place names, present a particular challenge to those studying northeast China. Mukden, for example, was the name the Manchus gave to their capital. In the early twentieth century, this city was known as Fengtian to the Chinese. Today, it is called Shenyang. Some of the changes are a result of differing systems of transliteration between Chinese, Japanese and English, but Russian nomenclature and Japanese governance also adds to the confusing mix. In an effort to simplify things, I have generally used one designation for a placename (preferably the one used in 1938 by the Japanese), even when this use may be technically anachronistic. It is also worth noting that I use "Manchuria" to designate the geographical region and "Manchukuo" to designate the political entity.

[14] This stage name was Ri Kōran in Japanese.

a young, proud Chinese woman, who after various trials and tribulations would fall in love with a wise, principled, problem-solving Japanese man. The not-so-subtle metaphor of these films was that with Japan's guidance and leadership, Asia would overthrow the last vestiges of Western imperialism and discover a new era of honor and power. As a transnational diva, Yoshiko as Li Xianglan became a symbol of an optimistic future for a newly constituted world.

Illustration 63: Yamaguchi Yoshiko with Kazuo Hasegawa in Song of the White Orchid, 1939.

Illustration 64: Map of the Japanese Empire, Manchukuo and environs in c. 1935

Illustration 65: Liaotung Peninsula c. 1935.

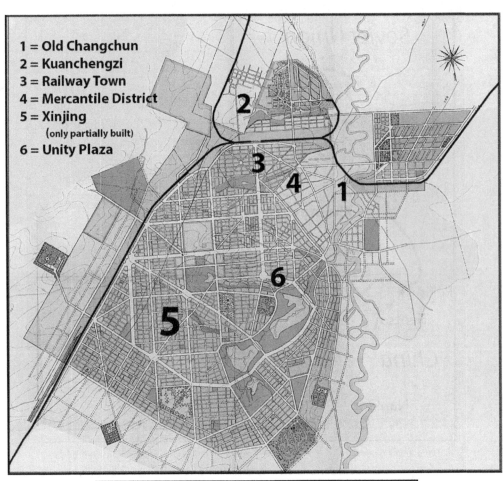

1 = Old Changchun
2 = Kuanchengzi
3 = Railway Town
4 = Mercantile District
5 = Xinjing
   (only partially built)
6 = Unity Plaza

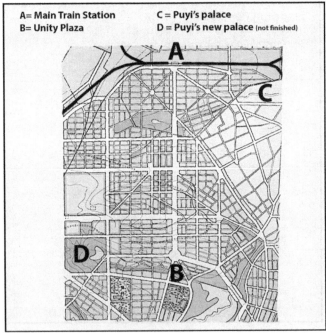

A = Main Train Station
B = Unity Plaza
C = Puyi's palace
D = Puyi's new palace (not finished)

Illustration 66: Maps of Xinjing and its environs (top) and central Xinjing (bottom).

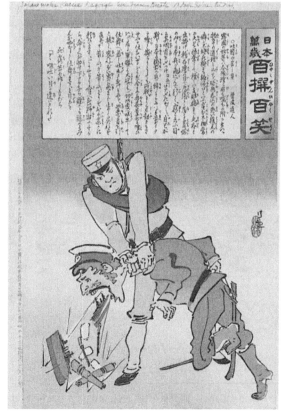

Illustrations 67 and 68: "Russia's War with Japan 1904," (above), and Kiyochika Kobayashi, "Japan Makes Russia Disgorge her Brave Threats of Days Before the War," 1904 (right)). These two propaganda posters dramatically depict in racist terms what their nation will do to the enemy in the Russo-Japanese War.

A Little Historical Context:

In late May 1905, Japan shocked the world by routing the Russian navy at the Battle of Tsushima. This engagement off the southern coast of Korea marked the first time that an Asian nation had convincingly defeated a European one in the modern era.[15] This symbolic shift showed that Japan was emerging as an international power. The battle also brought about a quick end to the hostilities. The resulting Treaty of Portsmouth recognized Japanese preeminence in Korea, transferred Russia's lease of the tip of the Liaotung Peninsula to Japan, and gave Japan control of Russia's Manchurian railroads south of the city that was to be named Xinjing. Significantly for the future, Japan was allowed to protect these tracks with troops. The treaty also granted Japan the southern half of Sakhalin Island, a favorable trade status, compensation for expenses related to prisoners of war, and fishing rights north from Japan to the Bering Sea. But because Russia had not been made to pay an indemnity, much of the Japanese public was aggrieved by the diplomatic settlement. Protests erupted. Over time, this resentment with the treaty's terms helped fuel the way for future conflict in East Asia.

Japan's empire building began in the late nineteenth century with the occupation of the Ryukyu Islands to its south (1872) and the Kuril Islands to its north (1875). Taiwan was subjected to colonial rule in 1895; Korea followed in 1905. Interest in Manchuria grew rapidly in the aftermath of the Russo-Japanese War. Underpopulated, vast, and full of natural resources, Manchuria beckoned for a host of social, economic, and political reasons. Here was a place where Japan's surplus population could emigrate, a place whose coal could power Japan's factories, and a place yearning for peace and stability after decades of warlord rule. Feeding the rise in Japanese nationalism, the domination of Manchuria also came to be seen as a necessary bulwark in Japan's national defense and proof that Japan was an equal participant in the imperialist community. Indeed, Manchuria was a place that the Japanese could modernize and civilize, much as the British, French, and Americans claimed to be doing elsewhere around the world. Eventually, Manchuria became such an idealized place that it was referred to in Japan as the "Kingly Way Paradise Land."

Between 1906 and 1931, the Japanese government relied on the South Manchurian Railway (SMR) to exploit the region's potential. Modeled after the British East India Company, SMR was a private, joint-stock company buoyed by extensive government participation. In fact, the Japanese government owned fifty percent of SMR's shares, Japan's prime minister appointed the corporation's president, and a Japanese military garrison, the Kwantung army, protected the

Illustration 69 and 70: Postcards of the exterior (left) and interior (right) of the South Manchurian Railway Station in Xinjing, c. 1934.

---

[15] The Russo-Japanese War is often referred to as the first time a non-European nation defeated a European one in the modern era, but this does not account for Ethiopia's defeat of an Italian army in the Battle of Adwa in 1896.

railroad's infrastructure. SMR administered everything from schools to coal mines, from public utilities to hotels, from factories to libraries. This power not only made Japan's largest corporation a state within a state, but it also became the mechanism by which Japan could achieve its colonial goals while portraying its presence in Manchuria as a mutually beneficial enterprise. As one key official admitted, SMR had "the appearance of a commercial company but really functions as an organization of the state to carry out colonial rule and colonization."

The illusion of Japan's benevolence ended on the night of September 18, 1931, when a group of Kwantung army officers, acting without proper authorization, placed explosives near the railroad track north of Mukden. Their staged detonation did not do substantial damage to the track, but the army blamed Chinese troops for sabotaging vital Japanese infrastructure. Then they attacked the Chinese garrison in Mukden and began to occupy the country. By December, two-thirds of Manchuria was under direct Kwantung control. Fearing a *coup d'état*, the timid civilian government in Tokyo refused to intervene in what became known as the Manchurian Incident. This event, the resulting seizure of northeast China, and the failure of Japan's civilian government to act had profound consequences. Not only did the event affirm the military's domination of Japanese domestic politics, but it also isolated Japan diplomatically from much of the world community. Indeed, the combination of domestic militarism and international belligerence resulted in the Second Sino-Japanese War (1937-1945) and, more generally, World War II. It also led to the creation of the Japanese puppet state of Manchukuo, which was founded on March 1, 1932.

Illustration 71: Emperor Puyi in Manchukuo uniform, c. 1934.

The nominal head of the Manchukuo government was Puyi, who had been the last emperor of China's Qing (Manchu) Dynasty. Puyi was deposed as a six-year old in 1912, but continued to live in a part of the Forbidden City until 1924, when he was expelled by a warlord who captured Peking. Puyi moved to Tientsin in 1925 and lived as a dandy and dilettante in the city's Japanese concession during his early twenties. As early as May 1928, newspapers were reporting the rumors that the Japanese were planning to place Puyi on a throne in Manchuria, but his inauguration as regent of Manchukuo only came in 1932.[16] The event was orchestrated with considerable pomp, which Puyi remembered vividly: "Even before the train stopped, I could hear the sounds of military music and the cheers of people on the platform." As he stepped off the train, he noticed former Forbidden City bannermen carrying the Qing Dynasty's yellow dragon flags and the sea of color that brought customary Chinese, Japanese and Western attire together. Every hand waved a small flag in welcome. During the inauguration ceremony, which followed "classical Manchu rites" and was performed in a makeshift throne room, Puyi was presented with golden seals, one of the state and one of his office. A gala event followed with "parades, dancing, music, theatricals and other entertainments."

Since there wasn't time to build a new palace, Puyi lived and worked in a compound of eclectic, repurposed buildings. Qinmin Hall, where the throne room was located and where Puyi received diplomats, was a particularly anomalous structure. Its second-story veranda suggested it belonged to the tropics, while its green catenary dome with a bulbous finial evoked the mosques of Samarkand. Romanesque windows on the ground floor brought light into the sumptuous rooms of red carpeting and gold fabrics. Nearby stood the Jixi Building, which

---

[16] In addition to "regent" Puyi's title in 1932 was also translated in the American press as "dictator," "chief executive," and "president-designate."

provided the living quarters for Puyi, his wife, and his concubines. It had originally been built as the central office for a transportation company. With its dark gray stone and Doric-columned portico, this building looked like it had been uprooted from a laird's estate in the Scottish Highlands. Its interior blended royal baroque trappings with art deco furnishings. These architectural details are worth noting because their inherent incongruity serves as a potent metaphor for the lack of harmony between Puyi, the people of Manchuria, and the realities of Japanese imperialism.

The city surrounding the temporary palace had four main neighborhoods in 1932. The oldest was the walled district of Old Changchun, an area with a labyrinth of muddy streets, cramped residences, and worn shops. Modernist city planners and architects considered it squalid instead of quaint. In 1898, the Russians built the second neighborhood, Kuanchengzi, to service its newly-completed railway to Harbin. This district was always a rather inconsequential place. After the Russo-Japanese War, Japanese officials with the Southern Manchurian Railway (SMR) decided to build a new depot and develop the necessary infrastructure south of Kuanchengzi to serve passengers and freight moving between the city and their new ports of Dairen and Ryojun. This new depot area became known as Railway Town. It was dominated by the art nouveau Yamato Hotel, the SMR office, and a circular intersection from which three broad avenues radiated to the southwest, south, and southeast. In between Old Changchun and the Railway Town, a commercial area emerged in the 1910s and 1920s; this Mercantile District mainly combined modern storefronts with Western office buildings like those that had been commandeered for Puyi's palace, but the quarter also housed small factories and warehouses, a prison, and the city's main prostitution district.

When the Japanese decided to make this city the new capital of Manchukuo in 1932, they envisioned creating a vast extension of the municipality. As with other purpose-built capitals like Brasilia, Canberra, or New Delhi, Xinjing's designers believed that the new capital would alleviate an array of past problems and offer an inspiration for a prosperous future. It was to be a modern, ideal city with wide, paved boulevards full of automobiles; underground power and water lines; efficient housing with indoor plumbing in all buildings; and an abundance of parks and open space. The master plan also called for separating industrial areas from commercial and residential zones to reduce noise and pollution, limiting building heights to maintain greater livability, banning electric trams because of their unattractive wires, raising a dam to provide new water sources, and constructing a new airport to accommodate the rapidly emerging mode of transportation. The Japanese wanted Xinjing to be a municipal showcase—proof that Japan could lead the world. Indeed, Xinjing's planners sought to make the city a symbol of the ideology that eventually became known as the Great East Asian Co-Prosperity Sphere. This philosophy asserted that with close Japanese guidance, Asia could do more than overthrow European imperialism; instead, Asia would lead, becoming the world's superior civilization. As SMR economist Miyazaki Masayoshi proclaimed in 1936, Japan will create "a great Oriental society of world-wide universality based on the new Oriental culture (a culture of the rule of righteousness.) The Western establishment in the Orient will be destroyed, and as time goes on its remnants will be absorbed into the new Oriental order."

Xinjing c. 1938:

When Yamaguchi Yoshiko arrived in Xinjing in 1938, she found a distinctive, bustling city that had in just six years assembled many of the necessities for a modern middle class lifestyle. Indeed, much of the city's master plan was rapidly falling in place. Not only were 6,000 buildings less than a year old, but Xinjing had miles of grand boulevards, all with sidewalks and lined with willows and elms. The capital boasted of public restrooms, effective sanitation systems, and two hospitals; new shopping areas, hotels, cinemas, and three theaters; newly-constructed schools, a newly-founded university, and thirty-two Shinto shrines. There were also abundant recreational facilities available, including swimming pools, golf courses, tennis courts, sumo dohyo, ice skating rings, eight large parks, a botanical garden, a race track, and a zoo. The city's nightlife boasted women in the latest fashions, dancing to orchestras in dinner jackets and listening to actors and actresses sing recent songs from Broadway shows or Hollywood movies. In other words, Xinjing visibly and tangibly proclaimed that it was a civilized city, one ready for the future. This was a message that impressed visitors, for it came as a surprise at a time when so much of the rest of the world was suffering from the Depression.

Construction on Puyi's imperial palace began in September 1938, after six years of debate over the specifics, including its location. Puyi, who was installed as the "Emperor of Manchukuo" in 1934, wanted the palace to honor Chinese traditions and be situated like the Forbidden City in Beijing: the focal point from which all power and energy emanated. He wanted the capital to reflect the fact that he was once again a Qing Dynasty emperor—a king who had successfully obtained the Mandate of Heaven by following ancient rituals and being enthroned in the traditional yellow dragon robes. While willing to accommodate Puyi in ceremony, the Japanese were not willing to give him any meaningful authority. Therefore, despite numerous discussions involving multiple options, the capital's final design reflected Japanese interests: the central railroad station and the prominent government buildings around Unity Plaza provided the central axis for the city. What Puyi and Japanese authorities could agree upon, however, was that the palace should have modern conveniences for a head of state, including parking garages and a bomb shelter.

Illustration 72, 73 and 74: Top left: postcard of the Supreme Court and Judiciary Building, c. 1939. Top right: part of the facade of that building in 2013. Bottom: postcard of Ministry of Foreign Affairs and Trade, Xinjing, c. 1940.

The decade had also seen the construction of important government buildings, the newest of which was the Supreme Court. Opened in 1938 in an area a mile and a half south of the approved site for Puyi's new palace, it was one of five government structures designed to showcase Xinjing as the home of Asian Revivalist architecture. This style reflected Japanese adaptability and blended Western and traditional elements to create buildings that would represent Japanese prowess while honoring Chinese sensibilities. The three-story Supreme Court and Judiciary Building sought to accomplish this with a pagoda roof that towered over curved exterior walls that spread out like a bird's wings; two more bulky, curved buttresses at the main entrance formed a portcullis. From the park across the street, it looked as if a guard tower on the Great Wall of China had been built by an Art Nouveau designer. That the Supreme Court and the other four government structures were built with steel frameworks and reinforced concrete only proved their bold modernity. But Xinjing's new architecture also occasionally gave a nod to Western classicism: the two-story Ministry of Foreign Affairs and Trade, which also opened in 1938, featured a Doric colonnade.

All of these indicators of Xinjing's prosperity came as a result of six years of enormous Japanese subsidies and a clear governmental economic philosophy:

> In order to avoid the baneful effects which capitalism, when unbridled, may exert, it is necessary…to apply a certain amount of national control…and to utilize the fruits of capital so that a sound and lively development of all branches of the people's economy may be realized.

In other words, Xinjing's bureaucrats and their counterparts in Tokyo proclaimed that they wanted to "prevent any privileged class of people from monopolizing the benefits of the exploitation of natural resources. Realistically, this meant blocking the domineering influence of Japan's single-family monopolies (*zaibatsu*), like Mitsubishi or Mitsui, and ensuring considerable government intervention in the economy. Therefore, the Japanese officials in the Manchukuo government were the ones who oversaw the construction of new railways, harbors and roads; vast hydroelectric projects; and a remarkable growth in the production of iron ore, coal, magnesite, limestone, soya beans, corn, rice, timber, cotton and wool. They also introduced a new currency, founded an experimental agricultural station to increase yields, and merged telegraph and telephone corporations to improve communication systems and efficiency. The government even proved able to reach a compromise with Nissan's founder Auyukawa Yoshisuke, who moved his company's headquarters to Xinjing in 1937 in order to help manage the coal, iron, steel, automobile, aircraft, and other industries for the state.

The capital was, however, also a city with problems. It grew by 80,000 people each year between 1937 and 1940. Despite the speed of construction in the city, this rapid growth created a severe housing shortage for the growing bureaucracy, and there weren't enough hotel rooms to handle the overflow. This deficiency made the cost of living expensive. That planners envisioned a metropolitan area with one million inhabitants only intensified the pressures. Xinjing was also a segregated city, for the resources and amenities the capital offered were largely meant for Japanese emigrants, not its Chinese or Manchurian residents. Rickshaws sharing the streets with automobiles served as a metaphor for the city's economic disparities; the poor often continued to live as they had, in thatched houses on crowded streets with poor sanitation. And because Xinjing's residents were assigned to housing on the basis of their ethnicity, the likelihood of improving the living conditions for non-Japanese inhabitants was slim. This led one journalist to conclude that resentments against the Japanese were growing, even as the military situation

Illustration 75: Chinese man pushing a wheelbarrow with happy Japanese and Manchurian children and bags of rice. The image's propagandistic message was to promote harmony and prosperity between the Japanese, Chinese, and Manchurians, but the reality in Xinjing was far less harmonious.

was becoming increasingly complex: the Japanese "in six years of rule have managed to antagonize" the Manchurians "so much that every Japanese not blinded by army blinkers recognizes that only the threat of force prevents an eruption in Manchukuo" against the puppet state. With the outbreak of the Second Sino-Japanese War in 1937, the capital acquired an increased military character. At its most innocuous, this involved cadets from the nearby Manchurian Military Academy proudly wearing their uniforms as they walked through town admiring the statues of military heroes. At its most sinister, the outskirts of Xinjing hid the 680 men who worked at Unit 100, a biological research station dedicated to developing weapons to kill livestock and contaminate crops. There was also experimentation on humans at Unit 100, including Russian POWs and Chinese convicts.

While Unit 100 remained a top secret operation in 1938, international suspicion about Manchukuo's government and Japanese intentions grew. In fact, by the end of the year, Manchukuo had only received diplomatic recognition from a handful of countries, including Japan, Mussolini's Italy, Hitler's Germany, Franco's Spain, El Salvador and the Dominican Republic.[17] This is why the State Department established specific protocols for the American ambassador to Japan: he could attend diplomatic receptions hosted by Japan, even if Puyi was also present, but he could not attend any function that was hosted by Puyi or which sought to honor him. Because Manchukuo remained officially unrecognized, the same American ambassador resorted to using quotation marks whenever referring to Manchukuo in his

---

[17] Because the USSR sold the China Eastern Railway to Manchukuo in March 1935, it offered de facto recognition to the state. The Vatican offered a formal blessing and sent high-ranking officials to Manchukuo, but it stopped just short of establishing formal diplomatic relations. The other nations to recognize Manchukuo were states which joined the Axis Powers (Bulgaria, Hungary, Romania, Thailand) or were colonies of or conquered by the Axis Powers (Somalia, Libya, Poland, Vichy France).

confidential reports to the State Department. This diplomatic distancing frustrated officials in Xinjing, who repeatedly sought recognition from the world community, despite the League of Nations' clear position that Manchuria was a part of the Republic of China.[18] As Japan's client state, Manchukuo could not hope to find the legitimacy it wanted, which meant that all of Xinjing's ambitions to be the capital of the future were doomed.

A Short Postscript:

Xinjing was so isolated from the hardships of World War II that it successfully hosted the Greater East Asian Exposition in 1942 to commemorate the founding of Manchukuo. That isolation suddenly changed on August 9, 1945, when the Soviet Union declared war on Japan and the Red Army began its invasion of Manchukuo. As part of that offensive, Soviet airplanes bombed the capital in a pre-dawn raid. The surprise of the Soviet attack, combined with the evacuation of Japanese military families, set off widespread panic in the capital. Through the course of the next week, the Japanese found themselves fighting all those who sought revenge for past wrongs: Russians, Manchurians, and Chinese all pillaged and raped, imprisoned and executed. By the end of the month, Puyi had been captured and imprisoned by the Soviets, 600,000 Japanese were on their way to work camps in the USSR, and the Red Army had begun removing Manchuria's desirable industrial equipment. The Soviets also changed the city's name back to Changchun.

Neither Soviet conquest nor Emperor Hirohito's broadcast announcing Japan's surrender brought peace to Changchun. Instead, it became the site of an intense battle between the Chinese Nationalists led by Chiang Kai-Shek and the Chinese Communists led by Mao Zedong. Chiang and Mao had put aside their differences to fight a common enemy in 1937, but with the Japanese defeat, the Chinese Civil War resumed in earnest. In March 1947, the Nationalists controlled Manchuria's railroads and all of its key cities except Harbin, while the Communists controlled the countryside and the food supplies that entailed. After a year of seesaw fighting that produced another stalemate, the Communists renewed their attention on Changchun in March 1948 and a decisive siege of the city had begun. By the end of May, the Communists had captured one of the city's two airfields, severed the Nationalists' rail link to the south, and cut off the city's water supply. By mid-August starvation was killing 500 a day and people began eating grass and bark; others resorted to cannibalism as fresh corpses were sold on the black market. The Nationalists finally surrendered in late October, but by that time 250,000 people had already died.

The communist victory brought changes to Changchun with new architectural styles, renamed streets, and new civic monuments. Most of all, there was a drive towards industrialization, for although initially designated Changchun as an "old city with little industry," Beijing officials in the 1950s sought to transform the city into an industrial center. By choosing

---

[18] This League of Nations position came from an investigative delegation to Manchukuo in 1933. The Lytton Report concluded that the creation of Manchukuo was due to the organized intervention of Japan.

Illustration 76: Changchun residents, December, 1978. Note the billboard in the background. It depicts Mao, who died in 1976, looking over the people with his appointed successor, Hua Guofeng, at his side.

Changchun as the home of the nation's first automobile plant, the People's Republic could change the city's character and erase some of Manchukuo's colonial legacy. This intention bore fruit, for today Changchun is a heavily industrialized city with nine million residents, and automobile manufacturing remains central to the city's economic base. Despite this transformation, remnants of Xinjing persist. The basic layout of the city follows the plans developed in the early 1930s, and most of the key government buildings constructed during Puyi's era are still used for similar purposes. This can especially be seen around Unity Plaza, which is now called People's Square. What was once the Manchukuo Central Bank on the northwest side of the great roundabout is now the State Administration of Foreign Exchange. Similarly, the original Manchukuo Telephone and Telegraph Company building on the west side of the circle is now the state-owned telecommunications operator China Unicom, while the Manchukuo Police Headquarters on the southwest side of the circle is now the Changchun Public Security Bureau. Other Manchukuo era buildings still stand, but have been completely repurposed. One such example is the Supreme Court, which is now a military hospital. Puyi's compound of eclectic, repurposed buildings officially became a museum in 1984, but suffered from decades of neglect and disinterest before then. Recent renovations have restored much of the compound's buildings and furnishings, allowing for a better understanding of Puyi's daily life and of Japanese rule. The site selected for Puyi's new palace is now the location of a geological museum and a large public square dedicated to cultural events. Changchun is, then, a city where glimpses of the past can be found, but whose energy rests elsewhere.

What Xinjing Teaches:

Urban historian Peter Hall once argued that, "it requires a rather drastic political change—the sudden and total dismemberment of an empire, the division of a country—to bring about a major shift in the role and the fortunes of a capital city." This was certainly the case for Changchun / Xinjing, for both its rise and fall occurred with astonishing speed. In the 1930s, the Japanese transformed a minor railroad depot into a notable, planned capital city; with Japan's defeat in World War II and the establishment of the People's Republic of China in 1949, the city's political importance fell to being one of three provincial capitals in Manchuria. Changchun / Xinjing's experience rose and fell as a result of world events and distant decisions. What this reveals is that a city's character is not determined by careful planning or organic evolution, as so many are wont to believe. Cities are not islands. Instead, they reflect a complex mix of political, economic, social, and environmental factors beyond local control.

Xinjing also shows how political legitimacy differs from political power. When the Japanese conquered Manchuria and created Manchukuo, they hoped to gain acceptance for the new government by constructing a magnificent, modern capital that would impress the world. The grand boulevards, stately buildings, and modern conveniences all pointed to prosperity and ingenuity, but these trappings failed to win the hearts of the city's Chinese and Manchurian residents, who largely remained second-class citizens. When the Japanese failed to engender, impose, or even fabricate the type of social contract between the rulers and the governed that philosophers as different as Confucius and John Locke said had to exist, they lost any hope of gaining political legitimacy. Instead, the government resorted to oppression, imposing the Japanese language in schools, conscripting teens into ideological associations overseen by the Kwantung army, issuing food rationing cards on the basis of ethnicity, forcing millions into compulsory labor, and censoring newspapers, books, and films to ensure that media aligned with government views and goals. Moreover, their failure to develop a social contract in Manchuria explains why the Japanese had to devote considerable attention to combatting rebellions in Manchukuo during their fourteen years in power. All of this meant that the Japanese were unable to alter international opinion and Manchukuo became nothing more than an ill-gotten colony to most of the world.

Another way Xinjing helps us measure the difference between political legitimacy and power involves Puyi. The last emperor of the Qing Dynasty may have only been a child when he was removed from his throne in 1912, but for monarchists Puyi still possessed a legitimate right to govern. Hundreds of years of Manchurian rule supported Puyi's claim, and that tradition gave him a credibility no new Chinese warlord—even a militarily powerful one—could possess. Similarly, as a Manchurian, Puyi could argue that he had a legitimate claim to govern Manchukuo, but the Japanese refused to allow him any authority to do so. In fact, Puyi's haplessness was so great that he couldn't even leave his palace compound without Japanese permission.

What Xinjing's experience shows is that the Japanese had power without legitimacy, and Puyi had legitimacy without power. Neither was a tenable position for the long term since effective leadership requires both a societal consensus and the authority to direct it.

Curated Bibliography for Chapter 6

Akagi, Roy Hidemichi. *Japan's Foreign Relations, 1552-1936: A Short History*. Tokyo: Hiduseido Press, 1936.

Baader, Gerhard, et al., "Pathways to Human Experimentation, 1933-1945: Germany, Japan, and the United States." *Osiris* 20 (2005). JSTOR.

Benson, John and Takao Matsumura, *Japan 1868-1945*. London: Pearson Education, 2001.

Billingham, A. J. "Hsinking is Transformed." *New York Times*. August 4, 1935, XX4. ProQuest Historical Newspapers.

Buck, David Buck. "Railway City and National Capital: Two Faces of the Modern in Changchun," *Remaking the Chinese City: Modernity and Nationalism, 1900-1950*, Joseph W. Esherick (ed.). Honolulu, HI: University of Hawai'i Press, 1999.

Cambridge History of Japan, Vol. 6: The Twentieth Century. New York: Cambridge University Press, 1988.

"China Hunger Toll Cited: 500 Dying Each Day In Or Near Changchun, Paper Reports." *New York Times*, August 10, 1948, 7, ProQuest Historical Newspapers.

Crane, Burton. "Japanese May Seek Aid Here in Growth." *New York Times*. November 21, 1937. ProQuest Historical Newspapers.

Dikötter, Frank. *The Tragedy of Liberation: A History of the Chinese Revolution, 1945-57*. New York: Bloomsbury Press, 2013.

Denison, Edward and Guangyu Ren. *Ultra-Modernism: Architecture and Identity*. Hong Kong: Hong Kong University Press, 2016.

DuBois, Thomas David. *Empire and the Meaning of Religion in Northeast Asia: Manchuria 1900-1945*. New York: Cambridge University Press, 2017.

"East Asian Federation." *Japan's Greater East Asia Co-Prosperity Sphere in World War II: Selected Readings and Documents*. Joyce C. Lebra (ed.). Kuala Lumpur: Oxford University Press, 1975.

Eckert, Carter J. *Park Chung Hee and Modern Korea: The Roots of Militarism, 1866-1945*. Cambridge, MA: Belknap Press/Harvard University Press, 2016.

Empire and Environment in the Making of Manchuria. Norman Smith (ed.). Vancouver, BC: University of British Columbia Press, 2017.

Fleming, Peter. *To Peking: A Forgotten Journey from Moscow to Manchuria*. London: Tauris Parke, 2009.

Gamsa, Mark. *Manchuria: A Concise History*. London: I. B. Tauris, 2020.

Grew, Joseph Clark. "The Ambassador in Japan (Grew) to the Secretary of State, No. 680, February 21, 1934." *Foreign Relations of the United States: Diplomatic Papers, 1934, Volume III: the Far East*. Washington, DC: Government Printing Office, 1950. HathiTrust Digital Library.

Gao, Yunxiang. *Sporting Gender: Women Athletes and Celebrity-Making During China's National Crisis, 1931-1945*. Vancouver, BC: University of British Columbia Press, 2013.

Guo, Qinghua. "Changchun: Unfinished Capital Planning of Manzhouguo, 1932-1942." *Urban History*. Vol. 31, No. 1 (May 2004). JSTOR.

Hall, Peter. "Seven Types of Capital City." *Planning Twentieth Century Capital Cities*. David L. A. Gordon (ed.). New York: Routledge, 2006.

Iguchi, Haruo. *Unfinished Business: Ayukawa Yoshisuke and U.S.-Japan Relations, 1937-1953*. Cambridge, MA: Harvard University Press, 2003.

Industrialization of Japan and Manchukuo, 1930-1940: Population, Raw Materials, and Industry. E. B. Schumpeter (ed.). New York: The Macmillan Company, 1940.

Japan and Manchoukuo. Vol. XXVIII (1935-1936). Tokyo: The New Japan Publishing Company, 1936.

Jowett, Philip. *China's Civil Wars: Rousing the Dragon, 1894-1949*. Oxford, UK: Osprey Publishing, 2013.

Kirsch, Griseldis. "Gendering the Japanese Empire: Ri Kōran as 'Transnational' Star." MDPI, 2019.

Koga, Yukiko. *Inheritance of Loss: China, Japan, and the Political Economy of Redemption after Empire*. Chicago, IL: University of Chicago Press, 2016.

Lieberman, Henry R.. "Changchun Loses Air Link To China: Communists Seize One Field And Increase Their Attacks Against Another." *New York Times*. May 28, 1948, 3. ProQuest Historical Newspapers.

Liu, Yishi. "Social Change in Changchun." *eScholarship*. University of California-Berkeley. 2011.

Lynch, Michael. *The Chinese Civil War, 1945-1949*. Oxford, UK: Osprey Publishing, 2022.

Manchoukuo: A Pictorial Record. Tokyo: Asahi Shimbun, 1934.

"Manchuria Plans Gala Inauguration: Pu-Yi To Be Inducted As Head Of New State Tomorrow With Ancient Manchu Ritual." *New York Times*. March 8, 1932, 5. ProQuest Historical Newspapers.

Meyer, Michael. *In Manchuria: A Village Called Wasteland and the Transformation of Rural China*. New York: Bloomsbury Press, 2015.

Negus, Keith, Hyunjoon Shin. "Eurasian Entanglements: Notes Towards a Planetary Perspective of Popular Music Histories." *Popular Music*. Vol. 40, No. 1 (February 2021.) ProQuest Central.

Nishio, Juzo. "The Status Quo of Manchou Tikuo." *The Japan & Manchoukuo*. Tokyo: Unknown, 1934.

"Occupy Presidential Palace." *New York Times*. March 9, 1932, 14. ProQuest Historical Newspapers.

Park, Sang Mi. "Ri Koran." *Theatre Journal*. Vol. 66, No. 2 (May 2014). ProQuest Central.

Pawlowicz, Rachel and Walter E. Grunden. "Teaching Atrocities: The Holocaust and Unit 731 in the Secondary School Curriculum." *The History Teacher*. Vol. 48, No. 2 (February 2015).

Peffer, Nathaniel. "Clouds Of Uncertainty Lie Over Manchukuo: Fate Of Japan's 'Promised Land' Bound Up With China Manchukuo Is Facing Uncertainty Manchukuo Uncertain." *New York Times*. December 5 1937, 161. ProQuest Historical Newspapers.

Pepper, Suzanne. *Civil War in China: The Political Struggle, 1945-1949*. Berkeley, CA: University of California Press, 1978.

Powell, John. "Chinese Fearful Japan May Set Up Ex-Boy King: Tokyo Seeks Virtual Manchurian Throne." *Chicago Daily Tribune*. May 20, 1928, 4. ProQuest Historical Newspapers.

Puppet State of "Manchukuo, The. Shanghai, China: China United Press, 1935.

"Pu-Yi Inauguration Will Be Held Today: New Leader And Wife Make Spectacular Entry Into City Of Changchun." *The Washington Post*. March 9, 1932, 4. ProQuest Historical Newspapers.

Pu Yi. *From Emperor to Citizen: The Autobiography of Aisin-Gioro Pu Yi*. W. J. F. Jenner (trans.). Oxford, UK: Oxford University Press, 1987.

Rea, George Bronson. *Manchukuo: Back to First Principles*. Geneva, Switzerland: Kundig, 1932.

Rea, George Bronson. *The Case for Manchoukuo*. New York: D. Appleton Century Company, 1935.

Robertson, Douglas. "Modern Capital For Manchukuo." *New York Times*. September 11, 1938, 163. ProQuest Historical Newspapers.

"Secretary of State to the Ambassador of Japan, The." No. 686 (February 5, 1935).41-42. HathiTrust Digital Library.

Sewell, Bill. *Constructing Empire: The Japanese in Changchun, 1905-1945*. Vancouver, BC: University of British Columbia Press, 2019.

Sungmoon, Kim. "Self-Transformation and Civil Society: Lockean vs. Confucian." *Dao: A Journal of Comparative Philosophy*. 8 (2009). https://doi.org/10.1007/s11712-009-9136-7

Takasima, Shizuo. "Nissan Legend 1: Yoshisuke Aikawa: A Modern Man with Insight." *Nissan Corporation*. http://usa.nissannews.com/en.

Trani, Eugene P. *The Treaty of Portsmouth: An Adventure in American Diplomacy*. Lexington: The University Press of Kentucky, 1969. EBSCOhost.

Udagawa, Masaru. "The Move into Manchuria of the Nissan Combine." *Japanese Yearbook of Business History*. 1990.

Van de Ven, Hans. *China at War: Triumph and Tragedy in the Emergence of the New China*. Cambridge, MA: Harvard University, 2018. EBSCOhost.

Vitello, Paul. "Yoshiko Yamaguchi, 94, Actress in Propaganda Films." *New York Times*. September 23, 2014, B17. ProQuest Central.

Wang, Yiman. "Between the National and the Transnational: Li Xianglan/Yamaguchi Yoshiko and Pan-Asianism." *International Institute for Asian Studies Newsletter*, No. 38 (September 2005). www.iias.asia/the-newsletter.

Woodhead, H.G.W. *A Visit to Manchukuo*. Shanghai, China: The Mercury Press, 1932.

Yamaguchi, Yoshiko and Fujiwara Sakuya. *Fragrant Orchid: The Story of My Early Life*. Chia-ning Chang (trans.). Honolulu, HI: University of Hawai'i Press, 2015.

Yamamuro, Shin'ichi. *Manchuria Under Japanese Dominion*. Joshual A. Fogel (trans.). Philadelphia, PA: University of Pennsylvania Press, 2006.

Yasuo, Nagaharu. "Manchukuo's New Economic Policy." *Pacific Affairs*. Vol. 11, No. 3 (September 1938). JSTOR.

Ying, Xiong. *Representing Empire: Japanese Colonial Literature in Taiwan and Manchuria*. Leiden, The Netherlands: Brill, 2014.

CHAPTER 7

ENUGU
REPUBLIC OF BIAFRA

Monday, May 29, 1967 was a fairly typical school day at the Queen's School[19] in Enugu, Nigeria. The girls, dressed in their school uniforms, began their classes as usual on the boarding school's flower-filled, hillside campus at 8:00 a.m. and ended them at 1:00 p.m., when the tropical midday heat became too oppressive for practicable learning. The school's standard classrooms, which were made of fretted concrete walls, were furnished with student desks, a blackboard, a bulletin board, and a teacher's desk, but a recent influx of students from northern Nigeria had put classroom space at a premium. This shortage is why Rosina Umelo, a White woman from England who married a Nigerian and moved to Enugu in 1965, held her last classes as a Nigerian teacher in one corner of the school's assembly hall.

At 3:00 a.m. the next morning, the military governor of the Eastern Region, Chukwuemeka Odumegwu Ojukwu, summoned the American, British, and Cameroonian diplomats stationed in Enugu to inform them that he would soon announce the secession of the Eastern Region from Nigeria and then proclaim the establishment of the Republic of Biafra. In a 65-minute radio address a few hours later, Ojukwu outlined the reasons for secession in melancholy tones and a new national anthem played. As the sun rose in the sky, the new capital city burst into celebration with spontaneous parades and dancing in the streets. Like her math and science colleagues at the Queen's School, Umelo tried to hold her Latin and English classes as usual that morning, but it was pointless: with too much excitement and anticipation in the air, the principal agreed to cancel classes and let the girls march down the road into town. They did so waving palm fronds with broad smiles on their faces as they passed through a double line of great trees. Few could have imagined what was in store for them or their new country.

---

[19] Some sources refer to the institution as "Queens School," but regardless of the correct punctuation, it was founded in 1954 as the only government-sponsored secondary school for girls in eastern Nigeria. Admission was very competitive.

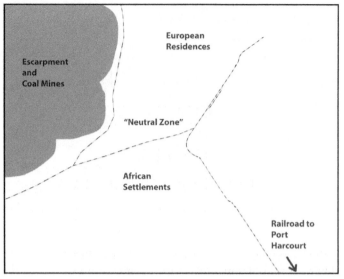

Illustration 77: Neighborhood map of Enugu in 1917.

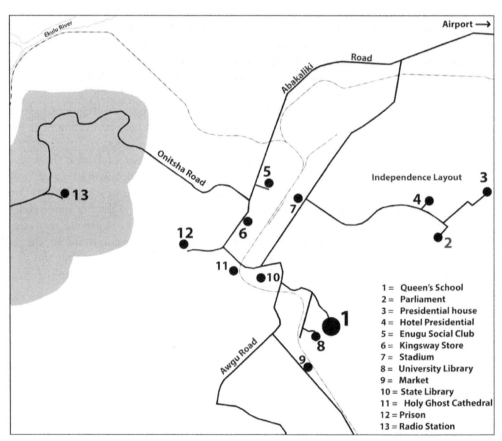

Illustration 78: Map of Enugu in 1967.

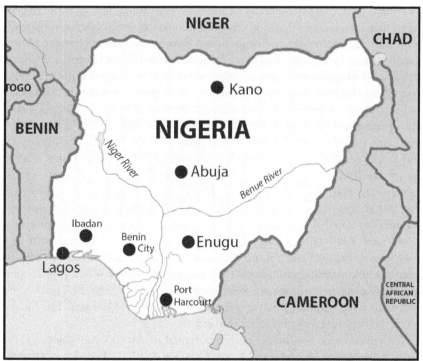

Illustration 79 and 80: Map of Republic of Biafra in 1967 (top) and map of modern Nigeria (bottom).

Enugu was founded as a British colonial mining town after the discovery of bituminous coal along an escarpment in 1909 by two itinerant Australian geologists. The area was a rather lightly populated part of the Igbo tribe's homeland, which meant that it offered the potential to become a model colonial city. This opportunity attracted the attention of Governor General Frederick Lugard, who visited Enugu in February 1915. He saw in Enugu a place which might exemplify Britain's Victorian mix of ambition and duty, for as Lugard once wrote, "Europe is in [tropical] Africa for the mutual benefit of her own industrial classes and of the native races in their progress towards a higher plane....It is the aim and desire of civilized administrations to fulfill this dual mandate." In other words, Enugu's coal would be exploited to benefit the demands of British industry, while British colonial administrators would guide Igbo miners in order to "further" their human development. The result was the creation of a paternalistic and segregated town in which Europeans lived in first or second class compounds with fixed lot sizes and regulated tree heights on higher ground, while Africans lived in overcrowded, unplanned shelters 500 feet below.

Illustration 81: Caricature of Frederick Lugard, 1895.

These two areas were also separated by a mile-wide "Neutral Zone" in order to create a sanitation corridor so that Europeans "might not be exposed to the attacks of mosquitoes" or suffer "the inconvenience" of "drumming and other noises dear to the Native" lest their "rest is disturbed," Lugard maintained. Enugu also had two hospitals (one for Blacks, one for Whites), three prisons, colliery offices and coal storerooms, a general store, and a parade ground. A railroad connecting Enugu to Port Harcourt and greatly facilitating exports opened in May 1916. Production increased in Enugu's mines six-fold as a result, from 24,000 tons to 145,000 tons between the railroad's opening and the end of World War I. By the end of World War II, 668,000 tons of coal were being pulled out of the earth every year. Despite this growth, mining conditions were poor and wages remained consistently low throughout the colonial period as miners worked barefoot by candlelight, without any protective gear from the coal dust. In addition, many workers were the victims of forced labor. These circumstances led to a persistent resistance to authority, just as had occurred between 1884 and 1914 when the British sought to control the Nigerian interior. The Enugu mines witnessed protests, slow-downs, or outright strikes in 1925, 1937, 1947 and 1949—industrial actions which the colonial government regularly saw as expressions of nationalism and a direct threat to British rule, instead of the repeated calls for fair pay and reasonable working conditions that they largely were. When police opened gunfire on unarmed striking mine workers, on November 18, 1949, killing 21 and wounding 51 more, perceptions changed radically; in fact, the Enugu Colliery Massacre can be seen as a major stimulus of the Nigerian independence movement.

With great hope for the economic potential of Africa's most populous nation, Nigeria became an independent federal republic on October 1, 1960. But this optimism was undercut by a political structure that benefitted some far more than others. When the British created the amalgamated Colony and Protectorate of Nigeria in 1914, they artificially brought 240 distinct language groups together, while allowing each of the largest tribes to control one region: the Yoruba in the West, the Igbo in the East, and Hausa-Fulani in the North. This policy marginalized other ethnic groups and created considerable ethnic tensions. Because the predominantly Muslim Northern Region was larger in both size and population than all the other regions combined, the Hausa-Fulani were able to control the federal government over the vigorous objections of the Yoruba and Igbo. Political opportunism, fraud, and corruption quickly became commonplace as tribalism[20] eclipsed nationalism in the young nation.

1966 proved to be a watershed year for Nigeria. The first of two *coups d'état* came in January and was led by six mid-level Igbo officers and one Yoruba officer. Before it was suppressed, the January coup attempt resulted in the deaths of numerous civil and military leaders, including the prime minister. Most of the victims were Northerners. Major-General Johnson Aguiyi-Ironsi, who was Igbo, proved able to restore order, but once he was in office he made the momentous decision in May to abolish political parties and replace the country's federalist system of government with a highly centralized state. Northerners saw this move as an Igbo plot to take over Nigeria and responded with repeated waves of anti-government violence. In late July, a second coup, which was led by aggrieved Northerners, toppled Aguiyi-Ironsi and installed a thirty-one-year-old lieutenant colonel, Yakubu Gowon, as head of state and commander of the armed forces. Gowon was a Christian from the North and, therefore, offered at least a symbol, and perhaps a promise, for Nigerian unity. One of Gowon's first acts was to reinstall the federalist governmental system in order to soothe Nigeria's regional tensions. Unfortunately, this effort was not successful. Instead, Northerners, who were stoked by false news reports that Muslims were being massacred in the Eastern province, began attacking Igbos living in the North. As the violence spread and intensified, Igbo homes were looted and then burned, hundreds of thousands of Easterners were maimed and raped, and perhaps 50,000 Igbos were killed in what was quickly identified as a pogrom.[21] Perhaps two million Nigerians became refugees as a result of the conflict, as members of the nation's various ethnic groups migrated back to the security of their tribal homelands. While Ojukwu, the military governor of the Eastern Region, initially saw Gowon as being sincere in his efforts to bring peace to all of Nigeria, the pogrom irrevocably changed his perceptions. Ojukwu described Northern actions in September and October 1966 as one of "unprecedented bestiality." Many Igbo became convinced that living even in a federated Nigeria with Hausa-Fulani and Yoruba was an intolerable proposition. As one journalist noted a few months later,

> The great cause of the present crisis is not political or economic but psychological. The Ibo [sic] people were struck a shattering, murderous blow last year, when thousands of them were massacred in the northern region of Nigeria. Most Ibos have fled home to Ibo land in the eastern region and barricaded themselves against the rest of Nigeria. So fearful and angry that they seem truculent…you can sense the intensity of Ibo feeling as soon as you enter Enugu.

Ojukwu and Gowon shared many commonalities, even if they were born into very different circumstances. Ojukwu was from one of Nigeria's most elite families: his father, Sir Louis Ojukwu, had made a fortune developing a transportation network and was knighted by Queen Elizabeth II for providing shipping services for British war supplies during World War II. The

---

[20] "Tribalism" is a controversial word, but it is one that Nigeria's famous author Chinua Achebe finds apt to describe the nation, partially as a result of British colonial policy. He notes that in Nigeria "tribalism is endemic."

[21] Estimates for the number of deaths during the pogrom range quite broadly, from 7,000 to 100,000. It is unlikely that an accurate figure will ever be able to be calculated, but all agree that perceptions changed, regardless of the exact number of deaths.

younger Ojukwu received a privileged education, attending secondary school in England and then Lincoln College, Oxford, where he graduated with a Master's degree in history in 1956. As a student, he had a reputation for debating, stylish dress, and driving a red MG too fast. In other words, he was a very smart playboy. Upon his return to Nigeria, Ojukwu soon joined the army, breaking with his father's expectations that he become a lawyer and work for the family conglomerate. After receiving additional military training in Britain, Ojukwu returned to Nigeria in 1957 and quickly attained the rank of Major, for he was one of the few Nigerian soldiers with a university degree. Overall, he was a man full of confidence, if not arrogance, who saw success and achievement as his birthright, and who spoke with a "polished Oxford accent." Gowon, on the other hand, was raised by Christian missionaries, attended a Nigerian secondary school, and

Illustration 82: Elizabeth I and Gowon during state visit in England in June, 1973.

entered the Nigerian army in 1954. Also buoyed by a personal connection to the British royal family,[22] Gowon's talents allowed him to attend the Royal Military Academy Sandhurst. He was an excellent soldier and a charismatic leader, who had the power to ingratiate, but he lacked Ojukwu's intellectual prowess, social ease, and essential creativity. Indeed, Gowon was a devout, by-the-book soldier who neither smoked or drank.

In early January 1967, Lieutenant Colonel Ojukwu, the military governor of Eastern Nigeria, and Lieutenant Colonel Gowon, the supreme commander of the Nigerian armed forces and head of state, met in Aburi, Ghana in an attempt to avert a looming civil war. Accompanied by the military governors of the Western, Mid-West, and Northern regions and other key officials, Ojukwu and Gowon hoped to draft a statement of principles which might hold the nation together. As the meeting opened, Ojukwu proposed a resolution to "renounce the use of force as a means of settling the present crisis" and to uphold the principle that "discussions and negotiations [are] the only peaceful way of resolving the Nigerian crisis." This pledge was quickly adopted and embodied what came to be called the "Spirit of Aburi." The problem, however, was Ojukwu and Gowon emerged from the summit with different understandings of what had been agreed to in terms of a reorganization of the army, the character of Nigerian federalism, compensation for displaced persons, and the repatriation of non-Easterners from the Eastern region. Perhaps most fundamentally, Ojukwu's refusal to acknowledge Gowon's authority as supreme commander stood at the center of the dispute. As Ojukwu proclaimed in a February 25 radio broadcast:

> I did not go to Aburi as an Easterner. I went there as a Nigerian seeking a satisfactory solution to a Nigerian problem. I did not go to Aburi to seek powers myself, nor did I go there for a picnic. I went there to work in order to save the country from disintegration….[The decisions made at Aburi were] accepted without equivocation [because] we all saw them as the *only* formula that can keep Nigeria together….On Aburi We Stand. There will be no compromise!

With these words, as well as with Gowon's statement a few days later that "we…live in a situation where we may be forced to take preventative measures to avoid disaster," meant that war was imminent.

---

[22] Gowon's connection was religious, rather than economic. His parents had been Christian missionaries in a Muslim town in northern Nigeria and the family's commitment made Yakubu Gowon " a particular favorite of the queen and other members of Britain's royal family," according to Chinua Ahebe.

Enugu 1967

"Enugu" means "hilltop" or "top of the hill." By 1967, the city was a sprawling community of about 140,000 people, surrounded by an escarpment of "burning orange-red," to borrow Rosina Umelo's words. It was divided into districts by railway lines and the topography of three small but deep valleys. The vibrant commercial district, centered at the intersection of the roads leading to the towns of Onitsha, Abakaliki, and Awgu, had wide, paved streets with storm drains and sidewalks, but also a plethora of potholes. These thoroughfares were lined with a combination of single-story shops and brightly-painted two-story houses with shops underneath. Most noticeable were the electronics stores, which blared Nigerian Highlife music day and night. Car dealerships, a social club, and a Kingsway department store catered to wealthy Nigerians and European expatriates, while a slew of mid-range pharmacies, bookstores, grocery stores and clothing boutiques offered fixed prices and no haggling. These businesses contrasted with the chaotic atmosphere of the city's largest public market, which teamed with the energy of on-going dickering, as customers looked for the best prices on everything from fabrics to yams, pots to plantains. Its vendors made money by buying goods in bulk in times of plenty and then selling them at inflated prices in times of scarcity. It was a delicate balance of supply and demand that not everyone could manage well.

To the east of the main commercial district was Enugu's largest residential area. Many of its houses did not have flush toilets, there were no sidewalks, yards were full of rubbish and abandoned vehicles, and water came out of the yard tap like "a smoky crystal or a rich brown soup." It was a neighborhood that existed in stark contrast with walled, verdant compounds of Enugu's elite. In these homes, there were servants and clear social expectations: trousers were always worn after seven-thirty and cigars with brandy typically followed the evening meal. On the city's northern edge stood the residential community for government workers and the city's newly-designed Independence Layout, featuring the Premier's Lodge (where Ojukwu lived), the House of Assembly, and the offices and large homes of government ministers. Nearby stood the city's pride: a new, five-story, 100-room hotel, the Hotel Presidential. Modernist in design yet plush in sensibility, it offered one of the few air-conditioned public spaces in Enugu. The city was also home to a branch of the University of Nigeria, boasted the oldest public library in Nigeria, and served as the broadcasting center of one of Africa's most powerful radio and television stations. Like so many cities in the developing world in the 1960s, Enugu was a place partly stuck in the past that was slowly inching towards modernity.

When a *New York Times* reporter landed in Enugu's airport in mid-March 1967, he found the capital preparing for war. The runways were lined with oil drums "ready to be rolled out to block the strip in the event of an air attack." Inside the small terminal building with its corrugated iron roof, "plainclothes policemen search every arriving passenger and his baggage, as if this were an independent country where all newcomers had to submit to customs." Police checkpoints monitored people's movements, demonstrations clogged Enugu's streets, youths stood in line to enlist in the army, and government newspapers featured articles telling readers what to do when war came. A not-entirely reassuring poster issued by the Authority of Civil Defense Committee proclaimed:

BE PREPARED AND AVOID PANIC

From the look of things, it would appear that the people of Eastern Nigeria would be forced by external violence to surrender their birthright. If this is attempted, there should be no panic. Eastern Nigeria is fully prepared for any action. Should any group of people make this attempt by attacking us, the public will be duly alarmed. When you hear any of the following alarms, know that the enemy is around:

> i) Prolonged sounding of horns, trains, loco and fire Unit;
> ii) Prolonged vehicle horns;
> iii) Continuous toll of school and church bells;
> iv) Market Masters and Town Criers bells or gongs;
> v) Bugle alarm calls.

DO NOT PANIC BUT TAKE THE FOLLOWING PRECAUTIONS

A. If you are in the open, immediately take cover and observe any enemy shooting. Thereafter, hurry by the safest means to your home or to the nearest building or to the nearest trenches.	K. If you come across guerilla forces, you must get away from them quickly and report to your own people, otherwise they will arrest you.
B. If in the building, pregnant women and nursing mothers, children, old or otherwise disabled men and women should lie on the floor indoors, preferably at the corners.	L. If an enemy catches you and interrogates you, on no account must you give him any information, his inhuman methods notwithstanding. Remember that after giving the enemy the information he requires, he must still kill you, and that any information given out may endanger the security of the whole populace.
C. Shut all doors and windows leaving only small gaps for observation. If at night, put lights out.	M. Obey any emergency regulations that may be made and enforced by your Government.
D. If you are in possession of a shot-gun, take suitable firing position inside or outside the building and shoot to kill the enemy.	N. You must deny the enemy the use of essential supplies and services.
E. If you have no gun, collect other implements of self-defense such as cutlasses, bows and arrows, pestles, missiles, etc. and fight back.	O. Do not indulge in "loose talks" and do not let the enemy know your plans. Walls have ears and careless talks cost lives.
F. In Schools and Colleges, children should lie down in the class-rooms until they can be evacuated home in small groups. Teachers should organize themselves into fighting groups using any available implement under able leadership. There is an evacuation team in your zone. Call for its assistance.	P. Always move fast and out of the view of the enemy.
G. People in mountain areas will ensure that hills dominating approach routes are manned under cover by people who will hurl down stones and other implements on the aggressor to kill him or impede his move.	Q. You should be able to identify your own troops from the enemy troops.
H. If you are wounded, do not panic or despair. There are trained teams to give you medical care and evacuate you to a safe area. They will come round immediately.	R. From the very time an alarm is given indicating the approach of the enemy, you should not stampede and scramble out for your home towns and villages as this will create traffic problems and impede the quick movement of your combatant Forces.
I. In the event of the enemy gaining control of your building or area, take as much food and water as you can carry and await your evacuation to a safe areas. Before vacating your building or area for the enemy, destroy all food or pour away water that may be left behind, and alternatively render such food and water unsafe for the enemy to use.	S. Whenever the alarm is given, all motorists should clear their vehicles out of the highway to allow free movement for the combatant forces.
J. After destroying the enemy or after they shall have fled, you should resume your normal life. Remove and bury all water and food that was left behind and made unfit for consumption. Also do not eat any food or drink any water left by the enemy. Do not touch any equipment or article left by the enemy.	

Be Prepared

If you have not a gun, get a cutlass, a bow and arrow or anything that can kill now and be ready. A few tins of canned food may be useful. NO NOT PANIC. No enemy can overcome you. We are proud to be Easterners and we must exist.

Be Prepared. Save the East

Issued by Authority of Civil Defense Committee, Enugu

102

By the end of April, Ojukwu had signed a decree taking control of all ports, railroads, post offices, coal mines, and telegraph and broadcast services; Enugu's cricket pitch was being used for military drills; and two Nigerian Airways planes had been confiscated in order to convert them for military purposes. Tensions continued to grow until May 27, when Gowon declared a state of emergency and jettisoned the existing four-province federalist structure, replacing it with twelve smaller states. He did this in order to win the support of Nigeria's smaller tribes and to undercut Igbo power in the East. As Gowon told the nation, "I am satisfied that the creation of new states [is] the only possible basis for stability and equality [and] is the overwhelming desire of the vast majority of Nigerians." Because Gowon's plans would result in the Igbo losing 60% of the Eastern Province's agricultural resources and 95% of its petroleum revenues, Ojukwu rejected the plan outright. He would not allow the Igbo to become landlocked and impoverished. Three days later, Ojukwu officially declared independence and the Republic of Biafra was born.

It was important for the new nation to have the symbols of an independent state, and all of these were first unveiled in Enugu. Biafra's flag, which was blessed by a Catholic bishop, was a horizontal tricolor of red, black and green that utilized the colors of Marcus Garvey's Pan-

Illustration 83 and 84: Flag of Biafra (right) and Biafra postage stamps from 1970 (left).

Africanist Movement. In the middle of the central black stripe rose a yellow sun, whose rays represented the eleven districts of the new republic. The new national anthem, "The Land of the Rising Sun," used poetry by Nigeria's first president and borrowed its somber tune from a Finnish composer Ojukwu admired.[23] In Enugu, street names and newspaper mastheads were quickly changed to eliminate references to Nigeria, post offices used new Biafra rubber stamps to cancel letters, car license plates received new emblems and designations, and telephone operators considered calls to Nigeria to be international ones. In a new nation, appearances mattered, especially since Biafra was so ill-prepared for war.

Indeed, Biafra didn't have the equipment it needed to fight. While Ojukwu had been secretly stockpiling arms since October 1966, there weren't enough rifles or ammunition to supply its soldiers, there were no ships for a navy, and its air force consisted of two World-War II bombers, six helicopters, and the two Nigerian Airways planes. While Biafra had more experienced officers than Nigeria, it did not have any tanks or much heavy artillery. All of this meant that when fighting broke out along Biafra's northern border on July 6, the breakaway republic was fortunate to meet an untested foe that was easily confused in the heat of battle. Although the Nigerians moved to within twelve miles of Enugu on July 12, the Biafrans proved able to repel the Nigerians' assault with smoke bombs and very limited mortar fire. The proximity of the combat

---

[23] The anthem's words were written by Nnamdi Azikiwe and the tune was that of Jean Sibelius' *Finlandia*.

was enough to put the capital on a high alert, and roadblocks and checkpoints appeared, annoyingly close together. As the Igbos' suspicion of foreigners and those with minority tribal affiliations grew, the British High Commission decided to order the evacuation of most of Enugu's male expatriate community, thereby having them join the women and children, who had been evacuated in early June. On the morning of July 16, some 200 foreign nationals, including citizens of Cameroon, Germany, Great Britain, India, Israel, Italy, Lebanon, and the United States, assembled at the Enugu Sports Club. Instead of playing tennis, enjoying the swimming pool, or quaffing beers at the cad's bar, as normally happened at the members-only club, the expatriates formed a convoy of cars and headed south to Port Arthur. Enugu was left to the Biafrans. Rosina Umelo may have been the only White woman left in town.

War brought Biafrans together: by August, when the first air raid on Enugu hit and as supplies were becoming more difficult to obtain as a result of Nigeria's increasingly effective blockade of Biafra, a call went out for those who knew how to knit to come to the Club to make sleeveless V-necked sweaters for soldiers. "A very gay colored army we shall have," one woman doubtfully commented as she knit from her geranium-colored yarn. "I mean, you could hardly call this a camouflage color, could you?," she joked. It was all a part of making do, of recognizing that something was better than nothing in times of war. This spirit of cooperation also led to the expansion of other volunteer organizations in town, including those dedicated to repairing uniforms or distributing needed food, toiletries, and blankets to soldiers and families. Indeed, as money became tight and prices soared, Enugu's residents based their wartime footing upon improvisation and resourcefulness.

As dawn broke on September 22, Enugu witnessed the execution of Victor Banjo, a non-Igbo colonel in the Biafran army, and three of his associates for treason. Six weeks before, under Ojukwu's orders, Banjo had led an audacious offensive deep into Nigerian territory. The invasion plan called for Banjo to march his rag-tag army directly to Lagos and overthrow Gowon, but Banjo stopped in Benin City and declared the creation of his own Yoruba state, the Republic of Benin. He also contacted the British High Command in Lagos seeking support for his endeavor. For disobeying orders, betraying the Biafran cause, and perhaps throwing away the best chance Biafra had to win the war, Ojukwu had Banjo court-martialed and shot. As Ojukwu said in an address a few weeks later, "Hardly could we know that a number of officers within our army did not share the aspirations of their people....Those in position of trust...shamelessly betrayed that trust...[in] acts of sabotage and treachery."

On September 26, Rosina Umelo heard the loudest explosion she had yet and decided with her husband John to flee Enugu with their four children, a nephew, and three servants. With ten in the car and "no space for luxuries," just "a suitcase with everyday clothes...tinned food...a small box of medicines" and a photo album, the family headed south. They were far from the only ones, for given what had happened to Igbos in northern Nigeria a year before, the fear of mass slaughter was palpable. As Ojukwu declared, "the Gowon junta...[is] waging a hideous and vicious war...the real purpose [of which] is the destruction of a

Illustration 85: Statue of Ojukwu, 2022.

104

people and a nation." It's "genocide behind the facade of maintaining Nigerian unity." Consequently, Ojukwu vowed not to abandon the capital and urged Biafrans to fight: "let us be prepared to die so that our children may live. Let us come out in force and destroy the enemy so that we may live and order our affairs in peace....To fail would mean the certain end of us as a people." But these words were mere bravado; Ojukwu, who escaped capture by federal troops by disguising himself as a household servant, understood that the fall of Enugu would not bring about the end of the war as Gowon and the Nigerians hoped. Instead, by moving the Biafran government south to Umuahia, Ojukwu would be able to fight another day. Therefore, the Nigerian capture of Enugu on October 4, 1967 had more symbolic than strategic meaning.

When journalists visited Enugu at the end of the month, they found a town full of rubble and broken glass and "inhabited only by federal troops and some 500 Eastern civilians either too old, too young, or too infirm to have left." Stores, homes, consulates, and the Hotel Presidential had been ransacked for items soldiers wanted, but much was simply ignored. Overall, the once-vibrant city felt like a ghost town.

A Short Postscript

The first five months of 1968 saw a series of events that galvanized world attention, including the seizure of the *U.S.S. Pueblo*, the Tet Offensive, the Prague Spring, the My Lai Massacre, the assassinations of Martin Luther King Jr. and Bobby Kennedy, and the near-collapse of the French government. Because of these events, awareness of the on-going Biafran War faded outside of Africa. That situation changed in June 1968, when an Irish priest working in Biafra for the order of Holy Ghost Fathers showed British journalists groups of children starving to death as a direct result of the intensity of the Nigerian blockade and the chaos of war. When *The Sun* and the International Television Network (ITN) exposed the story of Biafra's skeletal children with distended stomachs, the humanitarian crisis shocked the world. The haunting pictures appeared on the covers of American and European magazines like *Der Spiegel, Stern, L'Express*, and *Life* furthered the outrage and calls for action. There were predictions that as many as two million Biafrans would die by the end of the year.

Illustration 86: Protest march urging government action in The Hague, Netherlands, November 20, 1969.

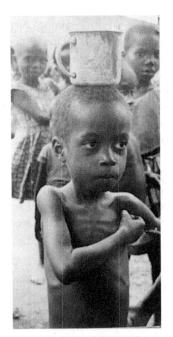 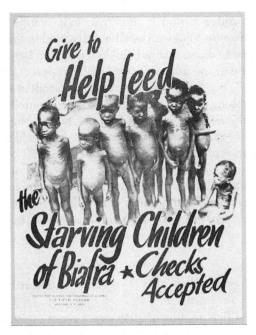

Illustration 87 and 88: Left: Malnourished child, Biafra, July 8, 1968, and, right, fundraising poster, New York City, April 13, 1969

Famine relief efforts were repeatedly undercut by politics. Until April 1968, no nation recognized the Republic of Biafra,[24] which meant that many of the best avenues for aid were legally unavailable. When the Nigerians insisted in January 1968 that all relief flights be routed through Lagos so that the planes could be inspected for illegal arms shipments, Ojukwu refused the condition as an affront to Biafra's sovereignty. In addition, the International Red Cross' early missions were cut short because as signers of the Geneva Convention, the organization had to obtain the permission of all parties in order to be able to operate in a conflict. This constraint meant that the Red Cross only flew 30 flights to Biafra between April 9 and July 15. Then, in August, an independent Swedish aviator, Carl Gustov von Rosen, broke the diplomatic posturing with a heroic mission: by flying at tree-top level from the then-Portuguese island of Saõ Tomé to Biafra's only functioning airport at Uli, von Rosen pierced Nigeria's blockade. A variety of Catholic and Protestant organizations then quickly followed suit, organizing what became the largest private airlift in history: 7,800 flights transported 100,000 metric tons of food and medical supplies to Uli's airstrip. It was an effort that saved untold lives, and yet it is also clear that one million Biafran civilians died of starvation during the war, most of whom were children or elderly.

Defying all-but-their-own expectations, the Biafrans continued to fight throughout 1968 and 1969. In March 1968, they destroyed a major supply column near Awka with a single mortar: it hit a gasoline truck and set off a chain reaction as other fuel and ammunition carriers exploded into flames. This attack set Nigeria's invasion back months. As the summer rainy season set in, the Biafrans successfully employed guerrilla war tactics to keep the Nigerians at bay and the war became a military stalemate. Ojukwu was able to boast on February 10, 1969, "Today, I am happy to report that their miscalculations have persisted. Rather than destroy our gallant people…we have stabilized the fronts; we have built up our forces and seized certain initiatives, and the future prospect is one that can generate confidence." A change of Nigerian commanders

---

[24] On April 13, 1968, Tanzania became the first nation to recognize Biafra. Eventually, Gabon, Ivory Coast, Zambia, and Haiti also did so.

and the arrival of British-made tanks, however, ended the stalemate and the optimism: federal troops entered Biafra's second capital, Umuahia, on April 22, thereby splitting remaining Biafran territory in two and separating the retreating government from the remaining food-producing areas. By fall 1969, there were serious signs that the end was near. In addition to fraternization between Biafran and Nigerian troops on the battlefield, there were increasing social tensions between the millions who lacked enough food and the elite, who enjoyed access to all they needed. With broken morale, the Igbo people lost their faith in Biafra. As one senior official later said,

> "Biafra was collapsing under its own weight of corruption. Relief goods were not getting to the people, army officers were commandeering property....If we could have introduced a more just and humane and equitable society, then it would have been possible...to extend the conflict."

Biafra's surrender came on January 12, 1970, just days after Ojukwu fled with his family for the Ivory Coast. Significantly, Gowon issued a general amnesty on January 15, saying in a radio broadcast that he welcomed "our brothers who were deceived and misled into armed rebellion against their fatherland." He pointedly declared there were to be "no victors, no vanquished." This declaration meant that Nigeria never held a victory celebration and that its troops proved to be well-disciplined in the war's aftermath. The rumors of rape, abduction of children, and wholesale looting proved to be untrue. There were certainly no massacres as so many Igbo had feared would come. Instead, Eastern Nigerians focused upon trying to rebuild their lives. It was not an easy task, for most of Biafra's towns lay in waste from the conflict, with its bridges, businesses, hospitals, residences, and schools all left in ruins. All of the buildings at the Queen's School in Enugu were roofless, its library had no books, and the double line of trees at the school's entrance had all been cut down for fuel. Things were no better in the center of town or in the coal mines—all of which had been flooded and vandalized during the war.

Today, fifty-five years since the Biafran War, Enugu's recovery is still not complete. The city is still a capital, but instead of being the government center for one of Nigeria's four provinces (as it was in 1966), or the capital of one of Nigeria's twelve states (as it was in 1971), today Enugu is just the headquarters of one of Nigeria's thirty-six states. This change means that Enugu's economic standing, political clout, and national importance have faded significantly. These changing circumstances can be seen in the fact that Enugu state ranks as Nigeria's twenty-sixth poorest, its housing quality is far below national averages, and its average resident only has an eighth grade education. Additionally, growing crime rates have led to a sense of urban insecurity, which has had an adverse impact on the city and the state's economic development. Optimists can point to the fact that Enugu has witnessed a dramatic drop in its infant mortality rate in the past five years; has a new, ambitious governor[25] who is committed to improving water supplies, doubling electricity generation, and founding a teaching hospital; and the region has enjoyed remarkable ethnic harmony since the war ended. On balance, however, Enugu feels like a city that has been left behind.

---

[25] The governor is Peter Mbah, who was elected in 2023.

What Enugu Teaches

The capture of a capital in war often marks the culmination of the conflict: the Fall of Constantinople in 1453, the Fall of Saigon in 1974, and the Fall of Kabul in 2021 are poignant examples of this pattern. Enugu, however, stands as an exception to this archetype. Its occupation occurred early in the Nigerian Civil War and yet the Biafrans continued to fight. In this way, Enugu's experience is akin to what happened in Washington, DC in the War of 1812: the British captured the city and leveled a great blow to American pride, but the Americans continued to fight and the subsequent peace preserved the *status quo ante bellum*. Similarly, the Biafrans persisted in their resistance, despite the loss of their symbolic center, and the war ended without a change of international borders.

Tellingly, the Biafran tenacity that so surprised Gowon and the Nigerian military offers several important historical lessons. The first is that propaganda works. Like advertising, propaganda is most effective when it presents a novel concept or approach that captures the public's imagination and leads to what has been described as a "sudden sense of deep understanding." When the Biafran government moved from Enugu to Umuahia in late October 1967, it created a Directorate of Propaganda and staffed it with professors from the University of Nigeria. Its purpose was to convince the world that the Nigerians were hellbent on the mass slaughter of the Igbo people and that the world had to intervene in order to prevent genocide. To facilitate this effort, the Biafran government hired an American-owned public relations firm based in Switzerland, which issued pro-Biafran press releases and made arrangements to transfer journalists behind the battle lines and witness Biafran suffering. These efforts proved quite effective, for as early as February 1968, *Time* published a story that showcased the effectiveness of Biafran resistance: the [Igbo] are proving as adept at the business of defending their homeland as they have always been at trade and commerce." The Igbo are "not only vigorously and successfully resisting invading federal Nigerian troops, but are maintaining high morale and a surprising amount of normalcy while doing so," the publication said. As a result of Biafran press releases, the *Washington Post* called for the Nigerian government to "ease off its military campaign" in order to "save itself uncountable cost and suffering, and earn the respect of decent men everywhere." Later, after *The Sun* and the International Television Network published their stories in June 1968 and the world came to visualize the true depth of Igbo suffering, the Nigerian-Biafran crisis became the world's first public relations war. Graphic, full-page advertisements in the *New York Times* provoked moral outrage and called upon readers to join protests. Benefit concerts quickly followed, featuring Joan Baez, Judy Collins, and Jimmy Hendrix. There were also protest rallies in Washington, DC, London, and The Hague. This response, which proved the efficacy of Biafran messaging, allowed Ojukwu to proclaim in 1969, "The world is now alive to our cause, and our struggle has become the topic of common discussion and concern in practically all countries of the world. World leaders have spoken out; a number of countries have given us diplomatic recognition." Indeed, thanks to his successful propaganda campaign, Ojukwu won over world opinion and saved countless lives in the process, even if he was never able to marshal the military might that was necessary to create an independent Igbo nation.

A second lesson is that civil wars are rarely resolved by foreign military intervention. Instead, civil wars end either because one side wins a decisive victory on the battlefield or because the two sides eventually decide to put aside their differences, compromise, and commit themselves to building a mutually beneficial future. Indeed, multiple economic studies show that foreign interventions in civil wars not only extend the duration of the conflict, but also reduce the likelihood of a lasting settlement. Afghanistan, Iraq, and Somalia stand as glaring examples of how recent foreign interventions failed to produce a viable peace. This contrasts with conflicts like the Nepali Civil War (1996-2006), which ended with a lasting settlement without foreign military involvement. This occurred because the combatants in Nepal negotiated the agreements themselves and subsequently committed themselves to building a new, integrated nation. Arriving at such a commitment is essential for a durable peace. In the case of the Nigerian Civil War, Portugal and France did provide military supplies to Biafra, just as Great Britain did for Nigeria, but their troops were never on the ground. The region did not become a Cold War conflict like Angola did because both Nigeria and Biafra had a fiercely anti-communist disposition and because the Soviet Union did not want to risk a repetition of the failed intervention in the Congo earlier in the 1960s. Similarly, African leaders also chose not to intervene, fearing that supporting a separatist movement in Nigeria might provoke corresponding movements in their own countries. Indeed, the combatants were largely left to resolve the conflict themselves, thereby ensuring that Nigeria would not become another Vietnam.

Curated Bibliography for Chapter 7

Achebe, Chinua. *There Was A Country: A Personal History of Biafra*. New York: Penguin Press, 2012.

Agbo, Chibuzor. *The Encyclopedia of the Coal City: Enugu 100 Year, 1909-2009: The Mother Capital City of Eastern Nigeria*. Enugu, Nigeria: San Press Ltd., 2011.

Akpala, Agwu. "The Background to the Enugu Colliery Shooting Incident in 1949." *Journal of the Historical Society of Nigeria*. Vol. 3, No. 2 (December 1965). JSTOR.

Aniago, Humphrey. *Sunrise in Enugu: A History of the Advent and March of Western Civilization in an Igbo City*. Enugu, Nigeria: Divine-Ark Konsult. 2019.

Baxter, Pete. *Biafra: The Nigerian Civil War, 1967-1970*. Solihull, UK: Helion & Company, 2014. EBSCOebook.

"'Be Prepared and Avoid Panic': Public Poster Displayed in Enugu, March 1967." *Crisis and Conflict in Nigeria: a Documentary Sourcebook, 1966-1969, Volume 1: January 1966-July 1967*. A. H. M. Kirk-Greene (ed.). London: Oxford University Press, 1971.

Bird, S. Elizabeth and Rosina Umelo. *Surviving Biafra: a Nigerwife's Story*. London, Hurst & Company, 2018.

"Blockaded Biafra Facing Starvation: Blockaded Biafrans are Facing Mass Starvation." *New York Times*. June 30 1968, 1. ProQuest Historical Newspapers.

Brown, Carolyn A. *"We Were All Slaves"': Africans, Miners, Culture and Resistance at the Enugu Government Colliery*. Portsmouth, NH: Heinemann, 2003.

Cana, Frank R. "Reviewed Work: *The Dual Mandate in British Tropical Africa* by F. D. Lugard." *The Geographical Journal*. Vol. 60, No. 1 (July 1922). JSTOR.

Currey, James. *Achebe and Friends at Umuahia: The Making of a Literary Life*. Rochester, NY: Terri Ochiagh, 2015.

"Display Ad 43: 6000 Children Starve Daily." *New York Times*. August 24, 1968, 23. ProQuest Historical Newspapers.

Doran, Roy. "Introducing the New Lens of African Military History." *Journal of African Military History*. Vol. 3 (2019).

"Eastern Nigeria Secedes; Central Government Mobilizes." *Chicago Tribune*. May 31, 1967, B2. ProQuest Historical Newspapers.

"Eastern Nigeria Takes Over Federal Services: Move Threatens to Isolate Rebellious Ibo Region." *New York Times*. April 20, 1967, 9. ProQuest Historical Newspapers.

Eze, Dons. *Enugu: 1909-2009: A Century in Search of Identity*. Enugu, Nigeria: Linco Press Ltd., 2009.

Eze, Jacintha U. "Staff Training Programmes in Nigerian Public Libraries: the Case of Enugu State Public Library." *Library Philosophy and Practice*. July 2012, Gale General OneFile.

Eze, Jonas. "Urbanization in Nigeria, Enugu (the Coal City) as an Urban Town: A Historical Review." *Cities*. Volume 113 (June 2021). Science Direct.

"Enugu Will Generate, Distribute Electricity by 2026, Gov Mbah Declares," *The Guardian* [Lagos], March 24 2024, ProQuest Central.

Falola, Toyin and Matthew M. Heaton. *A History of Nigeria*. New York: Cambridge University Press, 2008.

French, Howard W. "The Creation of Nigeria." *New York Review of Books*. Vol. LXX, No. 10 (June 8, 2023).

Garrison, Lloyd. "Biafra vs. Nigeria: The Other Dirty Little War." *New York Times*. March 31, 1968, SM36. ProQuest Historical Newspapers.

Garrison, Lloyd. "The Crisis in Nigeria: Regional Riots Put Nation to Biggest Test thus Far." *New York Times*. June 1, 1966, 8. ProQuest Historical Newspapers.

Garrison, Lloyd. "Eastern Nigeria in Tension's Grip: Mood Like That of a Nation on the Brink of War." *New York Times*. March 12, 1967, 19. ProQuest Historical Newspapers.

Garrison, Lloyd. "Top Nigerian Ibo Bars Surrender: But Eastern Governor Says Conciliation Is Necessary." *New York Times*. August 11, 1966, 9. ProQuest Historical Newspapers.

"GDL Area Profile Report: Enugu (Nigeria)." *Global Data Lab*. 2022, https://globaldatalab.org

Gould, Michael. *The Biafran War: The Struggle for Modern Nigeria*. London: I.B. Tauris, 2012. EBSCOhost.

Gowon, Yakubu. "Broadcast to the Nation, Dividing Nigeria into Twelve States." May 27, 1967. *Crisis and Conflict in Nigeria: a Documentary Sourcebook, 1966-1969, Volume 1: January 1966-July 1967*. A. H. M. Kirk-Greene (ed.). London: Oxford University Press, 1971.

Heerten, Lasse. *The Biafran War and Postcolonial Humanitarianism: Spectacles of Suffering.* New York: Cambridge University Press, 2017.

Inyang, Etiido Effiong. "Echoes of Secession: The Hero, the Rebel, and the Rhetoric of Might in Nigerian Civil War Pictorial Propaganda." *African Studies Quarterly.* Vol. 17, No. 3 (November 2017).

Jaja, S. O. "The Enugu Colliery Massacre in Retrospect: An Episode in British Administration of Nigeria." *Journal of the Historical Society of Nigeria.* Vol. 11, No. ¾ (December 1982-June 1983). JSTOR.

Jennings, J. H. and S. O. Oduah. *A Geography of the Eastern Provinces of Nigeria.* Cambridge, UK: Cambridge University Press, 1966.

Louchheim, Donald H. "Realist Ojukwu Has No Illusions about Reforms: Reappoints Father," *The Washington Post /Times Herald.* February 14, 1966. ProQuest Historical Newspapers.

Malis, Matt, Pablo Querubin and Shanker Satyanath. "Persistent Failure? International Interventions Since World War II." *Handbook of Historical Economics.* Alberto Bisin and Giovanni Federico (eds.). London: Academic Press / Elsevier Science, 2021.

"Mbah's Leadership in Enugu Worthy of Emulation–PDP Govs." *Vanguard.* March 17 2024. ProQuest Central.

McAlister, Melani. "Picturing the War 'No One Cares About'." *National Endowment for the Humanities,* May 18, 2023, https://www.neh.gov

Mcfadden, Robert D. "Odumegwu Ojukwu, breakaway Biafra leader, dies at 78." *New York Times.* November 27, 2011, A30. Gale General OneFile.

Meisler, Stanley. "Crisis in East Nigeria Believed Psychological: Barricaded Ibo People Fearful, Angry; Prepared for Secession or Civil War." *Los Angeles Times.* April 16, 1967, 1. ProQuest Historical Newspapers.

Meisler, Stanley. "Nigerian Troops Open Siege of Biafra Capital." *Los Angeles Times.* October 1, 1967, 1. ProQuest Historical Newspapers.

Niven, Rex. *The War of Nigerian Unity, 1967-1970.* Totowa, NJ: Rowman & Littlefield, 1971.

"Nigeria: the Art of Resistance," *Time,* February 9, 1968, 38.

Nigeria-Biafran War, The: Genocide and the Politics of Memory. Chima J. Korieh (ed.). Amherst, NY: Cambria Press, 2012.

"Nigeria's Destiny." *The Washington Post/Times Herald.* February 4, 1968, 1. ProQuest Historical Newspapers.

"Nigerian Civil War Makes Enugu a Ghost Town: Captured Secessionist City is Deserted and Despoiled Federal Radio Fails to Bring Back Biafrans Who Fled." *New York Times.* October 24 1967, 20. ProQuest Historical Newspapers.

Nwankwo, Arthur Agwuncha and Samuel Udochukwu Ifejika. *The Making of a Nation: Biafra.* London: C. Hurst & Company, 1969.

O'Connell, James. "The Ending of the Nigerian Civil War: Victory, Defeat, and the Changing of Coalitions." *Stopping the Killing: How Civil Wars End.* Roy Licklider (ed.). New York: New York University Press, 1993.

Obienyem, Valentine. *Ojukwu: The Last Patriot.* Ibadan, Nigeria: Wisdom Publishers, 2005.

Odoemene, Akachi and Olufemi Olaoba, "Explaining Inter-Ethnic Harmony in Enugu City, South-Eastern Nigeria, 1970 – 2003." *Accord.* July 20, 2010, https://www.accord.org.za

Okoye, T. O. *The City in South-Eastern Nigeria.* Onitsha, Nigeria: University Publishing Company, 1996.

Omaka, Arua Oko. "Humanitarian Action: The Joint Church Aid and Health Care Intervention in the Nigeria-Biafra War, 1967-1970." *Canadian Journal of History.* Vol. 49 (Winter 2014).

Omaka, Arua Oko. "Through the Imperial Lens: The Role of Portugal in the Nigeria-Biafra War." *Journal of Global South Studies.* Vol. 36, No. 1 (April 1, 2019). EBSCOhost.

Onyinye, Chime Jessie. "Urban Insecurity and Economic Development in Enugu State." *Journal of Policy and Development Studies.* Vol. 14. No. 2 (2023).

Ojukwu, C. Odumegwu. *Biafra: Selected Speeches and Random Thoughts.* New York: Harper & Row, 1969.

"Ojukwu Waves Final Good Bye." *AllAfrica.com.* March 2, 2012. Gale General OneFile.

Omenka, Nicholas Ibeawuchi. "Blaming the Gods: Christian Religious Propaganda in the Nigeria-Biafra War." *The Journal of African History.* Vol. 51, No. 3 (2010). JSTOR.

"Performance at the Scene Raising Funds for Biafra." *New York Times.* August 28, 1968, 38. ProQuest Historical Newspapers.

Perspectives on the Nigerian Civil War. Siyan Oyeweso (ed.). Lagos, Nigeria: Campus Press, Ltd., 1992.

Post, K. W. J. "Is There a Case for Biafra?" *International Affairs*. Vol. 44, No. 1 (January 1968), JSTOR.

Riesel, Victor Riesel. "Nigeria Worthy of American Help." *Los Angeles Times*. August 3 1964, 1. ProQuest Historical Newspapers.

Rotibi, Akinola. "Eastern Nigeria Boasts Powerful TV Service." *The Washington Post/Times Herald*. December 13 1964, 1. ProQuest Historical Newspapers.

Ryeland, Kenneth C. *The Up-Country Man: A Personal Account of the First One Hundred Days Inside Secessionist Biafra*. Unknown: Ogun's Fire, 2022.

Sampson, Cynthia. "'To Make Real the Bond Between Us All': Quaker Conciliation During the Nigerian Civil War." *Religion, the Missing Dimension of Statecraft*. Douglas Johnson and Cynthia Sampson (eds.). New York: Oxford University Press, 1994.

Shen, Wangbing et al. "What Makes Creative Advertisements Memorable? The Role of Insight," *Psychological Research*. Vol. 85, No. 7 (October 2021). EBSCOhost.

Stent, Angela. "The Soviet Union and the Nigerian Civil War: A Triumph of Realism," *Issue: A Journal of Opinion*. Vol. 3, No. 2 (Summer, 1973). JSTOR.

Tarantola, Daniel. "Unforgotten Biafra 50 Years Later." *American Journal of Public Health*, 108(3) (March 2018). doi: 10.2105/AJPH.2017.304289.

Stremlaw, John J. *The International Politics of the Nigerian Civil War, 1967-1970*. Princeton, NJ: Princeton University Press, 1997.

"Thunder Road to Umuahia." *Time*. Vol. 92, No. 14 (October 4, 1968), 36.

Venter, Al J. *Biafra's War 1967-1970: A Tribal Conflict in Nigeria That Left a Million Dead*. Solihull, UK: Helion and Company, 2015. EBSCOebooks.

Walter, Barbara F. Walter. *Committing to Peace: the Successful Settlement of Civil Wars*. Princeton, NJ: Princeton University Press, 2002.

Waters, Ken. "Influencing the Message: The Role of Catholic Missionaries in Media Coverage of the Nigerian Civil War." *The Catholic Historical Review*. Vol. 90, No. 4 (October 2004). JSTOR.

Zerby, Lewis and Margaret. *If I Should Die Before I Wake: The Nsukka Dream: A History of the University of Nigeria*. East Lansing, MI: Michigan State University Press, 1971.

CHAPTER 8

BANJA LUKA
REPUBLIKA SRPSKA

At 3:00 a.m. on Saturday, May 8, 1993, Banja Luka's residents awoke to trembling walls and shattering windows. Perhaps the front lines of the Bosnian Civil War had come far more quickly than was expected. Or perhaps Banja Luka had been hit by an earthquake, like the one that leveled the city in 1969. Regardless of the cause, few went back to sleep.

When dawn broke, Banja Luka's Muslims learned the horrible truth: the Ferhadija Mosque, which was built in 1579 and which was widely considered the finest mosque in Bosnia-Herzegovina, lay in rubble. Dynamited by Bosnian Serbs intent on a policy of ethnic cleansing and erasing the region's multicultural history, Ferhadija's fate soon befell Banja Luka's 15 other mosques. Similarly, Bosnia's oldest clock tower was also demolished. With the destruction of these cultural icons, Bosnian Serbs were constructing a new ethno-national narrative: because Banja Luka had no mosques, it could be defined as a purely Serbian city. Four hundred years of tradition vanished overnight.

Illustration 89: Ferhadija Mosque in 1989.

Illustration 90: Banja Luka Clock Tower, c. 1967

113

Illustration 91: Map of Yugoslavia in 1988, showing the borders of its six major constituent republics.

B = *Brčko District*
RS = *Republika Srpska*

Illustration 92: Map of Bosnia-Herzegovina, showing the borders of its two components: the Federation of Bosnians and Croats and the borders of Republika Srpska in white.

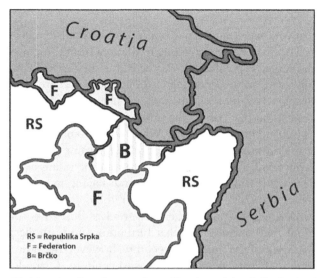

Illustration 93: Map detailing the complicated borders of the Brčko Region in 2024.

A Little Historical Context

In the late nineteenth century, four towering spires dominated central Banja Luka's skyline, each representing a different element of Bosnian society. The oldest was the proud minaret of the Ferhadija Mosque, which was built in 1579 by an Ottoman general and governor, Ferhad Pasha Sokolović, and which called the Muslim faithful to prayer five times a day. The second, a wood steeple with a homage to an onion dome underneath the lantern, rose a half a mile to the northeast. It was the tower of an Orthodox Christian church, which served as the center of Banja Luka's largest religious community. Nearby stood a Catholic church, also made of wood, whose more-stout, square pinnacle had Gothic windows. Lastly, quite near the mosque, arose a stone municipal clock tower, which had been built by Ferhad Pasha Sokolović in 1587. This square campanile, the oldest in Bosnia-Herzegovina, symbolized his hope that the newly-converted Bosnian Muslims, the Orthodox Serbs and the Catholic Croatians—all of whom were ethnically Slavs—could live aside one another in peace. After all, all three communities shared a love of minced, grilled meat (*ćevapčići*) and intense Turkish coffee.

Illustration 94: Banja Luka Orthodox Church, 1879.

Illustration 95: Banja Luka Catholic Church, late 1800s.

115

Bosnia-Herzegovina has long been a borderland—a transitional zone where conflicts seek their resolutions. The Slavs began migrating to the area from present-day Poland in the late sixth and early seventh century as polytheists. By the end of the first millennium, they had largely converted to Christianity, with some becoming Catholics, some becoming Orthodox Christians, and still others choosing to form their own independent Christian church. These three denominations disagreed about the Trinity, the primacy of the Pope, the celibacy of priests, and a host of other theological and liturgical issues. When the Ottomans conquered Bosnia in 1463 and made Banja Luka the provincial capital, the situation became even more complex as many Bosnians voluntarily converted to Islam to be able to join the ruling class. By the eighteenth century, with the independent Christian Bosnian church having faded away, Bosnia was 33% Muslim, 43% Orthodox, and 20% Catholic. All of these people were ethnic Slavs, who essentially spoke the same language and who called themselves Bosnians. All that really separated them was their choice of faith and the fact that Orthodox and Catholic peasants usually had Muslim landlords. By the end of the nineteenth century, however, the power of nationalism and national identity movements began creeping into Bosnian culture. Orthodox Bosnians began to identify as Serbs since the independent nation of Serbia was unequivocally Orthodox. Catholic Bosnians began to identify as Croats since semi-autonomous Croatia was fervently Catholic. This change left Bosnia's Muslims isolated because, unlike other ethnic groups in the Balkans, they did not have an historic or a modern political state, aside from Bosnia, with which to identify.

Bosnia remained under Ottoman control until 1878, when it became a protectorate of the Austro-Hungarian Empire. Formal annexation followed in 1908. Before World War I, the new imperial rulers created a contemporary central square and park for Banja Luka, which was ringed by government buildings and anchored a growing commercial district. Grand new houses, a new railway station, a hospital, banks, schools, and a military command center also advanced Banja Luka's infrastructure and modernized its appearance considerably. Many of the city's historic buildings date to the urban design efforts of the Austro-Hungarians. For Bosnia as a whole, however, the Austro-Hungarian period was economically difficult: its mountainous terrain discouraged development, its hereditary lease-holding peasants were the most exploited in the empire, its exports were barred from the Adriatic Sea by regulation, and its vast timber resources only produced wealth for businesses in Vienna and Budapest.

Illustration 96: Mansion in central Banja Luka built during the period Austro-Hungarian rule.

The nineteenth century's nationalism, romanticism, and radicalism all met in the imagination of Gavrilo Princip, a poor Bosnian Serb teenager who joined the underground organization Young Bosnia in 1911. The revolutionary group was dedicated to the creation of a unified Slavic state by violent means. On June 28, 1914, with the help of Serbian army officers and a bit of luck, Princip assassinated the heir to the Austro-Hungarian throne, Archduke Franz Ferdinand, and his wife, Sophie, in Sarajevo. The murder wasn't the cause of World War I, but it was the catalyst that sent ten million men to their deaths before an armistice came on November 11, 1918. The resulting Treaty of Versailles brought the South Slavs together into a kingdom that became known as Yugoslavia, but Bosnians, Croats, Serbs, Slovens, Macedonians, and Montenegrins struggled to reach a mutual understanding.

Ethnic resentments grew in the Bosnian region as a result of World War II. When the Germans and Italians conquered Yugoslavia in 1941, they created the Independent State of Croatia and installed an ardent Croatian fascist to subjugate most of Croatia and Bosnia. Ante Pavelić and his followers, known as the Ustaše, killed between 300,000 and 400,000 Serbs[26] and forced hundreds of thousands of other Serbs to convert to Catholicism in the few years they were in power. The Jasenovac concentration camp fifty miles north of Banja Luka, where so many Serbs died, was every bit as gruesome as those camps Jews faced in Poland, and this is why the war fueled Croat-Serbian animosity for generations. Bosnia's Muslims had a more complicated relationship with the Ustaše regime, for while some, including a group from Banja Luka, condemned Croatian treatment of Serbs in 1941, there were certainly other Muslims who enthusiastically welcomed the Nazis and their puppets. 21,000 Bosnian Muslims even joined the Waffen SS in an effort to combat two resistance groups: the royalist, Serbian-dominated Četniks and the communist Partisans, who were led by Josip Broz Tito. This active collaboration and support for the Nazis and their allies fed Serbian antipathy for Muslims as well. In fact, of the 86,000 Bosnian Muslims who died in World War II, the vast majority did so at the hands of the Četniks, who wanted to "cleanse Bosnia of everything that is not Serb," according to the minutes of a Četniks meeting held in June 1942.

Illustration 97: Memorial monument at the site of the Jasenovac concentration camp,

Banja Luka witnessed bitter fighting during the war as the city changed hands six times between April 1941 and April 1945. Combat was particularly intense in early 1944 with house-to-house fighting, but the more lasting scar came at the start of the war in Yugoslavia, when German bombs destroyed the city's newly-inaugurated Orthodox cathedral. That Catholic and Muslim places of worship emerged largely unscathed from the war also contributed to lasting ethnic bitterness between Catholic Croats, Orthodox Serbs and Bosnian Muslims.

Tito emerged victorious in the post-war struggle for power. He managed to suppress nationalist feelings and hold communist Yugoslavia together until his death in 1980. Over the next eight years, however, the long-simmering resentments between many of Yugoslavia's religious groups increasingly bubbled to the surface. By the time the Berlin Wall collapsed and the Cold War ended in 1989-1990, the road to Yugoslavia's dissolution had become quite short. This began with Slovenia's push to create a federated republic for Yugoslavia in 1989 that was democratic, pluralistic, and based upon voluntary membership. This move was a direct threat to the power of Serbian leader Slobadan Milošević, who sought a centralized nation that the Serbs could dominate. In June 1991, both Slovenia and Croatia declared their independence. It was

---

[26] The Ustaše also were responsible for the murder of the vast majority of Bosnia's 14,000 Jews and numerous members of the region's Roma and gay communities.

one thing for Slovenia to do so because it had well-defined borders and few minorities, but Croatia, with its large Serbian minority, was another matter for Milošević entirely. A vicious, six-month war ensued with the Serbs capturing large portions of Croatian territory and driving half a million people from their homes. A negotiated January 1992 cease-fire barely kept the hostilities at bay since Serbs remembered the crimes of the Ustaše regime and Croats mourned the destruction of historic cities like Dubrovnik and Vukovar.

Illustration 98: Radovan Karadžić in 1994.

This was also an important transitional period for Bosnia-Herzegovina. In late September 1991, the Bosnian parliament began proceedings to create an independent Bosnia state, with the major Muslim and Croatian political parties championing the move. The leader of the Bosnian Serbs, Radovan Karadžić, objected vigorously, however, saying that he "would never accept a document that took [Bosnian] Serbs out of Yugoslavia." He predicted that "succession could ignite the flame of civil war in Bosnia" and that this "hell" would "possibly [cause] the Muslim nation to disappear, for the Muslim people will not be able to defend [themselves] if it comes to war." When the parliament ignored Karadžić's warning, the Bosnian Serbs chose to create their own assembly, the Assembly of the Serb People of Bosnia-Herzegovina, on October 24. On January 9, this assembly met in Banja Luka and declared the majority-Serbian regions of Bosnia-Herzegovina to be independent of the rest of the country. This political entity became known as Republika Srpska (RS). When 99.7% of Bosnia's Muslims and Croats voted in a February 1992 referendum to separate from Serbian-dominated Yugoslavia, the Bosnian Serbs began pursuing military options to secure their position.

On May 12, 1992, the RS assembly passed a resolution at Karadžić's behest that outlined the Bosnian Serbs' major objectives for the war. The overarching goal was to separate Serb institutions, land, and people from the rest of Bosnia. Because of the way in which Muslims, Catholics, and Orthodox Christians had lived side by side for centuries in Bosnia, the only way to accomplish this goal was to rid Republika Srpska of all non-Serbs. The ethnic cleansing of Republika Srpska soon began.

Banja Luka c.1993

As the new year opened, the head of the Red Cross' mission in Banja Luka noted that the physical ravages of war had yet to come to the city. This was because local authorities sought to preserve it as a model community and capital. Indeed, visitors to Banja Luka in early 1993 were struck with how different it felt from Sarajevo, Mostar, and other cities in Bosnia- Herzegovina. There were "no shell craters, no pitted and gouged walls, no boarded-up shop fronts, no fire-gutted houses," an interpreter for a British military commander noted. Instead, the scars of war were psychological, for the city's Muslims lived in constant fear that the next knock on the door would result in tragedy: a Serb coming to take the house, rape a daughter, or murder a spouse. By 1993, harassment had turned to terror. In fact, the fear had become so pervasive (and the desire to leave so great) that Muslims were arriving at the Banja Luka's Bureau for the Removal of Populations and Exchange of Material Goods armed with documents to prove that they had surrendered the deed to their house and forfeited the contents of their bank accounts. All they wanted was a seat on one of the bus convoys. It didn't matter where they ended up as long as they were still alive. An orderly exit was, of course, exactly what the Bosnian Serbs in Banja Luka wanted. By the end of the year, of the 350,000 Muslims who once lived in the Banja Luka region, only 40,000 remained. Two signs explained the situation succinctly. The first, hung in a Muslim neighborhood proclaimed, "Avoid the hardships of winter. Leave the area now." The second, near the door of the local office for the United Nations High Commissioner for Refugees, said, "Welcome to the Dark Side of the Moon..."

Even in their desperate evacuation, the Muslims begged Bosnian Serb authorities to be allowed to collect and preserve the rubble of the Ferhadija Mosque. They hung onto the hope of one day being able to reconstruct it, but permission was refused. Instead, the remnants of the treasured building were dumped in the Vrbas River, taken to landfills, or hidden in secret locations. The site was then bulldozed into a parking lot. For the city's Serb leaders, there was to be no going back: all evidence of Muslim participation in what was once known as Bosnia's "common life" was to be permanently erased. That is what ethnic cleansing meant in Banja Luka.

As Muslims left, displaced Bosnian Serbs began to arrive from other parts of the country, for war had forced them to move as well. These refugees happily moved into the newly-evacuated Muslim homes, relieved to find in-tact residences with fully equipped kitchens and bedrooms. As one American journalist noted, "the toys they found...were an unexpected bonus."

Illustration 99: Recovered fragments from the original Ferhadija Mosque, April 2023.

Just as the Republika Srpska government began to feel confidence in its ability to create a new life for Bosnian Serbs, a surprising challenge arose. In September 1993, one corps of the Bosnian Serb army seized key municipal buildings, police stations, and communication centers and closed all of the major roads into Banja Luka. This renegade unit demanded better pay from the government, as well as the end to the wartime profiteering by well-connected politicians. The soldiers wanted to benefit from some of the illegally-obtained wealth flowing into Bosnia, which one study valued to be 23% of all humanitarian aid. This graft didn't anger the general public, however, for they remained largely unsympathetic to the soldiers' cause. Instead, most Bosnian Serbs expected them to continue to sacrifice for the Bosnian Serb cause. Indeed, most of Banja Luka's residents would have applauded a soldier who told *Time*:

> This is a very personal war. It will decide who I shall live with, and we can never live with the Muslims again. I do not mind spending the rest of my life in the trenches if it will finally settle the question of who owns the land. Then my children can live in peace.

Without public support, the tank unit found itself in an untenable position. This fact helped RS president Radovan Karadžić quell the crisis quickly upon his arrival in Banja Luka. His ability to do so also allowed Karadžić to be generous: while he had a few of the ringleaders arrested, most soldiers returned to duty without punishment.

With the local military situation secure and the city becoming more homogeneously Serbian, Republika Srpska officials saw an opportunity to celebrate Serbian identity and values while restoring Banja Luka's cultural heritage. War had destroyed the city's Orthodox cathedral in 1941, but now there was the opportunity to build something triumphant—a poignant symbol of Serbian faith and the Serbian vision for Bosnia's future. The new cathedral would be like a phoenix rising out of the fire, full of hope. Symbolically, the architectural plans specifically called for the inclusion of a campanile that was taller than either Ferhad Pasha Sokolović's minaret or his municipal clock tower. In an elaborate ceremony watched by more than 10,000 people, the Cathedral of Christ the Savior's foundations were consecrated on October 17, 1993. In one address, the patriarch of the Serbian Orthodox Church noted that:

> Once a sin is committed, a new sin always begets. That's why everything tragic that happens in these times is a consequence of the events during the Second World War. Hence the destruction of the synagogue and so many deaths in this unfortunate war. The causes of this present-day tragedy…did not arise overnight.

Illustration 100, 101, and 102: Facade and dome of Christ the Savior Orthodox Cathedral, Banja Luka, April 2023.

In other words, history weighs heavily and prominently in the minds of those living in the Balkans. It is omnipresent, which is why cultural symbols hold such importance. For Banja Luka, the destruction of the Ferhadija Mosque in May and the consecration of Christ the Savior in October stand as 1993's bookends to what can only be described as an enormously complicated, repeatedly tragic history.

A Short Postscript

The Bosnian Civil War raged on through the rest of 1993, all of 1994, and most of 1995 with Muslims fighting Croats, Croats fighting Serbs, and Serbs fighting Muslims at different times in different parts of the country. Atrocities continued to be committed by all sides, but what happened in the UN "safe town" of Srebrenica in July 1995 remains one of the war's most potent symbols. The attack was ordered by Republika Srpska president Radovan Karadžić and resulted in the systemic murder of approximately 8,000 Bosnian Muslim men and boys, as well as the rape of an untold number of Muslim women. Karadžić later boasted of his decision, but the massacre in Srebrenica and the capture of other UN-protected communities proved to be a serious miscalculation. The horrors were such that NATO and President Bill Clinton were finally pushed into meaningful action. After a Bosnian Serb mortar exploded in a Sarajevo market on August 28, NATO began bombing RS positions around the city. This major assault was combined with the launching of thirteen Tomahawk missiles on the Bosnian Serb army's command center outside of Banja Luka and the unexpectedly quick advance of the Croat army to within twelve miles of Banja Luka. These developments convinced Yugoslavian president Slobodan Milošević that he had to intervene more directly and purposefully. He subsequently forced Karadžić to sign an agreement to allow Milošević to represent the Bosnian Serbs at the negotiating table.[27]

The decisive peace talks to end the Bosnian Civil War were held at an American air force base outside of Dayton, Ohio in November 1995, with Croatian President Franjo Tudjman representing the Bosnian Croats, Alija Izetbegović representing the Bosnian Muslims, and Milošević representing the Bosnian Serbs. The leading American diplomat, Richard Holbrooke, selected the site over cities like Paris or Geneva because he wanted to control the press, keep the negotiators in close proximity, and offer few distractions. The sparse accommodations would also help ensure that no one would want to linger. This worked, for by the third week of the negotiations, everyone was "sick of the confinement and the artificiality of it," as one American official noted. That the three leading delegates—Izetbegović, Milošević, and Tudjman—hated each other also meant that everyone was eager to conclude an agreement as quickly as possible.

The final accord split Bosnia-Herzegovina into two political entities: Republika Srpska with 49% of the territory and its capital of Banja Luka and the Bosnian-Croat Federation with 51% of the territory and its capital of Sarajevo. Both entities were to be governed by a joint

---

[27] Karadžić's political career came to an end shortly after surrendering to Milošević's demands. He remained in hiding for many years, but was finally arrested and put on trial for war crimes and genocide. In 2016, Karadžić was found guilty by the International Criminal Tribunal for the former Yugoslavia (ICTY) and was sentenced to life imprisonment.

legislature and a presidency that rotated between the three major ethnic groups. An Office of the High Representative and 60,000 UN peacekeeping troops would enforce Dayton's terms and ensure the peace. Because no agreement could be reached on the Brčko District, the matter was referred to arbitration.

The Dayton Agreement successfully ended the civil war, but it also created a de facto partition that some today see as rewarding the aggressors and supporting genocide. Others hold that the agreement was the best that could be achieved at the time, given the multitude of factors and perspectives. What is clear is that the serpentine borders dividing RS from the Federation (which is composed of separate Muslim and Croat cantons) make little geographical sense, for neither RS or the Federation have a contiguous border. Instead, the lines on the map reflect Bosnia's multicultural history, ethnic cleansing, the territorial swaps made at the negotiating table, and troop positions at war's end. It is also clear that over two million people were displaced from their homes during the conflict, 36,700 civilians were killed, and 68,000 soldiers died because of the ways in which ethnic prejudices were fueled by virulent propaganda campaigns by all sides. Even more tellingly, the various parties have never been able to reach a final agreement on the strategic Brčko District, for the governments of Bosnia-Herzegovina struggle to be effective as a result of overlapping jurisdictions, vested interests, residual suspicions, economic barriers, corrupt courts, and the nation's fundamental constitutional structure. As one historian put it, Bosnia-Herzegovina is a "two-headed monstrosity," within which lives a "second hybrid entity— the Muslim-Croat federation—that existed mainly in the minds of foreign diplomats." Indeed, the war and the Dayton Accord destroyed any hope for a unified multicultural nation. The great consequence of the victory of ethnic-religious nationalism is that Bosnia-Herzegovina has yet to develop into a mature democracy with a modern economy.

Shortly after peace came to Bosnia-Herzegovina, about 500 Muslim refugees returned to Banja Luka. They quickly expressed their desire to rebuild the Ferhadija Mosque, using recovered original stones wherever possible. City officials balked at issuing a building permit, with the mayor saying in 1998 that the mosque was a symbol of Turkish occupation and oppression: rebuilding it "would be perceived by the Serbs as the darkest humiliation, which would open the old wounds and bring far-reaching consequences." When the cornerstone was finally laid in 2001, on the eighth anniversary of the mosque's destruction, it was clear that the mayor wasn't exaggerating. The ceremony sparked a violent reaction from several thousand Serbian nationalists, who committed acts of arson and vandalism and imprisoned 300 people in the city's Islamic Center, including representatives from the UN and ambassadors from Britain, Sweden, and Pakistan. By the end of the day-long riot, thirty people had been injured, including local police officers who had been unable to maintain the peace. One Muslim died two weeks later, having been beaten with his prayer rug until comatose. Dayton may have brought an official peace to Republika Srpska and its capital of Banja Luka, but the region's long-standing prejudices continued to percolate.

Construction of the mosque proceeded in spite of the riot and the continued threat of violence, and on May 7, 2016 nearly ten thousand Bosnian Muslims gathered in front of the reconstructed Ferhadija Mosque to witness an inspiring demonstration of religious and political unity. Guarded by over a thousand Bosnian Serb police officers, an array of secular and religious officials came together to commemorate the mosque's reopening after twenty-three years. The dignitaries included Bosnia-Herzegovina's head of state, the nation's Grand Mufti, the American ambassador, European bureaucrats, and representatives of the region's Catholic, Jewish, and Orthodox Christian communities. Turkish Prime Minister Ahmet Davutoğlu gave the ceremony's main address, which highlighted Turkey's and Bosnia-Herzegovina's shared cultural heritage. He proclaimed:

Those who bombed and destroyed Ferhadija Mosque 23 years ago not only destroyed a mosque, they also destroyed humanity's conscience. Today by rebuilding this mosque, we are in fact rebuilding the conscience of humanity. Let it be known that as long as this mosque is here, prayers voicing humanity's conscience will speak to the skies in Banja Luka."

It was a day of optimism, joy, and reconciliation for a city and a country struggling to come to terms with its complicated past. The air seemed full of new possibilities and new opportunities, thanks to the inspired speeches, poignant handshakes, and common prayers. As the Grand Mufti concluded, "Ferhadija was, is, and will be the magnificent witness of faith in the unity of the Creator."

Illustrations 103 and 104: Left: Ferhadija Mosque in 1989, and, right, the mosque from a similar angle in 2023. The attention to detail in the reconstruction is clear.

Reality returned quickly enough. The next day, on May 8, a group of nationalistic Bosnian Serbs chanted a particularly hateful slogan in front of the mosque during morning prayers: "Nož, žica, Srebrenica! Nož, žica, Srebrenica!" Rhyming in Serbian, "The Knife, the Barbed Wire, Srebrenica!" is a chant that glorifies one of the civil war's most notorious atrocities. As the hateful words ricocheted off the carefully reconstructed walls and the mosque's single, soaring minaret, Ferhadija once again became a symbol of ethnic division in a still-troubled land.

What Banja Luka Teaches

The first thing that Banja Luka showcases is the way in which works of architecture hold enormous power as symbols of identity. Just as the Parthenon symbolizes Greece, the Giza

Pyramids represent Egypt, and the Great Wall denotes China, the Ferhadija Mosque embodied Banja Luka's Muslim community. After the war, the mosque's absence personified everything that had been lost: homes and neighbors, friends and family, wealth and well-being. By rebuilding the mosque, the city's Muslims sought to honor their past, celebrate the present, and convey their hopes for the future. They wanted to express their long-standing civic membership, as well as the promise of future civic participation. But because architecture is a material expression of power, this objective sparked a violent reaction from radicals within Banja Luka's Serbian community, who wanted to define citizenship as being exclusively Orthodox. As with Mostar's Old Bridge, Ferhadija's destruction and eventual rebuilding became a potent representation of the conflict and its partial resolution.

The second lesson shows how binary thinking limits understanding. Americans are particularly prone to this trap, for they tend to categorize their world as being one thing or the other: good or bad, black or white, North or South, domestic or foreign, Democrat or Republican. This was particularly true during the Cold War because of the way the threat of nuclear annihilation was added to the mix. The problem for American officials in the early 1990s was that having lost the Cold War as an organizing principle, they were paralyzed with indecision. Unable to determine decisively who was an ally and who was an enemy in a nation with three adversaries, American officials dithered as the Bosnian Civil War developed. They didn't see the conflict as being important enough to risk American lives. They especially struggled to read the lay of the land because Catholics, Orthodox Christians, and Muslims could all point to multiple atrocities having been committed against them, as well as to evidence of members of their own communities overcoming circumstances and prejudice to help people of different faiths in times of crisis. Were the Americans able to overcome the limitations of binary thinking and come to a consensus faster, as their NATO allies begged them to do, Bosnia-Herzegovina would be a happier place today.

Illustration 105: Memorial to the Bosnian Serb police officers who died during the civil war, which stands in front of Banja Luka's main police station.

Curated Bibliography for Chapter 8

2016 European Islamophobia Report. Enes Bayrakli and Farid Hafez (eds.) Istanbul: SETA, 2017.

Andrić, Ivo. *The Bridge on the Drina.* Chicago, IL: University of Chicago Press, 1977.

Bal, Mustafa. "Romantic Piers of *The Bridge on the Drina.*" *Serbian Studies.* Vol. 21, No. 1 (2007).

Barnes, Edward. "Behind the Serbian Lines." *Time.* May 17, 1993, 32-35.

Battling Over the Balkans: Historiographical Questions and Controversies. John R. Lampe and Constantin Iordachi (eds.). New York: Central European University Press, 2020.

Bennett, Christopher. *Bosnia's Paralysed Peace.* New York: Oxford University Press, 2016.

Biondich, Mark. "Religion and Nation in Wartime Croatia: Reflections on the Ustaša Policy of Forced Religious Conversions, 1941-1942." *The Slavonic and East European Review.* Vol. 83, No. 1 (January 2005), JSTOR.

Björkdahl, Annika and Johanna Mannergren Selimovic. "A Tale of Three Bridges: Agency and Agonism in Peace Building." *Third World Quarterly.* Vol. 37, No. 2 (2015).

Bose, Sumantra. *Bosnia After Dayton: Nationalist Partition and International Intervention.* New York: Oxford University Press, 2002.

"Brčko." *Columbia Electronic Encyclopedia.* 6th Edition (2021). EBSCOhost.

Broz, Svetlana, Laurie Kain Hart, and Ellen Elias-Bursać. *Good People in an Evil Time: Portraits of Complicity and Resistance in the* Bosnian War. New York: Other Press, 2004.

Carney, James. "Finally, the Leader of NATO Leads." *Time.* September 11, 1995, 54.

Chazan, Yigal. "Vice Tightens in a Town of Hard Choices: Banja Luka In Bosnia Has Escaped the Worst of Serbian Ethnic Cleansing, but the Pressure is Growing on the Muslims and Croats There." *Guardian* [London]. January 8, 1993. Gale Health and Wellness.

Church of Christ the Savior, Banja Luka. https://hhsbl.org/sr/istorijat-hrama?start=9

Čuvalo, Ante. *Historical Dictionary of Bosnia and Herzegovina.* Lanham, MD: Scarecrow Press, 2007.

"Davutoğlu Attends Reopening of Historic Bosnian Mosque." *Daily Sabah.* May 07, 2016.

"Details about the Opening of Ferhadija in Banja Luka." *Sarajevo Times.* May 7, 2016.

Donia, Robert J. *Radovan Karadžić: Architect of the Bosnian Genocide.* New York: Cambridge University Press, 2015.

Drašković, Branislav. "Urban Expansion of the Largest Cities in Bosnia and Herzegovina Over the Period 2000-2018." *Geographica Pannonica.* Vol. 25, No. 4 (December 2021).

Duggal, Hanna. "Infographic: 30 years since the Bosnian War." *Al Jazeera.* April 6, 2022.

Dzidic, Sanin. "Homage to Prof. Dr. Ismet V. Tahirovic: Some Structural Undertakings for Preservation of Historical Monuments in 20th Century Bosnia and Herzegovina." *Research Gate,* 2017.

Fedarko, Kevin. "A Bosian Peace Deal in Dayton is 'Inches Away.'" *Time.* November 27, 1995, 40-41.

Fedarko, Kevin. "Louder Than Words." *Time.* September 11, 1995, 50-59.

Glenny, Misha. *The Balkans: Nationalism, War, and the Great Powers, 1804-1999.* New York: Penguin Press, 2001.

Gordon, Michael R. "U.S. Finds Serbs Skimming 23% Of Bosnian Aid." *The New York Times.* January 13, 1993. Gale Opposing Viewpoints.

Hamilton, Daniel S. "Fixing Dayton: A New Deal for Bosnia and Herzegovina." *NextEurope.* No. 1 (November 2020).

Hayden, Robert M. *Antagonistic Tolerance: Competitive Sharing of Religious Sites and Spaces.* New York: Routledge, 2016.

"Half of Nazi Base Is Seized by Tito." *New York Times.* January 4, 1944, 6. ProQuest Historical Newspapers.

Husarska, Anna. "Without A Prayer?: Rebuilding a Muslim Temple is a Test of Bosnia's Peace." *The Washington Post.* May 10, 1998. C1. ProQuest Historical Newspapers.

Jankovic, Aleksandar. "Nationalism as a Structural Obstacle to Democratization of Bosnia and

Herzegovina Society." *Sociologija*. 61 (2019). ResearchGate, 10.2298/SOC1901087J.

Jankovic, Aleksandar. "On the Road From Socialism to Capitalism: Attitudes of Young People in Bosnia and Herzegovina on Economic Role Of The State." *Sociologija*. Vol. LXVI, No. 2 (2024).

Jelavich, Barbara. *History of the Balkans: Eighteenth and Nineteenth Centuries*. Vol. 1. New York: Cambridge University Press, 1983.

Jones, Paul. *The Sociology of Architecture : Constructing Identities*. Liverpool, UK: Liverpool University Press, 2011). EBSCOhost.

Judah, Tim. *The Serbs: History, Myth, and the Destruction of Yugoslavia*. New Haven, CT: Yale University Press, 2009.

Kann, Robert. A. *History of the Habsburg Empire, 1526-1918, A*. Berkeley, CA: University of California Press, 1974.

Kaplan, Robert D. *Balkan Ghosts: A Journey Through History*. New York: Picador, 2005.

Karčič, Hikmet. "Uncovering the Truth: The Lake Peručac Exhumations in Eastern Bosnia." *Journal of Muslim Minority Affairs*. Vol. 37, No. 1 (2017).

Levy, "'The Last Bullet for the Last Serb': The Ustaša Genocide Against Serbs, 1941-1945." *Nationalities Papers*. Vol. 37, No. 6 (November 2009).

Maass, Peter. *Love Thy Neighbor: A Story of War*. New. York: Alfred A. Knoff, 1996.

Motadel, David. "The 'Muslim Question' in Hitler's Balkans." *The Historical Journal*. Vol. 56, No. 4 (December 2013). JSTOR.

Muslims of Bosnia-Herzegovina, The: Their Historic Development from the Middle Ages to the Dissolution of Yugoslavia. Mark Pinson (ed.). Cambridge, MA: Harvard University Press, 1996.

Palowitch, Stevan K. *Tito: Yugoslavia's Great Dictator: A Reassessment*. Columbus, OH: Ohio State University Press, 1992.

Packer, George. *Our Man: Richard Holbrooke and the End of the American Century*. New York: Alfred A. Knopf, 2019.

Pejanović, Mirko. *Through Bosnian Eyes: A Political Memoir of a Bosnian Serb*. West Lafayette, IN: Purdue University Press, 2004.

Perić-Romić, Ranka. "Rehabilitation of Urban Heritage in the Service of Ethno-National Divisions on the Example of Sarajevo and Banja Luka." *Politeia*. Vol. 10, No. 20 (2020).

Robinson, Guy M. and Alma Pobric. "Nationalism and Identity in Post-Dayton Accords: Bosnia-Hercegovina." *Tijdschrift voor Economische en Sociale Geografie*. Vol. 97, No. 3. Blackwell Publishing.

Strachan, Hew. *The Outbreak of the First World War*. New York: Oxford University Press, 2004.

Stokes, Gale. *The Walls Came Tumbling Down: Collapse and Rebirth in Eastern Europe*. 2nd ed. New York: Oxford University Press, 2012.

Stankovic, Milos. *Trusted Mole: A Soldier's Journey into Bosnia's Heart of Darkness*. New York: HarperCollins, 2000.

"Tito Expelled from Banja Luka by Strong Nazi Reinforcements." *New York Times*. January 8 1944, 4. ProQuest Historical Newspapers.

Toal, Gerard and Carl T. Dahlman. *Bosnia Remade: Ethnic Cleansing and Its Reversal*. New York: Oxford University Press, 2011.

Thurow, Roger. "Desperate Muslims Eek Way Out Bosnia: Poster Urging People To 'Avoid The Hardships Of Winter. Leave The Area Now' May Sound Like A Travel Promotion. But The Real Message Is One Of Life And Death." *Globe & Mail*. November 23, 1993. Gale Health and Wellness.

Wald, Patricia M. "Forward: War Tales and War Trials." *Michigan Law Review*. Vol. 106:901 (April 2008).

"Yugoslavs Battle Foe in Banja Luka." *New York Times*. January 5 1944, 5. ProQuest Historical Newspapers.

CHAPTER 9:

HARGEISA
SOMALILAND

Hargeisa's Waheen Market had been the economic center of the city for decades, but on the evening of April 1, 2022, a fire tore through the massive *souk*. Fed by numerous flammable goods that were difficult to extinguish and expedited by a lack of sprinkler systems, the fire reduced the warren of 2,000 shops and makeshift stalls to ashes by the time the sun rose the next day. Amazingly, no one died that night in the 24-acre conflagration in the heart of the city, but the damage devastated anyway: Hargeisa's Chamber of Commerce observed that the third largest market in Africa accounted for as much as 50% of the city's economic activity. The mayor later estimated the losses to be $2 billion or about 60% of Somaliland's gross domestic product.

What these statistics meant on an individual level confounded, especially for so many of Hargeisa's women. Amina Mahmud was a well-respected forty-one-year-old woman, who operated a butcher's shop and a thriving housewares store in the market prior to the fire. Dressed each day in a colorful *garbasaar* or shawl that covered her shoulders and head, she made more than $2,700 a month selling camel meat and household merchandise. This income was enough to raise her seven children. But when Mahmud lost $10,000 worth of property in the inferno, she lost much of her social standing as well. Resolutely set in front of a wooden table selling a few bananas and cabbages three weeks after the fire, Mahmud simply said, "my life is starting from scratch." Another woman, Nimco Husein Abdi, owned a business that sold bedding and clothes. After the fire, she found that there was nowhere to turn. She said, "all my things are gone....I just sit at home most of the time because there is nothing for me to sell." A third Hargeisa businesswoman, Ayaan Salaad Mohamed, owned a beauty services shop before the blaze. She noted, "nobody knows how this has impacted us. We weren't rich people, but we would make enough money to get through our daily affairs. [Now] our life has taken a drastic turn, but we will work with whatever God provides."

Recovering from losses this large, whether on the individual, municipal, or national level, would be a challenge anywhere, but Somaliland's status as an unrecognized state makes the task that much greater. Because of its diplomatic status, Somaliland is ineligible for loans from the World Bank or the International Monetary Fund, and it cannot participate in international markets and trading networks as recognized nations do. Somaliland's president, Muse Bihi Abdi, declared the Waheen Market Fire to be "an emergency of the highest magnitude" and pointedly said that "time is of the essence," but the fact was that he and his nation had to face the catastrophe with limited options. This is why Somaliland's paradoxical past remains so omnipresent in its daily life today, and it begs the question, how can a fully-functioning state not legally exist?

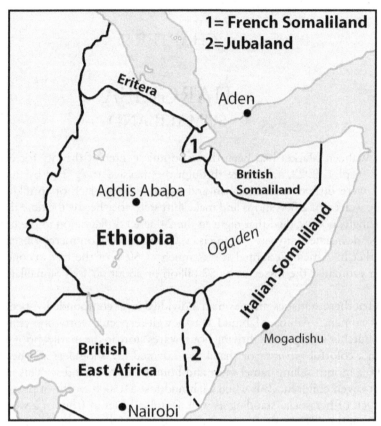

Illustration 106: Map by the author of the Horn of Africa in 1900

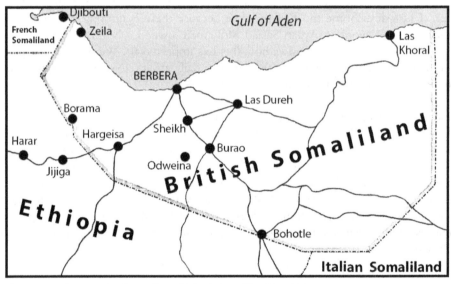

Illustration 107: Map by the author of British Somaliland in 1900.

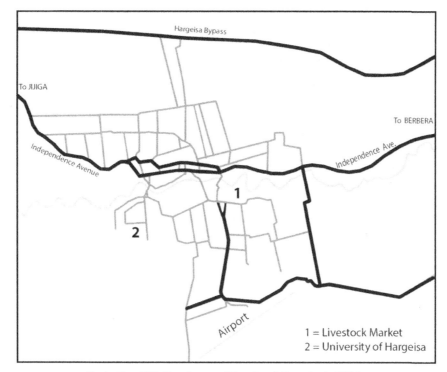

Illustration 108: Street map of the city of Hargeisa in 2024.

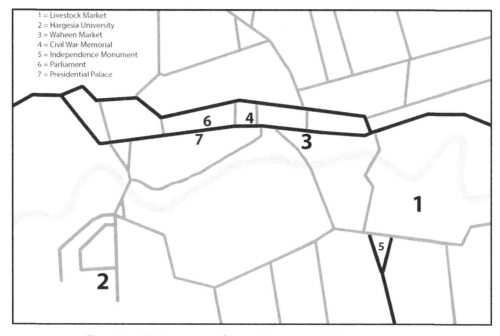

Illustration 109: Street map of central Hargeisa in 2024.

A Little Historical Context

Because the Somali people primarily inhabit arid steppes and deserts, they were largely pastoral nomads before colonization. Their clan-based society never formed a unified, centralized Somali state prior to the Scramble for Africa, [28] largely because livestock grazing in regions with minimal precipitation requires near-constant movement. Indeed, the expectations of modern statehood and the necessary individuality pastoralism engenders are difficult to reconcile. This situation, combined with multigenerational clan-based violence and internal turmoil, allowed the Europeans and Ethiopians to partition Somali lands into five parts by 1900. French Somaliland, British Somaliland, and Italian Somaliland were carved out to create colonies or protectorates, while Ethiopia absorbed the vast Ogaden region and the British incorporated much of Jubaland into the Northern Frontier District of British East Africa. [29] This critical partition, combined with

the endemic clan-based animosities within Somali society, stand at the heart of the tensions between the governments in Hargeisa and Mogadishu today.

The British and the Italians took very different approaches to their territories on the Horn of Africa. The British established British Somaliland in 1888 to help provide meat for the British soldiers stationed at the Aden naval base across the gulf. They wanted easy, dependable access to Somali herds, but ultimately their interest in the land itself (which offered few other resources) or its people (who were too mobile to serve as a dependable tax base) was minimal. [30] Consequently, the British didn't control the interior until the 1930s, didn't open a government school in the protectorate until 1938, or attempt to create a strong local bureaucracy in Somaliland as they did in other parts of Africa. [31] Conversely, the Italians looked to build a true colony in their part of Somalia. Not only did Italy's fascist government encourage migration and settlement to the colony in the 1920s and

Illustration 110: Stamp from the British Somaliland Protectorate, Edward VII issue, 1904.

1930s, but they developed a system of plantation agriculture in southern Somalia, cultivating bananas, citrus, cotton, and sugarcane. They also imposed a new tax structure, a new legal code, and a new administrative system that purposefully fueled Somali clan animosities by co-opting

---

[28] There were several important regional medieval sultanates, such as the Adal Sultanate (which nearly conquered Ethiopia in the early 16th century) and the Ajuuraan Sultanate (which participated in a vibrant Indian Ocean trade until 1700), but neither of these can be seen as uniting the Somali people into a single state. The "Scramble for Africa" is a term given to European imperialists competing to acquire colonies in Africa in the late 19th century.

[29] Jubaland was transferred to Italian Somaliland in 1925.

[30] The word "ultimately" is important here. The British led four military expeditions into the interior in the nineteenth century (1886, 1890, 1893, and 1895) and four more between 1901 and 1904 as part of their conflict with a Sufi sheikh and poet, Sayyid Muhammad Abdullah Hassan (known to the British as the "Mad Mullah"). Hassen led a persistent jihad against British rule from 1900 to 1920. In 1914, he even attacked and looted the British coastal capital of Berbera. When Hassan, who some see as the father of modern Somali nationalism, died of influenza in 1920, what was known as the Dervish War ended. In the 1930s, the British were finally able to establish control over much of the interior.

[31] This primary school was all-male. The first school for girls in British Somaliland didn't open until the 1950s, while the first secondary school, again only for boys, wasn't opened until 1955.

one group, the Rahanweyn, to become policy enforcers. The Italians also created urban plans to develop Mogadishu and other cities, replacing medieval centers with broad boulevards and modernist architecture. Indeed, the Italians were belated colonists in every sense, wanting to see Somalia (as well as Libya, Eritrea, newly-conquered Ethiopia, and the Aegean Islands of the Dodecanese) as a new Roman Empire.[32]

During World War II, Italy invaded British Somaliland in August 1940, forcing the British to evacuate their vastly outnumbered garrison to Aden.[33] It was the first British territorial loss in the war. The setback did not last long, however, for the British retook their protectorate just five months later, held it for the remainder of the war, and moved their capital to Hargeisa, where they began constructing government offices, shops, and housing in what had thus far been a simple village. This victory was accompanied by other attacks on Italian holdings in East Africa, including a force of South African and Nigerian troops under British command that captured Kismayo and Mogadishu in February 1941. These forces then turned west to Ethiopia, where they were joined by South African and Punjabi troops that had landed at Berbera. The combined imperial forces captured Addis Ababa on April 6, 1941, at which point it looked like Italian rule in East Africa had come to an end. Instead, after the British had carted off much of Somalia's useful infrastructure for their war effort, the United Nations voted in November 1949 to make Italy's former colony a U.N. Trust Territory under Italian supervision for ten years, until 1960. This was an unprecedented decision since Italy wasn't even a U.N. member until 1955. More significantly, Italian Somaliland's pre-war fascists, who ruled with the assistance of the Rahanweyn clan, quickly reestablished themselves. In Mogadishu, it was as if the war never happened: the Italians still ruled.

In Hargeisa, the British did not initially set a specific timetable for independence, but as the 1950s progressed, it became an increasingly difficult decision to avoid. In February 1959, British colonial secretary Alan Lennox-Boyd announced that the British government was in favor of the creation of a unified Somali state. This unrealistic proposal fueled already-growing Somali nationalism, both in the British and Italian-controlled regions. Romance quickly overtook practicality, for the idea of combining lands with such different administrative, accounting, educational, and legal systems, as well as currencies, official languages, trading patterns, and clan affiliations, bordered on the absurd.[34] In August 1959, pan-Somali leaders went even further and called for the creation of a single Somali state that would unite all of the regions inhabited by the Somali people, including Somali residents in Djibouti, Ethiopia, and Kenya. This idea of Greater Somalia was even more far-fetched since France had little reason to surrender its colony, Ethiopia refused to relinquish the Ogaden, and Britain was committed to keeping Kenya intact. That Somali leaders could propose such a grand union on the Horn of Africa shows how seduced they became with nationalistic sentiments.

Even the process of a limited Somali unification was messy. It also remains quite

---

[32] The Italians attempted to conquer Ethiopia in 1895, but suffered a devastating defeat at the Battle of Adwa on March 1, 1896 when its army proved ill-prepared and vastly outnumbered. The embarrassment of the defeat at Adwa festered in Italy until 1935, when Benito Mussolini ordered an invasion of Ethiopia. This time, buoyed with superior weapons, British and French consent, the League of Nation's incompetence, and the use of mustard gas, the Italians won and captured Addis Ababa in May 1936.

[33] The Italians invaded in three columns totaling 175,000 soldiers, most of whom were Somalis from Italian Somaliland. The British garrison consisted of 36,000 men. The invaders captured Zelia, Hargeisa, and Odweina within three days, and forced the British to retreat to the mountains near Sheikh. At the Battle of Tug Argan, the Italians pushed the British out of the mountains, but the British were able to conduct an orderly withdrawal from Berbera to Aden on August 19, 1940.

[34] Just within the British and Italian regions, there were, in fact, four legal systems involved: British Common Law, Italian law, Islamic sharia, and Somali customary law (*xeer*). The idea of adding French and Ethiopian systems into this mix made Lennox-Boyd's idea even more illogical, even if the Somalis share a common culture.

controversial. Britain granted Somaliland independence on June 26, 1960, and the new nation was quickly recognized by thirty-five countries. The next day, Somaliland's legislature in Hargeisa passed two bills: the Act of Union, and the Union of Somaliland and Somali Law. These acts were supposed to be endorsed by Somali representatives from Mogadishu as well, but this never occurred. Instead, on June 30, the Somali legislative assembly in Mogadishu sanctioned unification in principle, but the wording of the two unification agreements differed. Then, on July 1, the legislative assemblies of Somaliland and Somalia met in joint session in Mogadishu. The representatives elected a provisional president, who proclaimed the de facto union of the two sovereign states, even though the merger lacked a fully legal basis. Because this process was rushed and not as clean as it might have been, a national referendum to ratify the constitution was held a year later, in June 1961. By this time, northerners were beginning to have serious doubts about the wisdom of joining their southern cousins. They had become politically marginalized since the president, the prime minister, and ten of the fourteen cabinet ministers were from the former Italian colony. This also meant that the dominant clan in Somaliland, the Isaaq, had lost its influence to the southern clans. Therefore, in the national referendum, southerners supported the new constitution, but in the north, 63% voted "no." Somalilanders were beginning to realize that they had made a huge political mistake.

In October 1969, the president of Somalia was assassinated. Mohamed Siad Barre, the commandant of the army and an accomplice to the murder, then staged a *coup d'état* against the civilian government. Because so many Somali army officers had received their training in Soviet military schools, Barre turned to the Soviet Union for assistance. A month before his first visit to Moscow in November 1971, Barre declared that Somalia would adopt "scientific socialism" as the nation's official ideology. But Barre was not a true Marxist. Rather, he used a Marxist cloak as a guise for totalitarianism—complete with the suspension of the constitution and the judiciary, the creation of a KGB-styled secret police, the closure of the national assembly, and the execution of potential rivals. He also sought to undercut the position of clan leaders, and made it a crime to refer to one's clan affiliation. Perhaps Barre's greatest legacy was his declaration of war on Ethiopia in August 1977, for he hoped to realize the old dream of Greater Somalia and to take advantage of Ethiopia's political confusion in the aftermath of the military coup that toppled Emperor Haile Selassie. By the end of the year, Somali troops had not only taken the Ogaden, but had also advanced deep into Ethiopian territory, capturing Jijiga and laying siege to Harar. This drive angered the Soviets, who began supporting the new revolutionary government in Ethiopia instead of Barre. Boosted by

Illustration 111: Siad Barre arriving at Schiphol Airport, Amsterdam in 1978.

the assistance of more than ten thousand Cuban troops, the Ethiopians quickly recovered their early losses, turning the war into a rout of the Somali army by spring 1978. The speed of the Ethiopian advance triggered a refugee crisis as ethnic Somalis living in Ethiopian territory feared retribution and fled to Somalia. By early 1981, there were two million refugees in Somalia, 1.3 million of whom lived in camps. Many of these refugees were concentrated in Somaliland, which caused a population increase in the region by perhaps forty percent and put an enormous strain on resources in an ecologically inhospitable area.

These demographic and environmental pressures fostered the development of an opposition movement to Barre's rule. The most important of the opposition groups in the north was the Somali National Movement (SNM), which was founded in London in 1981 by a group of army officers, religious leaders and businessmen who were primarily members of the Isaaq clan. Operating from a base in Ethiopia, the SNM began guerrilla operations against the Barre regime, and in 1988 they took control of Hargeisa and Burao. Barre responded by unleashing his South African-funded air force against the cities and the refugee camps with the full intention of liquidating the Issaq clan altogether. 20,000 to 50,000 civilians were killed in the aerial bombardments, heavy artillery assaults, and ground attacks; cities were reduced to rubble; and rural wells were purposefully poisoned. 400,000 Somalis fled to Ethiopia.[35] In the battle's aftermath, Hargeisa and Burao when seen from the air "looked like a city of dry swimming pools;" it was only upon further inspection that one could see that these "pools" were actually the remnants of houses without rooftops.

Siad Barre was deposed in 1991, and Somalia slid into civil war with numerous regional and clan-based groups competing for control. Somaliland, which declared itself to be a separate country in May 1991, was never designated "a failed state" the way Somalia was, thanks to the lasting success of the Grand Conference of National Reconciliation, which opened in January 1993. Held in Borama, the transformative five-month summit produced a new constitution that balanced tradition and modernity, clan loyalties and national commonalities.[36] Entirely funded by local businessmen who were eager to bring stability to the region and attended by seventeen women observers who tangibly influenced the proceedings, the Grand Conference created a bicameral legislature with a non-elected upper house for clan elders and a popularly-elected lower house of representatives. This structure protected the prerogatives of powerful clan elders and embraced the advantages of a modern state. The summit also produced a National Charter that called for the drafting of a formal constitution to be ratified by plebiscite, and a Peace Charter that called for the demilitarization of the clans. Perhaps most importantly, the Grand Conference saw a transfer of leadership from the head of the Somali National Movement, who was a member of one Issaq subclan, to Mohamed Haji Ibrahim Egal, who was a member of a different subclan. These unprecedented negotiations, actions, and processes made the Borama Congress a participatory, grassroots endeavor of Somalilanders. By 2010, the nation had approved the constitution with a 97% approval rate and had witnessed the peaceful transfer of power between presidents three times.[37] Although the nation certainly experienced significant setbacks during its formative years,[38] the Borama delegates and observers built an organic political system that continues to meet their own political, socio-economic, and cultural needs. This resolution is a far cry from what happened in Somalia, where decades of internationally-organized negotiations and interventions have never produced anything resembling stability or peace.

---

[35] Many of these refugees struggled to get across the border, for the Somali army blocked the way and shot at anyone who approached. Clearly, there were many who lost their lives in attempting to flee the battle.

[36] There were 150 male representatives at the Borama Conference, who were drawn proportionally from the size of each clan and subclan, but the summit was attended by 2,000 observers, including seventeen official women observers. Women had been vocal in calling for peace prior to the Borama Conference and traditionally serve as inter-clan mediators in Somali society.

[37] The constitution, which was approved in 2001, specified a three-party system in an effort to pollinate cross-clan political alliances.

[38] These setbacks included major clashes from 1994 to 1996 between forces loyal to Egal and forces loyal to SNM leader and former president Abdirahman Ahmed Ali Tuur, and the postponement of elections in 2008, 2009, and 2017 due to political violence.

Hargeisa c. 2022

Situated in a highland valley and blessed with moderate temperatures for the region, Hargeisa is a city of about a million people that is growing 3.1% a year.[39] Its neighborhoods are segregated by clan and subclan affiliations, but to the outsider the capital appears quite amalgamated since ninety percent of the city's buildings have been built since 1988, the year of Siad Barre's devastating attack. Independence Avenue forms the backbone of the city, as it undulates through the city's center, roughly following the course of a wadi that began attracting Somali herders centuries ago. At one end, this avenue leads northeast to Berbera's port on the Gulf of Aden and at the other end, it leads southwest to Jijiga, Ethiopia. This puts Hargeisa at the center of a vital international trade link. Low-slung hotels, gas stations, financial offices, cafes, and shops—almost all of which are locally-owned and unaffiliated with international companies—line much Independence Avenue, giving Hargeisa a dusty strip mall feel. This mood is counterbalanced, however, by shiny, six-to-eight-story, modern and postmodern buildings that periodically rise from unpaved streets to break the skyline and give the capital city the sense of resiliency and freshness, determination and hope. The arrival of functioning traffic lights has aided the perception of urban progress, even as donkey-pulled carts continue to share the streets with Toyota Land Cruisers and motorcycles.

The businesses along Independence Avenue, which is one of the city's few paved streets, provide revealing windows into Hargeisan society. Cafes and coffeehouses, for example, are ubiquitous, for they serve as a primary male social gathering place in a country where alcohol is completely banned and there are no bars or nightclubs in the Western sense. These establishments—all of which close five times a day with the call to prayer and remain closed until Salah has finished—range from a few franchised outlets with a prescribed decor to family-operated holes-in-the-wall with plastic chairs. While there are a few establishments that are exclusively for women or offer separate seating for women, café culture as a whole is decidedly male. Indeed, even if women own the business, they do not interact with customers. This is because Hargeisa is a socially conservative place as a result of the nation's faith-based and clan-based customs.[40] Arranged marriages, childhood marriage, female circumcision, and polygamy are all still widely accepted practices, and women are expected to wear an abaya and hijab, if not a niqab, whenever they are in public.[41] There is also evidence that the city's social milieu is becoming more conservative in terms of allowing for individual expression in Somaliland. This is one of the reasons why Hargeisa's popular cafe, the Cup of Art Italian Coffee House, closed in 2016. Located near the Presidential Palace, the cafe offered poetry slams, fashion nights, rock concerts, and a whiteboard upon which customers could express themselves freely. Such

---

[39] Hargeisa (or Hargeysa) has an elevation of 4,377 feet and the environment is classified as subtropical steppe. Temperatures are typically in the mid-80s during the day and the mid-60s at night. Traditionally, Hargeisa received an average of 16 inches of rain a year, but climate change is lowering this amount, triggering droughts. The city's growth has been sudden: in 2012, Hargeisa's population was just 500,000.

[40] Islamic law, sharia, forms the basis of the legal system in Somaliland, but sharia works in conjunction with Somali clan-based customary law or *xeer*. Sharia is seen as being more progressive in protecting women's rights than xeer is.

[41] An abaya is a full-length, loose-fitting outer garment. A hijab is a headscarf that covers the hair and neck, but not the face. A niqab is a veil that covers the head and face, but allows the eyes to be seen. Burkas, which are not common in Somaliland, cover the entire body and hide the eyes behind a fabric mesh. Ninety five percent of Somaliland's women are subjected to female circumcision, which is often called female genital mutilation because there is often the complete removal of the external female genitalia.

behavior was considered out-of-step with the dominant cultural norms of a city that seems caught between wanting to honor conservative Muslim values and one whose girls are forming basketball and soccer leagues and demanding the right to play. This social tension and the future character of the city are things men consider throughout the day, sipping tea in cafes in the morning and chewing khat in the afternoon, as women work throughout the day.[42]

Perhaps the most important businesses along Independence Avenue are money transfer providers. At one end of the spectrum are large, government-recognized banks like Dahabshiil, whose green glassed, postmodern headquarters in the center of the city also serves as a popular shopping mall. At the other end are the underground banking agents, who operate under a system known as *hawala*. *Hawala* allows those in a trusted network of known associates to transfer money for customers, while bypassing conventional financial channels and record keeping. It's sort of like a friend of a friend sending you money and keeping a small fee for the services provided. The advantage of the *hawala* system for a Somalilander in Minnesota who wants to send money to a relative in Hargeisa is that the costs are a fraction of what banks or Western Union would typically charge. Significantly, both large financial institutions and private individuals

Illustration 112: Somaliland Women in Hargeisa celebrating Independence Day, May 18, 2016.

must operate in accordance with sharia law, for the Quran says, "God has laid His curse on usury." (2:276) Therefore, instead of charging interest for loans as Western banks do, all financial institutions in Somaliland utilize profit sharing, fees, and mutual trust to ground their transactions. The results of these transactions are Somaliland's lifeblood. Collectively, remittances from abroad accounted for 50% of Somaliland's gross national product or $1.4 billion in 2018. COVID-19 disrupted this cash flow into the nation, but by 2022 the crisis had abated and a fierce competition between banks, telecommunication companies, and *hawala* agents had emerged.

Remittances are what allow children to attend private schools, which are important institutions in Somaliland since primary education is not compulsory. In fact, only 33% of boys and 29% of girls aged five to twelve attend any type of school at all, and most who do so start later than the recommended age of six.[43] Ten percent of the children under five are malnourished, which is more than double the percentage in Kenya, and childhood vaccination

---

[42] Khat leaves contain a stimulant that when chewed releases dopamine, producing a mild sense of euphoria. It is also an appetite suppressant. It is estimated that 90% of the male population in Somaliland chew khat, while 20% of the women do. Most of these women only chew it in private, thereby limiting their consumption and having fewer side effects and health issues related to khat use.

[43] The percentage for children attending schools from minority groups (those who are not from the Isaaq clan) is only 20%.

rates are frighteningly low.[44] This profile stands quite in contrast with the existence of Hargeisa University. Founded in 2000 and serving about 6,000 students today, Hargeisa University offers undergraduate degrees in everything from business and engineering to education and health sciences. Instruction throughout the university is in English, except in the College of Islamic Studies. Significantly, the coeducational university also offers graduate-level programs in international relations, development, public health, ophthalmology, and peace and conflict studies. The educational contrasts in Hargeisa poignantly illustrate Somaliland's socio-economic stratification.

What income doesn't come from remittances largely derives from exporting livestock, mainly to Saudi Arabia. Hargeisa's Livestock Market, located south of Independence Avenue, serves as an important trade center in a commerce that has continued for centuries. Somaliland's

Illustration 113: Hargeisa camel market, May 2016.

nomadic and semi-nomadic groups—still some 55% of the total population—make their livelihood by raising goats, sheep, and camels in the hinterlands and selling them in the markets in Hargeisa and Burao. Hargeisa's middlemen then take the livestock to Berbera, where they are quarantined and inspected. From there, millions of goats and sheep are shipped to Saudi Arabia in time for the *hajj* to meet the needs of pilgrims.[45] In the first six months of 2022, for example, over 1.5 million animals were exported, earning a value of more than $148 million.

The city has two monuments to its short past. The first is the Independence Monument

---

[44] According to a 2011 study, 43% of the children in Somaliland had not received any childhood vaccination and only 7% were fully vaccinated.

[45] Saudi Arabia has repeatedly placed bans on the importation of Somaliland livestock (2000-2009, 2016, and during COVID-19) largely because of insufficient quarantine procedures. The economic consequences of these bans were such that Somaliland's government decided to build modern quarantine stations in Berbera.

on Airport Road. A three-tiered plinth supports a concrete pedestal painted in the colors of Somaliland's flag, red, white, and green. Rising out of this pedestal is hand and wrist, also painted in red, white, and green. The hand holds a map of Somaliland with its provinces and key cities shown. The statue evokes the clenched fist of protest, but its modest size, construction materials, and lack of upkeep mean that the statue fails to inspire. This was also once a problem with the city's second major monument, the Civil War Memorial, which sits in a public square just to the west of the site of the Waheen Market and just to the east of Dahabshiil Bank's rounded, postmodern headquarters. The memorial's centerpiece is a Soviet MiG-17 fighter jet that crashed during Siad Barre's bombardment of

the city. Originally balanced atop a rather shoddily-constructed pyramid that was decorated with folk art murals, the plane gained a new, grander venue in 2021. Today, the fighter sits upon a beige marble pedestal that is attached to a curved colonnade with two arches on each side. It looks far more like a conventional war memorial than its predecessor, and that formality fits with the government's yearning to be seen as a full-fledged, legitimate modern nation.

Illustration 114: War Memorial, Hargeisa, 2023.

Indeed, there is no issue more pressing for Somaliland than diplomatic recognition. In 1933, the Montevideo Convention on the Rights and Duties of States established the four criteria for the recognition of a new nation in terms of international law: a permanent population, a defined territory, a government, and the capacity to enter into relations with other states. Somaliland easily meets all four. In 1964, however, the Organization of African Unity, decided that in the interests of stability, the continent's colonial borders needed to remain in place. As Modibo Keita, the president of Mali, said at the time:

> We must take Africa as it is, and we must renounce any territorial claims, if we do not wish to introduce what we might call black imperialism in Africa....African unity demands of each one of us [have] complete respect for the legacy that we have received from the colonial system, that is to say: [the] maintenance of the present frontiers.

There have been two major exceptions to this policy. The first was in 1993, when Eritrea separated from Ethiopia and became a recognized, independent country. The second was in 2011, when South Sudan separated from Sudan to become Africa's newest nation. In both cases, the change in international boundaries occurred with the consent of the older, parent state. Were Somalia to agree to Somaliland's separation, Hargeisa's international recognition would come swiftly. Ironically, this is what the African Union recommended in 2005, and what has de facto happened, with Türkiye and Ethiopia having consulates in Hargeisa, the United Arab Emirates having an official Commercial Office in the city to facilitate trade and development, Denmark having a Program Office to work with local non-profits, and Taiwan having a Representative Office on Independence Avenue. There are also numerous NGOs in Hargeisa, including ActionAid, the African Relief Committee, CARE International, and UNICEF. In this way, Hargeisa feels like other capital cities.

These relief agencies, and others, like The International Federation of Red Cross and

Red Crescent Societies, provided critical assistance to Hargeisa and Somaliland's herders during the severe drought of 2022. During the crisis (which came in the wake of catastrophic droughts in 2011 and 2017), 60% of the pastoralists lost all of their livestock and were forced to move to cities, including Hargeisa, where they began living with family or settled into impermanent, makeshift camps surrounding the city. While there have been some efforts to anticipate the next drought and mitigate its effects, such as restoring traditional underground water cisterns, there has also been considerable criticism of the Somaliland government for not being sufficiently proactive in the face of the world's climate crisis. As an analyst with the Peace Research Institute in Oslo says,

> The state footprint in the rural areas is very limited....It is mainly Somalis in the diaspora and the international community who provide assistance....When the drought has ended, the whole discussion of droughts ends there. The government does not allocate a budget for future droughts despite droughts occurring every four years for decades. By the time they are able to raise funds for the drought response, people have already lost their livestock and people have already moved into the camps."

This means that while Somaliland's government is not effectively serving its citizens as the global climate crisis attacks the Horn of Africa, it is also true that Somaliland's officials face nearly unparalleled constraints because of the lack of diplomatic recognition.

Hargeisa is, then, a city of contrasts and contradictions. Just as there are dirt streets lined with vendors selling their wares from umbrella-covered stalls, there are bougainvillea reaching out from the beautiful gardens and walled compounds of the elite. Hargeisans retain deep connections to their nomadic heritage, and yet live in a city that is served by flights arriving from eight international destinations.[46] Thirty percent of Hargeisa's population lives on a dollar a day and yet the city boasts hotels that would be welcomed options for international travelers in major cities around the world. The facade of Somaliland's postmodern parliament building might be mistaken for the entrance to a movie theater in the United States, and yet its legislators are preserving democracy in a region full of anti-democratic regimes. And Hargeisa is reputed to be one of the safest capitals in Africa and the Middle East, but the U.S. State Department has issued a Level 4 Travel Warning for Somaliland ("Do Not Travel"), due to "crime, terrorism, civil unrest, health issues, kidnapping, and piracy."[47] In short, Hargeisa is still a capital searching for acceptance in the world.

Illustration 115: Parliament building, Hargeisa, 2015.

---

[46] The destinations are Addis Ababa, Djibouti, Dubai, Galkayo, Jeddah, Mogadishu, Nairobi, and Wajir in northern Kenya.
[47] Australia, Canada, Ireland, the United Kingdom, and other nations have similarly-worded travel advisories.

A Short Postscript

In July 2023, Somaliland's president, Muse Bihi Abdi, flew to Eswatini (Swaziland) to announce that the Inyatsi Construction Group had won the contract to rebuild what will now be called the Waheen Shopping Centre. Inyatsi's plan calls for a three-story, open-air modernist building with Islamic touches. The Centre will house nearly 800 small vendor shops, which will surround a large atrium with four fountains and palm trees.

This welcomed news was eclipsed in January 2024 at another press conference. Sitting behind two lavish bouquets of multicolored roses, Muse Bihi Abdi, and Ethiopia's prime minister, Abiy Ahmed, stunned the diplomatic world by announcing in Addis Ababa that they had come together to sign a Memorandum of Understanding (MoU) between their two governments. In doing so, Bihi Abdi and Abiy sought to end the decades of dysfunctionality in the Horn of Africa.

The specific wording of the agreement remains unpublished, but Somaliland's press release hailed the MoU as "a significant diplomatic milestone for our country," for "in exchange for 20km [of] sea access for the Ethiopian Naval forces...Ethiopia will formally recognize the Republic of Somaliland, setting a precedent as the first nation to extend international recognition to our country." Ethiopia's press release was more circumspect, but reported that the MoU "shall pave the way to realize the aspirations of Ethiopia to secure access to the sea and diversify its access to seaports. It also strengthens [Ethiopia's and Somaliland's] security, economic and political partnership...[and] indicates the pathway to bolster their political and diplomatic relations." In their direct comments to the press, Ethiopia's Abiy said, "This will be the starting point of our cooperation with the brotherly people of Somaliland, to grow and develop together in cooperation and ensure our common security. As we have repeatedly stated previously, we don't wish to use force on anyone. Rather, we will use what we have cooperatively." Somaliland's Muse Bihi then said, "We are very happy and we thank the Ethiopian prime minister as we sign the agreement here. We have allowed them 20 kilometers of our sea and they will also recognize us as an independent state. They will become the first state to recognize Somaliland after the signing of this Memorandum of Understanding."

While many in Somaliland and Ethiopia welcomed the news and shared in Muse Bihi and Abiy's enthusiasm, the president of Somalia, who sees Somaliland as an integral part of his nation's territory, was disdainful. In an interview on Al-Jazeera, Hassan Sheikh Mohamud accused Ethiopia of violating international law by "annexing part of Somalia and changing the borders of Somalia" with the January 1 agreement. He added, "Somalia is an independent, sovereign state. When such deals are taking place, it is...the federal government of Somalia who [has] the legitimate right to be discussing [them], not a breakaway...region of Somalia at all." Mohamud then smiled with a touch of amusement as he contemplated the very notion of giving Ethiopia a port on Somali soil with both commercial and military capacity. Perhaps his drollness came from knowing that key regional powers, including Egypt and Saudi Arabia, were standing with Somalia instead of with the government in Hargeisa.[48]

---

[48] There must have also been a certain sense of irony in Mohamud's mind. Just three days before the agreement between Somaliland and Ethiopia was signed, Mohamud and Abiy had put their signatures on an agreement to restart talks between Somalia and Somaliland over the latter's constitutional status. Abiy and Abdi's agreement, however, quickly ended all talks between Hargeisa and Mogadishu. Mohamud had been double-crossed by Abiy within the course of three days.

What Hargeisa Teaches

It is challenging to draw *historical* conclusions about what Hargeisa's experience in 2022 can teach us in 2024, as this book is about to be published. This is because historians require the passage of time to be able to offer valuable insight. They need distance to be able to evaluate what events and which people truly have significance. Like a fine wine, meaning only comes with maturation, reflection, and chronological detachment. For a historian to try to draw historical conclusions after just two years is, in many ways, to misunderstand the discipline's nature.

This said, it is also striking to see how much of Hargeisa's experience over the past thirty years reinforces the veracity of the historical lessons discussed in the preceding chapters. With Hargeisa, it is clear once again that the force of localism is powerful, that nomenclature holds meaning, that diplomatic recognition matters, that historical periods aren't experienced in the same way everywhere, and that binary thinking limits understanding. These patterns, repeated in such a different culture and at such a different time, go a long way towards proving their merit. As with the other lessons presented here, the universality and the repeated applicability validate.

The city also offers a chance to come full circle and to reexamine the historical lessons presented in the introduction. Will and Ariel Durant held, in part, that life is competition, war is certain, progress is dependent upon conflict, and nations die. These conclusions and the idea that history is the story of competition find their origins in the science of Charles Darwin and the philosophy of Georg Wilhelm Friedrich Hegel.[49] Applying these Western ideas to Islamic Africa is problematic in many ways, but the people of Hargeisa are proud of the fact that they endure against the odds. Their lives challenge assumptions about citizenship, self-governance, and international law. In terms of realpolitik,[50] they are quite different from Somalis in other parts of the Horn of Africa. Somalilanders have developed their own political system—one that balances tradition and modernity and minimizes the clan divisions that have caused so much suffering in human history. They may live in a world in which they cannot get credit cards, international loans, and national internet domains and telephone prefixes, but they have fashioned effective workarounds and developed an informal economy that functions for them. And Somalilanders have also forged an independent foreign policy, building new bridges with Ethiopia and the United Arab Emirates and working to show that they should be a recognized member of the international community. In other words, Somalilanders are survivors in life's competition, war's certainty, and progress' conflict. They do not seem to live in a nation that is going to die anytime soon.

---

[49] Charles Darwin (1809-1882) believed that Natural Selection was the essential evolutionary process; in the late 19th century, men like Herbert Spencer (1820-1903) sought to apply the idea of competition in the natural world to humans, arguing for the "survival of the fittest." This ideology was used to justify racism and imperialism and is known as Social Darwinism. Georg Wilhelm Friedrich Hegel (1770-1831) was a German philosopher who argued that all history began with a premise, that a reaction to that premise (the antithesis) would emerge over time and out of that conflict a new synthesis would emerge. For Hegel, this cycle of thesis – antithesis – synthesis is ongoing.

[50] Realpolitik or "realistic politics" is the practice of conducting diplomacy and other political affairs on the basis of practical issues instead of ideological, ethical, or moral considerations.

Curated Bibliography for Chapter 9

Aidid, Safia. "The Café Talkers of Somalia: Fighting While Seated." *Popula*. August 1, 2018. https://popula.com/2018/08/01/the-cafe-talkers-of-somalia/

Abdinur, Mustafa Haji. "Huge Fire Destroys Somaliland Market." *AFP International*. April 2, 2022.ProQuest Central.

Akou, Heather Marie. *The Politics of Dress in Somali Culture*. Bloomington, IN: Indiana University Press, 2011). EBSCOhost.

Bradbury, Mark. *Becoming Somaliland*. London: Progressio, 2008.

Briggs, Philip. *Somaliland: the Bradt Travel Guide*. Guilford, CT: Globe Pequot Press, 2019.

Capspersen, Nina. *Unrecognized States: the Struggle for Sovereignty in the Modern International System*. Malden, MA: Polity Press, 2012.

"Case Study: Women in Peace and Transition Processes: Somaliland." *Geneva Inclusive Peace & Transition Initiative*. July 2017.

Clapham, Christopher. *The Horn of Africa: State Formation and Decay*. New York: Oxford University Press. 2017.

Cotran, Eugene. "Legal Problems Arising Out of the Formation of the Somali Republic." *The International and Comparative Law Quarterly*. Vol. 12, No. 3 (July 1963). JSTOR.

Das, Sourav Kumar, Kishor Naskar and Chandra Sekhar Sahu. "Why Does Refugee Generates? An Empirical Perspective." *Refugee Crises and Third-World Economies: Policies and Perspectives*. Sourav Kumar Das and Nidhi Chowdhary (eds.). Bingley, U.K.: Emerald Publishing Limited, 2020. EBSCOhost.

"'Don't do it': Somali President Warns Ethiopia over Somaliland Port Deal." *Al Jazeera*. January 23, 2024. https://www.aljazeera.com

Drake-Brockman, Ralph E. *British Somaliland*. London: Hurst & Blackett Ltd. 1912.

Ducker, John T. *Beyond Empire: The End of Britain's Colonial Encounter*. London: Bloomsbury Academic, 2020. EBSCOhost.

De Waal, Alex. *The Real Politics of the Horn of Africa: Money, War, and the Business of Power*. Cambridge, UK: Polity, 2015.

"Ethiopia Signs Agreement to Use Somaliland's Red Sea Port." *Al Jazeera*. January 1, 2024. YouTube, https://www.youtube.com

Farah, Hibaq, "'It's all Gone': The Women Left Bereft when Somaliland's Largest Market Burned Down." *The Guardian*. April 25, 2022, ProQuest Central.

Fergusson, James. *The World's Most Dangerous Place*. Cambridge, MA: DeCapo Press, 2013.

Gele, Abdi A., Bente P. Bø, and Johanna Sundby, "Have We Made Progress in Somalia after 30 Years of Interventions? Attitudes toward Female Circumcision Among People in the Hargeisa District." *BMC Notes*. Vol. 6 (2013). ProQuest.

Hamilton, Angus. *Somaliland*. Westport, CT: Negro Universities Press, 1970.

Hamilton, Glenn S. "Italy Invades British Somaliland." *Great Events from History: The 20th Century, 1901-1940*. January 2007. EBSCOhost.

Harper, Mary. *Getting Somalia Wrong?: Faith, War, and Hope in a Shattered State*. London: Zed Books, 2012.

Hassan, Mohamed Aden, Ahmed Musa, Nauja Kleist & Mark Bradbury. "COVID-19 has Transformed Somaliland's Remittance Lifeline." *Danish Institute for International Studies*, April 22, 2021, https://www.diis.dk/en/research/

Hegazi, Sami. "Arab League Denounces Ethiopia-Somaliland MoU as 'Coup' against Somali Unity." *Daily News,* January 18, 2024. https://www.dailynewsegypt.com

Hensen, Rachel. "Hargeisa, Somalia; A City Rising from the Ashes." *World Literature Today*. 86, 1 (January/February 2012). ProQuest Central.

Hill, Martin. *No Redress: Somalia's Forgotten Minorities*. London: Minority Rights Group International, 2010.

Ingiriis, Mohamed Haji. *The Suicidal State in Somalia: The Rise and Fall of the Siad Barre Regime, 1969–1991*. Lanham, Maryland: University Press of America, 2016.

Jackson, Donna R., "The Ogaden War and the Demise of Détente." *The Annals of the American Academy of Political and Social Science*. Vol. 632 (November 2010). JSTOR.

Jeffrey, James. "The Art of Covering Up in Somaliland." *Inter Press Service News Agency*. June 10, 2016.

https://www.ipsnews.net

Kapteijns, Lidwien. *Clan Cleansing in Somalia: the Ruinous Legacy of 1991*. Philadelphia: University of Pennsylvania Press, 2013.

Kennedy, Merlin. *Somalia: Perspectives on Challenges and Lessons*. New York: Nova Science Publishers, Inc, 2014. EBSCOhost.

Kilcullen, David. "Hargeisa, Somaliland: Invisible City." *Brenthurst Foundation*. 2019. https://www.thebrenthurstfoundation.org

Lewis, Ioan M. *Understanding Somalia and Somaliland: Culture, History, Society*. New York: Columbia University Press, 2008.

Malasevskaia, Iana, Ahmed A Al-Awadhi, and Lubna Mohammed. "Tea in the Morning and Khat Afternoon: Health Threats Due to Khat Chewing." *Cureus*. Vol. 12, No. 12. (December 2020).

Musa, Ahmed M., Oliver Vivian Wasonga, and Nadhem Mtimet. "Factors Influencing Livestock Export in Somaliland's Terminal Markets." *Pastoralism: Research, Policy and Practice*, 10:1 (2020).

Njoku, Raphael Chijioke. *History of Somalia*. Santa Barbara: Greenwood, 2013.

Osman, Abdirizak Mohamoud. "Urban Poverty in Somaliland: The Case of State House Area in Hargeisa." *Somaliland Peace and Development Journal*. October 2018. https://instituteforpeace.org/

"One Year After the Waheen Market Fire: Lessons Learned and the Role of Danwadaag." VNG International. no date, https://www.vng-international.nl

Prunier Gérard. *The Country That Does Not Exist: a History of Somaliland*. London: Hurst & Company, 2021.

Renders, Marleen. *Consider Somaliland: State-Building with Traditional Leaders and Institutions*. Leiden: Brill, 2012.

Serunkuma, Yusuf. "'These Somalis are not Somalis'": Cup of Art Italian Coffeehouse, Authentic Identities, and Belonging in Hargeisa, Somaliland." *African Studies Review*. December 23, 2023. DOI:10.1017/asr.2023.105.

Seton-Watson, Christopher. "Italy's Imperial Hangover." *Journal of Contemporary History*, Vol. 15, No. 1 (January, 1980). JSTOR.

Somalia: A Country Study. Helen Chapin Metz (ed.). Washington, DC: United States Government, 1993.

"Somaliland Fire Leaves Traders Penniless and Market Destroyed." *AllAfrica.com*. April 22, 2022, ProQuest Central.

"Somaliland Launches $2 Billion Appeal After Market Inferno." *AFP International*. April 6 2022. ProQuest Central.

Somaliland Protectorate 1956 and 1957. London: Her Majesty's Stationery Office. 1959.

Statehood and Self-Determination: Reconciling Tradition and Modernity in International Law. Duncan French (ed.). New York: Cambridge University Press, 2013.

Smythe, Kathleen R. *Africa's Past, Our Future*. Bloomington, IN: Indiana University Press, 2015.

Stewart, Andrew. *The First Victory: The Second World War and the East Africa Campaign*. New Haven: Yale University Press, 2016. EBSCOhost.

"Storm Over a Port, A." *The Economist*, January 6, 2024. 35.

Tahir, Abdifatah Ismael. "Critical Infrastructures as Sites of Conflict over State Legitimacy: the Case of Hargeisa Airport in Somaliland, Northern Somalia." *Geoforum*. June 2021. Elsevier.

Tahir, Abdifatah Ismael. "The Production of Clan Segregation in Urban Somalia: Historical Geographies of Hargeisa," *Journal of Historical Geography*, April 2021, 53-62, Science Direct.

"Timeline: Breaking Down More Than a Decade of Drought in Somalia." *Concern Worldwide US*. October 22, 2022. https://concernusa.org

Touval, Saadia. "The Organization of African Unity and African Borders." *International Organization*, Vol. 21, No. 1 (Winter, 1967), 102-127, JSTOR.

Triprodi, Paolo. *The Colonial Legacy in Somalia: Rome and Mogadishu, from Colonial Administration to Operation Restore Hope*. New York: St. Martin's Press, 1999.

United Nations Trustee System, The: Legacies, Continuities, and Change. Jan Lüdert, Mara Ketzmerick and Julius Heise (eds.). New York: Routledge, 2023.

"'We Were Rich, Now We're Poor' - Life After Record Droughts in Somaliland." *AllAfrica.com*. February 22, 2024. ProQuest.

Wilson Eliot. "Recognize Somaliland as an Independent Nation." *The Hill*. February 12, 2024, https://thehill.com

"Women and Men in Somaliland: Facts and Figures, 2018," *Ministry of Planning and National Development*. 2018. https://www.somalilandcsd.org/

"Women in Peace & Transition Processes, Somaliland (1993), Case Study." *Geneva: Inclusive Peace & Transition Initiative*. July 2017. https://www.inclusivepeace.org

World Peace Foundation. "Somalia: Fall of Siad Barre and the Civil War." August 15, 2015. *Mass Atrocity Endings, Tufts University*, https://sites.tufts.edu/atrocityendings

Yasin, Gulled M. "Effect of Pedagogical Processes on Academic Performance of Pupils in Public Primary Schools in Hargeisa District." *Turkish Online Journal of Qualitative Inquiry*. Vol. 12, No.7 (July 2021).

SUGGESTED BOOK GROUP DISCUSSION QUESTIONS

Dutch historian Pieter Geyl once wrote, "To expect from history those final conclusions that may be found in other disciplines is to misunderstand its nature. History is indeed an argument without end." It is in this spirit that these questions are best considered.

1. Which chapter did you like the best? Why was this so?

2. If it were safe to travel to all of these capitals in three years from now, which one would you most want to visit? Why?

3. Think about an organization or institution with which you have been involved over time. Why is group cohesiveness so hard to maintain and longevity so hard to achieve? What does this have to do with the experience of some of the capitals discussed in this book?

4. To which are you most loyal: your nation, state, city or neighborhood? Why is this so? Why do you think people in different time periods or from different cultures have felt different loyalties?

5. Pick an historical event and a current event that all participants have experienced and compare how the group's understandings differ. Why don't we all experience history—or even the present—the same way?

6. If our life experiences are uniquely shaped by the culture in which we live, then how can it also be true that there are broad commonalities in the human experience?

7. Identify a cultural monument that is particularly important to you. Why does this hold such meaning? Why is it so hard for others to understand its importance?

8. Why do people so often come together in times of crisis, but struggle to do so otherwise?

9. The Enugu chapter argues that propaganda is effective. Is this always so? What are its limits?

10. Review Will and Ariel Durants' historical lessons from the Introduction. Which of these do you find the most compelling and which do you find to be the most objectionable? Have you developed any new historical conclusions of your own?

ILLUSTRATION CREDITS

1. Map by the author.
2. Map by the author.
3. Map by the author.
4. A. T. Agate and J. B. Neagle, "Mosque in their town of Sooloo," *United States Exploring Expedition During the Years 1838, 1839, 1840, 1841, 1842,* Vol. 5. (Philadelphia, PA: Lea and Blanchard, 1845), 354. Courtesy of the Biodiversity Heritage Library, Smithsonian Institution.
5. *J. Drayton and R. S. Gilbert, "Fort at Caldera," United States Exploring Expedition During the Years 1838, 1839, 1840, 1841, 1842, Vol. 5. (Philadelphia, PA: Lea and Blanchard, 1845), 328.* Courtesy of the Biodiversity Heritage Library, Smithsonian Institution.
6. Thomas Allom, "Amoy, from the Outer Anchorage," 1843, courtesy of The New York Public Library.
7. Louis Le Breton and Eugène Cicéri, "Entrée de la rivière de Solo," Plate 139, *Voyage au Pôle Sud et dans l'Océanie sur les corvettes L'Astrolabe et La Zélée exécuté par ordre du Roi Pendant les Années 1837–1838–1839–1840 sous le commandement de M. Dumont-d'Urville,* (1846), courtesy of Heritage Library of Gray, Haute-Saône, France, and Wikipedia
8. Louis Le Breton and Adolphe Jean-Baptiste Bayot, "Visite au sultan de Solo," Plate 138. *Voyage au Pôle Sud et dans l'Océanie sur les corvettes L'Astrolabe et La Zélée exécuté par ordre du Roi Pendant les Années 1837–1838–1839–1840 sous le commandement de M. Dumont-d'Urville,* (1846), courtesy of Heritage Library of Gray, Haute-Saône, France, and Wikipedia Commons.
9. Baltasar Giraudier, "Expedición a Joló," courtesy of Biblioteca Virtual del Patrimonio Bibliográfico, Madrid, and Wikimedia Commons.
10. John J. Pershing, "After the Battle at Mount Dajo on Jolo Island, Sulu province. March 7, 1906," (published in 1907), courtesy of the National Archives and Record Administration College Park, Maryland and Wikimedia Commons.
11. "A Man Absurdly Well-Prepared for the Cholera Epidemic of 1832," courtesy of the Wellcome Collection, London.
12. "A Woman Extravagantly Equipped to Deal with the Cholera Epidemic of 1832," courtesy of the Wellcome Collection, London.
13. Map by the author.
14. Map by the author.
15. Map by the author.
16. Map by the author.
17. Gold coin, courtesy of National Numismatic Collection of the National Museum of American History and Wikimedia Commons.
18. Crest of Arms, courtesy of Nerdoguate and Wikimedia Commons.
19. "Work on a Coffee Plantation in Guatemala."[Detail] Wood-engraving by G. Andrews, 1877, after E. Muybridge, courtesy of the Wellcome Collection, London.
20. Albert Carrington, c. 1866, photograph by studio of Charles R. Savage and George M. Ottinger, Courtesy of the Church History Library, Salt Lake City, and the Joseph Smith Papers.
21: Map by the author.
22. Map by the author.
23. Unknown artist's rendering of Joseph Smith, 1845 on display at LDS Church History Museum, Salt Lake City, photographed by the author June 2022.
24. Brigham Young daguerreotype, 1853, courtesy of Marsena Cannon and Wikimedia Commons.
25. President Millard Fillmore, photograph by Mathew B. Brady circa 1855-1865. Courtesy of the Brady-Handy Collection, The Library of Congress, LC-BH82- 7 C.
26. Photograph by the author, April 2021.

27. Photograph of Turman O. Angell on display at the Territorial Statehouse State Park Museum, Fillmore, Utah, photographed by the author, April 2021.
28. Drawing of Plan for Utah Capitol Building, Fillmore, by Truman O. Angell, c. 1852 on display in the Territorial Statehouse State Park Museum, Fillmore, photographed by the author, April 2021.
29. The South Wing of the Territorial Statehouse, photographed by the author, April 2021.
30. The South Wing of the Territorial Statehouse, photographed by the author, April 2021
31. Queen Emma, 1896, "Queen Emma Photo Collection," courtesy of the Papua New Guinea Association of Australia.
32. Map by the author.
33. Map by the author.
34. Map by the author.
35. Map by the author.
36. John H. Margetts, "Coconuts New Britain," *Picturesque New Britain: Snaps from a Missionary's Camera*, early 1900s, courtesy of the Papua New Guinea Association of Australia; and,
37. "Drying Copra in the Dutch East Indies," c. 1920, courtesy of Leiden University Libraries, KITLV 377647.
38. "SMS Hohenzollern," German postage stamp from German New Guinea, 1901, courtesy of Colnect.com and Wikimedia Commons.
39. "Haupfling mif zwei brudern -- Deu-Pommern," ("Chief with Two Brothers - German Pomerania,") by Hermann von Lichtdruck, *Nachrichten über Kaiser-Wilhelms-Land und den Bismarck-Archipel.* Berlin: Neu Guinea Compagnie, 1889.
40. Rabaul volcanoes, courtesy of Ian_0126, Flickr, and Wikimedia Commons.
41. "Rabaul Street," by John H. Margetts, *Picturesque New Britain: Snaps from a Missionary's Camera*, early 1900s, courtesy of the Papua New Guinea Association of Australia.
42. "Customs House, Rabaul," c. 1935, courtesy of Leiden University Libraries, KITLV 377796 .
43. "Chinese District, Rabaul," c. 1935, courtesy of Leiden University Libraries, KITLV 377802.
44. Governor's House , Rabaul, 1935. Courtesy of Leiden University Libraries, KITLV 377513.
45. "Albert Hahl (1868-1945), Gouverneur vu Dytsch-Neigunea 1901-14," 1905, courtesy of Archiv vu dr Uni Frankfurt zur DKG and Wikimedia Commons.
46. Political cartoon by A. G. Racey. c. 1914, courtesy of Wellcome Collection, London.
47. "Ash Rain During the Eruption of the Volcano near Rabaul,"1937, Courtesy of Leiden University Libraries, KITLV 377831.
48. Chris Reed, "Post Office," *Rabaul Eruption 1994 Photo Album*, courtesy of the Papua New Guinea Association of Australia.
49. Chris Reed, "Turanguna Street," *Rabaul Eruption 1994 Photo Album*, courtesy of the Papua New Guinea Association of Australia.
50. Erwin Piscator, 1929, courtesy A Piscator Archive (EPS, Sign.: 38991) and Wikimedia Commons.
51. Map by the author.
52. Map by the author.
53. Lutheran Church in Norka, January 1881, courtesy of https://enc.rusdeutsch.ru/ and Wikimedia Commons.
54. Camels with farmer and plow, courtesy of Steven Schreiber and www.norkarussia.info.
55. "Wattled Granary" c.1885, courtesy of the New York Public Library Digital Collections.
56. "Bone Grinding and Glue Plant in Engels," c. 1930, courtesy of Alexander Spack and https://wolgadeutsche.net/
57. Anti-Kulak Poster by Nikolai Ivanovich Mikhailov, c. 1930, courtesy of Wikimedia Commons.
58. Soviet poster, "Labor Will Be the Masters of the World," 1920, courtesy of The New York Public Library Digital Collections, b12358315.
59. Soviet poster, "Red Ploughman," 1920, courtesy of The New York Public Library Digital Collections, b12358315.
60. Lavrentiy Beria, c. 1940, courtesy of Wikimedia Commons.
61 and 62. Photograph of deportation and eviction card, 1937, courtesy of Steven Schreiber and www.norkarussia.info.
63. Song of the White Orchid photograph, 1939, courtesy of Toho Company and Wikimedia Commons.
64. Map by the author.

65. Map by the author.

66. Maps by the author.

67 and 68. Unknown artist, "Russia's War with Japan 1904," courtesy of Wikimedia Commons, and Kiyochika Kobayashi, "Japan Makes Russia Disgorge her Brave Threats of Days Before the War," 1904 or early 1905, courtesy of the Library of Congress, 2009630468.

69 and 70. Postcards, South Manchurian Railway Station, Xinjing, c. 1934, courtesy of Wikimedia Commons.

71. Emperor Puyi in Manchukuo uniform, c. 1934, courtesy of Wikimedia Commons.

72 and 73. Postcard of the Supreme Court and Judiciary Building, c. 1939, courtesy of Wikimedia Commons, and same building in 2013, courtesy of Dong Chenxing and Wikimedia Commons.

74. From "Set of 12 Postcards Depicting Views of Xinjing (i.e. Changchun, China) during the Manchukuo period," c. 1940, courtesy of Harvard-Yenching Library, Harvard University, J-0930-0034

75. Chinese man pushing a wheelbarrow, c. 1938, courtesy of The Manchukuo Collection, Harvard-Yenching Library, Harvard University.

76. Michael E. Arth, "Changchun, Manchuria, 1978," courtesy of Michael E. Arth and Wikimedia Commons.

77 and 78. Maps by the author.

79 and 80. Maps by the author.

81. Caricature of Captain Frederick Lugard by Leslie Ward, which appeared in *Vanity Fair* December 19, 1895, courtesy of Wikimedia Commons.

82. General Gowon and Queen Elizabeth, June 13, 1973, courtesy of Keystone Press and the Nationaal Archief, The Hague, Netherlands, 926-4815

83 and 84. Flag of Biafra, courtesy of Mysid and Wikimedia Commons and Postage Stamps, courtesy of Aart Rietveld collection, University of Leiden and Wikimedia Commons.

85. Sculpture of Odumegwu Ojukwu, September 17, 2022, courtesy of Iwuala Lucy and Wikimedia Commons.

86. Protest march in The Hague, Netherlands, November 20, 1969, by unknown photographer, courtesy of the Nationaal Archief, The Hague, Netherlands, 922-9928.

87 and 88. Left, malnourished child, Biafra, by unknown photographer, courtesy of the Nationaal Archief, The Hague, Netherlands, 921-5790, and, right, a flyer advertising a donation drive to help the starving children in Biafra, April 13, 1969, courtesy of Committee To Save The Children Of Biafra and the Smithsonian National Museum of African American History and Culture, 2015.97.27.47.

89. Ferhadija Mosque, 1989, courtesy of Georgi Coventry.

90. Photograph of Clock Tower, c. 1967, on display at the Museum of the Republika Srpska, photographed by the author, April 2023.

91. Map by the author.

92. Map by the author.

93. Map by the author.

94. Photograph of Orthodox Church, 1879, on display at the Museum of the Republika Srpska, photographed by the author, April 2023.

95. Photograph of Catholic Church, late 1800s, on display at the Museum of the Republika Srpska, photographed by the author, April 2023.

96. Mansion, Banka Luka, late 1800s, photographed by the author, April 2023.

97. Award-winning photograph of Jasenovac Memorial, February 2010, *courtesy of Petar Milošević / CC BY-SA and Wikipedia Commons.*

98. Radovan Karadžić, 1994, courtesy of Mikhail Evstafiev and Wikimedia Commons.

99. Ferhadija Mosque fragments on display at the mosque, photographed by the author, April 2023.

100, 101, 102: Orthodox Cathedral, Banja Luka, photographed by the author, April 2023.

103. Ferhadija Mosque, 1989, courtesy of Georgi Coventry

104. Ferhadija Mosque, photographed by the author, April 2023.

105. Bosnian Serb Police Officer Memorial, Banka Luka, photographed by the author, April 2023.

106. Map by the author.

107. Map by the author.

108. Map by the author.

109. Map by the author.

110. British Somaliland stamp, 1904, courtesy of de la Rue, Ltd, London and Wikimedia Commons.

111. Siad Barre, courtesy of Nationaal Archief, Den Haag, Netherlands, 2.24.01.05.

112. "Somaliland Women Hargeisa," May 18, 2016, courtesy of Clay Gilliland and Flickr.

113. "Camel Market Hargeisa, Somaliland," May 19, 2016, courtesy of Clay Gilliland and Flickr.

114. "War Memorial, Hargeisa, May 18, 2023," Courtesy of Dr. Calvin Sun, Monsoon Diaries, https://monsoondiaries.com/2023/05/18/hargeisa/

115. Parliament building, Hargeisa, 2015, courtesy of Vincent van Zeijst and Wikimedia Commons.

ABOUT THE AUTHOR

Derek Dwight Anderson is an independent high school history teacher and librarian who has dedicated his professional life—both as an educator and as a writer—to examining history in unconventional ways. In 2020, he published his first book, *Improbable Voices: A History Of The World Since 1450 Seen From Twenty-Six Unusual Perspectives*, and *Forgotten Capitals* continues his mission to help people reconsider whose history matters.

Anderson holds a B.A. from Bates College and a Master of Library and Information Science from San José State University. He also studied at the University of Edinburgh. A senior faculty member at Marin Academy in San Rafael, California, he currently teaches an interdisciplinary world history course that integrates history, art history, and studio art. A dedicated world traveler who loves museums both large and small, he lives with his partner in Sausalito.

Learn more at: **forgottencapitals.com**

Made in the USA
Las Vegas, NV
23 November 2024

12501686R00092